# ITALIAN PARTISAN
Weapons in WWII

Gianluigi Usai & Ralph Riccio

# ITALIAN PARTISAN

## Weapons in WWII

Schiffer Publishing Ltd
4880 Lower Valley Road • Atglen, PA 19310

Library of Congress Control Number: 2016950999



Cover & Interior designed by Matthew Goodman

Type set in Minion & ITC Franklin Gothic STD

ISBN: 978-0-7643-5210-2
Printed in China

Published by Schiffer Publishing, Ltd.
4880 Lower Valley Road
Atglen, PA 19310
Phone: (610) 593-1777; Fax: (610) 593-2002
E-mail: Info@schifferbooks.com
Web: www.schifferbooks.com

A replica of the car used by Commander Poli on the set of the 1999 Italian movie *Il partigiano Johnny*. *Car and photo Gianluigi Usai*

# CONTENTS

## CHAPTER IX
# PROFILES . . . 105

## Bolt-Action Rifles ........ 150



## Semi-automatic and automatic Rifles ........ 161



## Submachine Guns ........ 174

## Light and Heavy Machine Guns.......... 207

# ACKNOWLEDGMENTS

Archivio Storico Cristilli Clusone (BG)
Avv. Lorenza Balbo
Scott Benedict
Elida Biggi
Centro documentazione e Ricerche Storiche Gotica Toscana
Centro Studi Fenoglio, Alba
Bruno Chionetti
William Cogger
Jon Cohen
Comune di Ceva, via Signor Giorgio Gonnella
ILSREC Genova for permission to use photos from their collection
Luong Dang
Colin Doane
Patrick Egan
Al Gerth
James D. Julia Auctioneers, Fairfield, Maine
Elisabeth MacDonald
Robert Stephen MacDonald
Edward McLean
National Rifle Association, National Firearms Museum
Enzo Palma
Maxim Popenker
Fulvio Sasso
Honorable Umberto Scardaoni, president, Istituto Storico Resistenza Età Contemporanea Savona (†)
Emilio Scarone
Caroline Simms (NRA museums)
Don Angelo Siri (†)
Gianni Toscani
Charles Wagner
Lisa Warren (James D. Julia Auctioneers)
G. C. Garello
Giovanni Sanguineti
Michele Becchi

# INTRODUCTION

This book is not meant to be a history of the Italian resistance movement—covered in innumerable works—because we hope to address ourselves to a readership that is well aware of the various actions and all of the political background leading to the liberation of Italy at the end of WWII.

We have found that the subject of the weapons used by the partisans is still marked by serious gaps: a lack of documentation, especially during the early stages; a lack of attention in memoirs and a similar oversight by historians; and the highly fragmented nature of studies on the subject have all led to the perpetuation of a low level of knowledge of this subject which is dear to our hearts.

This book is not meant to be a technical catalog of all the small arms used during WWII; rather, it is an in-depth historical examination of what could be found in the hands of the Italian partisans during the resistance.

Our primary interest was to understand the mysterious means by which weapons were able to make their way from far-flung shores to Italian territory.

Who would ever imagine the commander of an Italian partisan division in the Langhe area would be photographed with an Argentine pistol on his belt, and what kind of journey did that pistol make prior to the moment the photograph was taken?

And yet there are many similar cases, and insofar as possible, we have sought to understand or discover how they may have happened.

If any readers are seeking detailed information or a technical/historical manual of all of the world's small arms, we can suggest the following two publications as reference works:

*Small Arms of the World*, by E. Ezell

*Military Small Arms of the 20th Century*, by Hogg & Weeks

Happy reading.

If any reader has any observations regarding this book, we would be most happy to receive comments, corrections, or additions sent to the following addresses: gusai47@hotmail.it or raphaelriccio@msn.com.

# CHAPTER I
# HISTORICAL BACKGROUND

## The Italian Resistance Movement

The Italian resistance movement—whose members were known as partisans—was, like many of the resistance movements in other countries in Europe during WWII, often marked by factional and ideological rivalry. The resistance movement began almost immediately following the September 8, 1943, armistice between Italy and the Allies. The brief period of resistance by regular Italian military units against Germans in Italy, the Aegean, and the Balkans, although fascinating, does not fall within the parameters of this work. Brief mention is in order regarding the failed defense of Rome September 9–11, 1943, by units of the *Regio Esercito*. The announcement on September 8 of the armistice between Italy and the Allies caught the Italian army high command somewhat by surprise and confusion was rampant as to what action to take against German forces in Italy; the Germans already had plans in place for such an eventuality and immediately began to take action against Italian units. Combat between Italian and German forces in Rome and outlying areas (Tor Sapienza, Monterosi, Bracciano, Manziana, and Monterotondo) began the morning of September 9. Despite the truly heroic efforts of some of the Italian units (Granatieri di Sardegna infantry, Piave motorized and Ariete II armored divisions, Lancieri di Montebello Regiment, and Carabinieri and police units), lack of clear orders from above and the superiority of German forces forced the Italians to cease resistance on September 10. Quite possibly the first group of non-military resistance fighters to actually take up arms against the Germans consisted of members of the Communist Movement, who supported the Italian units fighting inside Rome at Porta San Paolo.

Another noteworthy reaction against the Germans was the spontaneous popular insurrection in Naples September 27–30, 1943, that erupted as Allied forces were poised to liberate the city; the German withdrawal from Naples had in fact already begun. That insurrection was somewhat of an anomaly, as it occurred in southern Italy and was not part of the resistance movement itself; the German withdrawal from Naples put an end to any need for further action by armed Italians in the area.

The actual resistance movement had its beginnings immediately after the September 9 armistice in Rome, when the *Comitato di Liberazione Nazionale* (CLN – National Liberation Committee) was formed. The CLN consisted of six anti-fascist groups: the Italian Communist Party, Italian Socialist Party, Action

Party, Christian Democratic Party, Workers Democracy Party, and the Liberals. The CLN was an overarching political organization. The earliest partisan combat groups were organized and led by former Italian army officers and NCOs motivated by a variety of reasons running from hatred of the Germans to a desire to reclaim national dignity, and simply to escape capture and imprisonment by the Germans, to whom they refused to swear loyalty. By mid-September, there were an estimated 1,500 active partisans; among the most fervent were former alpine unit junior officers who were at home in the mountain environment of northern Italy, nursed a particular resentment against the Germans, and who had gained combat experience in Russia. By June 1944 (after D-Day and the liberation of Rome), these numbers had risen dramatically to an estimated 50,000, of which some 25,000 were communists ("Garibaldini"), 15,000 were "giellisti" (the left-wing *Giustizia e Libertà* of the Action Party), and 10,000 "autonomi."

There were two very broad categories of partisan units: those that essentially refused to model themselves along the lines of what they viewed as the discredited Italian army, and those that were organized by former Italian military personnel. The first category included communists, socialists, and other left-wing groups, while the latter included the "autonomous" units organized and led by former junior and mid-grade officers and had conservative or royalist sentiments. Except for the "autonomous" units, all partisan formations had a political commissar equal in rank to the military commander who was responsible for training and morale, as well as sharing operational responsibility with the military commander. Although at the political level there was a consensus to cooperate in the common anti-fascist and anti-German struggle, at the operational level in the field there were rivalries based on ideologies and personalities, among other factors; the partisan groups of the right deeply distrusted the power that a powerful, well-armed, and organized communist faction could wield in Italy once the Germans and fascists had been defeated.

The resistance movement was active in the areas of northern and central Italy (basically Piedmont, Lombardy, Emilia-Romagna, the Marches, and the regions of Abruzzi, Tuscany, Veneto, Friuli, and Venezia Giulia) under the control of the Germans and Mussolini's puppet regime, the Italian Social Republic (RSI). The majority of the partisans were members of brigades or divisions that operated in the mountains, but there were two other types of groups: the GAP (*Gruppi di azione patriottica*) and the SAP (*Squadre di azione patriottica*). The GAP were based in cities and carried out small-scale guerrilla attacks against the Germans and fascists, while the SAP were based in factories and carried out acts of sabotage.

The size of the armed partisan units varied considerably depending on demographics, logistics, and local support. Although the left-wing formations tried to disassociate themselves from military customs and traditions and attempted to be "democratic," inevitably all of the formations followed or adopted a military hierarchical structure. The basic formation was the squad (*squadra*: 25–30 men); three or more squads formed a detachment (*distaccamento*: 75–100 men); three or more detachments constituted a brigade (*brigata*: 250–300 men); and three or more brigades made a division (*divisione*: 750–1,000 men). Several divisions formed a divisional group, which was responsible for an operational zone.

Following is a brief description of the relationship between the Allies and the Italian resistance movement. Immediately following the September 8, 1943, armistice, the British SOE and US OSS began to support various anti-German resistance groups in the hope of obtaining assistance freeing Allied prisoners, encouraging sabotage behind enemy lines, and gaining information essential to the conduct of war. They began to send missions behind the lines consisting of Allied agents and Italian collaborators to guide the efforts of the insurrectionists. In the case of the British missions, these groups generally consisted of three men: an Allied chief of mission, an instructor/sabotage specialist, and a radio operator; while the US missions were much larger, in some cases reaching fifteen to twenty men. Allied higher headquarters had some reservations regarding the intentions of some of the resistance groups and sought to limit aid to them, especially with respect to arms and ammunition, fearing repetition of what was happening in Greece, where following liberation communist forces unleashed a guerrilla war in an attempt to install themselves as the government. This conduct led to favoring certain groups that seemed more reliable over others whose loyalty was doubtful, although this policy was not always observed in the field by all of the "missionaries" to the point that in some areas some of them that had "leftist" sympathies funneled most of the aid to the left-leaning "Garibaldini" formations, rather than to the more conservative "autonomous" formations. In the field this behavior was offset by theft and appropriation of various sorts.

Until December 1944, the conduct of these behind-the-line operations was under British control, whereas after January 1945, control passed into United States' hands. This may explain why until a certain date the weapons dropped or furnished to the partisans were mainly of British origin (even though they originated from various producers, among them the United States), while beginning in January, US weapons began to be supplied. Whereas the British had some difficulty finding members for their missions who could speak Italian, the situation was markedly different for the US missions. A large influx of Italian immigrants—mostly from southern Italy—in the early 1900s resulted in an Italian—or more precisely an Italian regional dialect—spoken in many households; this phenomenon lasted until at least the 1960s. Southern Italian dialects were markedly different from the language and local dialects spoken in northern Italy, and although the US missions were at times able to draw upon soldiers who spoke the regional dialect of northern Italy, even those who spoke the southern dialect were able to communicate effectively on a basic level with the partisans and engendered an enhanced degree of good will and cooperation.

Despite disagreements among themselves and the varying nature of their discussions with the Allies, the partisans were able to render the German rear areas extremely dangerous, forcing them to divert substantial combat forces from front-line duty, thus easing pressure on Allied liberation forces.

The information and photographs presented in this book relate to partisan formations in the region of Italy known as the Langhe, in Piedmont, and in

Liguria; this is the area to the west and northwest of Genoa. More specifically, the documentation and images refer largely to a number of Garibaldi formations, chief among them the 1st Garibaldi Assault Division "Gin Bevilacqua" and its subordinate units, the 3rd Garibaldi Assault Brigade "Libero Briganti," 4th Garibaldi Assault Brigade "Daniele Manin," and 5th Garibaldi Assault Brigade "Baltera." This regional focus is a function of the access Gianluigi Usai had to documentation and photographic sources in the area of Genoa and Savona; regarding the weapons used by partisans, the information is applicable and valid for the partisan movement throughout Italy, regardless of the political orientation of the formations involved. At the outset the partisans armed themselves with whatever was immediately available, usually weapons taken from Italian army arms rooms or depots, and progressively replaced those with more capable weapons either captured from the Germans or supplied by Allied missions. Standardization of weapons or of ammunition calibers was far from a hallmark of the partisan arms inventory.

## Weapons of the Partisans

An examination of weapons used by the partisans reveals an interesting range of worldwide small arms production in the years prior to WWII and includes what can only be described as museum pieces, such as pinfire revolvers going as far back as the 1870s. The only important thing was they were able to fire.

Bit by bit the oldest weapons—for which ammunition was difficult to obtain—were largely discarded in favor of the newcomer on the scene: the submachine gun.

We can subdivide the small arms used in Italian territory according to their origins:

The liberation of Florence: whomever has just fired used a black powder weapon, probably a pin-fire revolver like the one being held by the individual behind the cloud of smoke. *ISREC Savona*

- Nationally produced weapons
- Weapons furnished by the Allies during WWI
- Austrian war booty from WWI
- French, Greek, Yugoslav, and Russian weapons captured at the beginning of WWII
- Weapons captured from the Germans or their RSI allies
- Weapons supplied by the Allies either by air drops or directly across the lines

The first group includes all of the principal pistols issued to the Italian army: revolvers such as the Mod. 1874 and Mod. 1889, semi-auto pistols such as the Glis-

**REWARD FOR TURNING IN WEAPONS**

"To anyone who turns in or assist in turning in weapons formerly belonging to the Italian Armed Forces shall receive as a reward:

For each pistol ..........................................L. 100
For each rifle or carbine................................" 200
For each automatic rifle or machine gun.........." 500

"Such weapons must be reported and delivered to an Italian military command or to the Magistrate or the Carabinieri, and - in accordance with the orders of the German authorities of the area – their turn-in must be reported to the authorities themselves. The military authorities or the Magistrates will pay the above amount as soon as the weapon is turned in, and will request reimbursement from the Provincial Military Headquarters."

THE CHIEF OF STAFF OF THE ARMY
*Gambara*

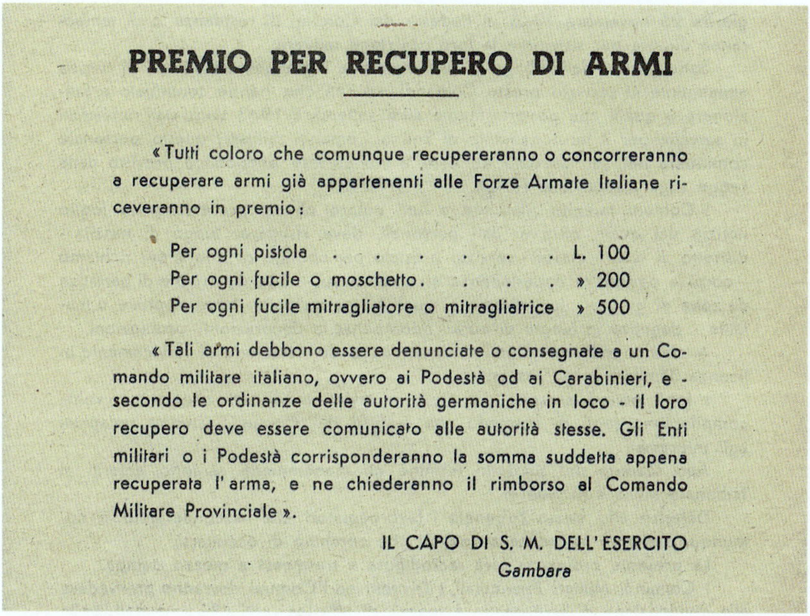

**PREMIO PER RECUPERO DI ARMI**

«Tutti coloro che comunque recupereranno o concorreranno a recuperare armi già appartenenti alle Forze Armate Italiane riceveranno in premio:

Per ogni pistola . . . . . . . . L. 100
Per ogni fucile o moschetto. . . . . » 200
Per ogni fucile mitragliatore o mitragliatrice » 500

«Tali armi debbono essere denunciate o consegnate a un Comando militare italiano, ovvero ai Podestà od ai Carabinieri, e - secondo le ordinanze delle autorità germaniche in loco - il loro recupero deve essere comunicato alle autorità stesse. Gli Enti militari o i Podestà corrisponderanno la somma suddetta appena recuperata l'arma, e ne chiederanno il rimborso al Comando Militare Provinciale».

IL CAPO DI S. M. DELL'ESERCITO
*Gambara*

A flier requesting weapons abandoned after September 8, 1943, be handed in to military or civil authorities. *G. Gonnella*

enti, and the entire range of Beretta pistols from the Mod. 1915 to the Mod. 1934. Then there are all of the variants of the Model 1891 rifle and carbines, along with the odd Vetterli-Vitali, both in its original caliber and those converted to 6.5 mm.

Initially, the only fully automatic weapon available was the Beretta Mod. 38A, while the reigning light machine gun was the Breda 30. Heavy machine guns consisted of the Fiat 35 and Breda 37. A few examples of the Fiat 1914 were still available, as were some SIA, Breda-SAFAT, and others.

The MAS 38 allegedly used to kill Mussolini recently discovered in a museum in Tirana, Albania.

Among the machine guns furnished by the Allies during WWI were the French Hotchkiss, Saint Etienne, and Chauchat, and some very old US Colts.

The chief Austrian weapon was undoubtedly the Schwarzlose machine gun, of which a number of examples were found in Italian territory, while most had been issued to colonial troops. Mannlicher M1895 rifles and Steyr pistols—mainly the Mod. 1912—could also be encountered.

The various territories that Italy occupied during the initial phases of WWII yielded a number of light machine guns, such as the Chatellerault M1924/29 taken in France, many French Mod. 1926 Hotchkiss light machine guns captured in Greece, and numerous Czech ZB 26/30 captured in Yugoslavia. The SACM 1935 semi-auto pistol and the 7.65L MAS 38 submachine gun, according to credible accounts, fired the fatal burst that killed Mussolini. The first Thompson submachine guns also came from France, having been furnished by the United States during the early months of the war.

The list of weapons captured from the Germans is very extensive; in addition to weapons actually produced by the Germans, the Wehrmacht was in possession of weapons from disarming the armies of half of Europe. As a result, in addition to classic German issue military weapons such as the Luger P08 , Walther P38, various Mauser rifles, and the MP40, MG34, and MG42 machine guns, we find a varied panoply of small arms of French, Belgian, Norwegian, and Czech origin. Weapons from almost all of Europe, including occupied nations and nations that in some way collaborated with Germany, such as Spain, which furnished over 100,000 pistols; and Finland, which furnished 3,000 Suomi M31 submachine guns, were also common.

The partisans also used some newly introduced weapons, such as the Gew. 41 and Gew. 43 semi-auto rifles and later the FG42 paratrooper's rifle, and finally the StG44 or MP 43, which was the forerunner of the modern assault rifle.

Among the weapons in this category two new Italian designs (TZ45 and FNAB43 submachine guns) can be included.

To add to the confusion, SS units acquired weapons independently and issued whatever they deemed adequate, which explains the presence of many MP 34 and 35 and many MP34(o), which was the Austrian version of the Steyr/Solothurn SI100, as well as old MP18 and MP28 submachine guns.

In this final group we can also number the weapon that became an icon of the resistance: the Sten—almost exclusively the MkII version—in addition to the Bren and Thompson—mainly the 1928 and 1928A1 versions that were

A partisan with a Lewis machine gun originally mounted on an aircraft. This is the only photograph we have found of a partisan armed with such a weapon, and we are unaware of any evidence the Lewis was used operationally by partisan forces. *Michele Becchi*

A 12.7 mm SAFAT aircraft machine gun on an improvised mount in use by RSI forces; this type of machine gun was also put to use by partisans. The wooden chest for Mod. 35 hand grenades in the background is likely filled with sand as part of the protective parapet. *Giancarlo Garello*

supplied to the British. From the United States, we find the Thompson M1 and M1A1, some M3 (but no M3A1), the UD M42 (furnished by British services), many M1903 bolt-action rifles and a small number of Garands, some M1 and M1A1 carbines with either full-length or folding stocks, Colt 1911A1 pistols, Colt and Smith & Wesson revolvers, BAR automatic rifles, and various models of Browning 1919 machine guns.

A considerable number of weapons of Argentine origin—such as the Ballester Molina—and Spanish weapons—such as the Llama, which were copies of the Colt 1911A1—were supplied by air drop.

The Allies essentially divided the areas of Italy in which they were to supply weapons so weapons that were very common in one area were completely unknown in others. A typical example was the Garand, many of which show up in areas contiguous to areas occupied by US forces, while they are not found at all only a few miles away.

In light of the Italian motto *non si butta via niente* ("nothing gets thrown away"), we have to mention the practice of salvaging machine guns from downed or damaged aircraft and fabricating improvised mounts for them. We find .30-caliber Browning 1919 and .50-caliber M2 machine guns from US aircraft, .303-caliber Brownings from British aircraft, various caliber Breda SAFATs and 7.7 mm Lewis guns from Italian aircraft, and the usual panoply of German machine guns, such as the MG13 and MG15. The latter pair had already been

**VAL PESIO BRIGADE**

30 July 1944

TO HEADQUARTERS "ALPI" ALPINE DIVISION HEADQUARTERS

For information
TO HEADQUARTERS DETACHMENT 6..... HEADQUARTERS
TO HEADQUARTERS DETACHMENT 7..... HEADQUARTERS

SUBJECT; Repairs to salvaged aircraft machine gun.-

It is urgent to repair the machine guns salvaged from the fallen aircraft; I therefore order that:

1) – all of the equipment that was salvaged or that is to be salvaged be brought to Pian Delle Gorre.
2) The non-commissioned machine gunner Robert, assisted by patriots Cartagenova Edilio and Ferro Eros will see to the repair of the above mentioned machine guns.
3) Robert-Cartagenova-Ferro will for some period of time move from Gias Madonna and transfer to Detachment No, 7 (Pian Delle Gorre).
4) Patriots Ferro-Cartagenova are charged with designing a tripod to be fixed to the body of the machine gun.
5) I be notified of any difficulties that may be encountered to carry out the above orders.

The Commander

*see page 20*

"recycled" by their previous users and can be found either modified by the Germans or in a more field expedient configuration done by the partisans.

All civilian weapons found in the area were also used, including shotguns, which were undoubtedly widely available despite numerous directives issued

Staff Sgt. Maurice LaRouche wearing the Silver Star. *Giancarlo Garello*

**Staff Sgt. Maurice "Robert" LaRouche** was reportedly born in Quebec, Canada, in 1918, and died in Florida in 2007. During the war he served with the US Army Air Corps, 15th Air Force, in the Mediterranean theater. On March 29, 1944, he was part of the crew of B-17 42-97152 of the 20th Squadron, 2nd Bomb Group—serving as a machine gunner—when the bomber was attacked by four Fiat G-55 fighters of the Italian Social Republic Air Force that shot the aircraft down over Cairo Montenotte. Of the ten crew members, all were taken prisoner except for Staff Sgt. Maurice LaRouche, who evaded capture and stayed with Italian partisan forces for several months; he was especially valued by the partisans for his ability to repair machine guns they had salvaged from downed aircraft. He subsequently joined the Allied mission headed by Capt. Long, ultimately making his way across the Alps to Ventimiglia and then by rowboat to Nice, France, and back to the 2nd Bomb Group. La Rouche was awarded the Silver Star for conspicuous gallantry and intrepidity in action for his work with the partisans.

BRIGATA VAL PESIO

li 30 luglio 1944-

AL COMANDO DIVISIONE ALPINA"ALPI" → SEDE

e.p.conoscenza AL COMANDO DISTACCAMENTO.....N° 6 SEDE

AL COMANDO DISTACCAMENTO.....N° 7 SEDE

OGGETTO: Sistemazione mitragliere ricuperate aereo.-

Urge la rimessa in efficenza delle mitragliatrici ricuperate dall'aereo caduto; pertanto dispongo:

1)- tutto il materiale ricuperato e da ricuperare sia portato al Pian Delle Gorre.

2)- il sottufficiale mitragliere Robert, coaudiovato dai patrioti Cartageneva Edilio e Ferro Eros, cureranno la rimessa in efficenza delle mitragliatrici suddette.-

3)- Robert-Cartageneva-Ferro dal Gias Madonna, per qualche tempo si trasferiranno al distaccamento n°7 (Pian delle Gorre)

4)- I patrioti Ferro-Cartageneva sono incaricati di studiare un treppiedi da applicare al corpo della mitragliatrice.-

5)- mi siano segnalate le eventuali difficoltà che potranno essere incontrate per mettere in esecuzione quanto sopra disposto

Il Comandante

by the Germans ordering the civilian population to turn in all firearms, including sporting weapons.

Finally weapons were stolen from other partisan units by disarming them or convincing them to "change the color of their neckerchief" (i.e., to switch their allegiance from one partisan band to another espousing a different ideology).

This document from an ideologically communist unit shows no qualms about authorizing outright theft to the detriment of another partisan unit, which in this case happens to be an ideologically conservative "autonomous" unit deemed more fortunate regarding their supplies while professing to promise cooperation by outlining the procedures for receiving the weapons.

COMITATO DI LIBERAZIONE NAZIONALE

CORPO VOLONTARIO DELLA LIBERTA

BRIGATA DASSALTO GARIBALDI(MARIO SAMBOLINO)

Oggetto Aumento armi ricuperate

Si segnala l'assegnamento del seguenti armi, ai Distacc. NINO,e BORREANI.
N°2 mitra Beretta con due caricatori,N°I parabello(Russo) con 55 colpi.N°I fucile semiautomatico(Russo)e8bombe a mano, N°8 moschetti Italini e due Tedeschi
Le sopradette armi sono state ricuperate a Partigiani sbandati.

ZONA X li 27-I-45 L'INTENDENTE

Visto

---

ITALIAN NATIONAL LIBERATION COMMITTEE
VOLUNTEER CORPS FOR LIBERTY

"MARIO SAMBOLINO" GARIBALDI ASSAULT BRIGADE

Subject Increase of recovered weapons

Assignment of the following weapons is noted to Detachments NINO and BORREANI.
2 Beretta submachine guns, with two magazines, 1 parabellum (Russian) with 55 rounds. 1 semi-automatic rifle (Russian) and 8 hand grenades. 8 Italian and two German carbines.
The above mentioned weapons were taken from partisan stragglers.

ZONE X dated 27-I-45 THE SUPPLY OFFICER

"LANGHE,,
NANNI ,,
RAGGRUPPAMENTO
" LUPO ,,

Zona 29/IO/44.

OMITATO DI LIBERAZIONE NAZIONALE
po Volontari della Libertà

ò: Diserzioni.

In riscontro alla V./ del 27/IO/44 posso affermare che una squadra proveniente da Ferrania o di ri= orno si è presentata a Cortemilia e quindi inviata a Castino in una formazione Mauri e precisamente nella seconda Divisione, al coman= do di Poli. - Ho sentito altre voci le quali parlano di circa 40- uomini provenienti dalla Liguria ma non posso precisare niente, cercherò di assumere informazioni esatte.

Oggetto: Lanci.

Lanci, assicuro nel modo più categorico che fino ad oggi non ho avuto nessun lancio.- Qualora vi trovaste nelle prossimità d'una formazione Mauri la quale riceva lanci, potrei darVI la possibilità di rubargliene alcuni, tengo però a precisarVi che soltanto da giorni ho potuto mettermi in contatto con persone a conoscenza dei loro segnali.

Fortuna e gloria alle N./ Brigate Garibaldine, morte ai nazifascisti.

IL COMANDANTE

Lupo

Comando Raggruppamento "Lupo"

9

GARIBALDI ASSAULT BRIGADE "LANGHE"
(indistinct) "NANNI"
GROUP
"LUPO"

Zone 29/10/44

ITALIAN NATIONAL LIBERATION COMMITTEE
Volunteer Corps for Liberty

Subject: Desertions

In reply to your letter of 27/10/44
I can not confirm that a squad coming from or returning to Ferrania made its appearance at Cortemila and was then sent to Castino in a Mauri formation and specifically in the Second Division, under the command of Poli. I also heard other rumors which spoke of about 40 men coming from Liguria but can add no specifics but will try to obtain more precise information.

Subject: Air drops

Air drops, I can assure you categorically that until today I have received no air drops. Whenever you are able to find yourself near a Mauri formation that receives supplies by air drop, it might afford you the opportunity to steal some of them, but I have to inform you that it has been only a few days since I have been able to be in contact with persons who are privy to their signals.

Fortune and glory to our Garibaldi Brigades,
Death to the Nazi-Fascists

THE COMMANDER
(signed Lupo – "Wolf")

## CHAPTER II

# HISTORICAL AND DOCUMENTARY REFERENCES

The relationship between partisans and the weapons they used is an interesting aspect of the history of the period. All of the sources we have consulted agree the contributions of deserters from the Italian divisions trained in Germany provided worthwhile assistance to the resistance movement, which had already obtained support from Italian soldiers who had abandoned the army following the September 8, 1943, armistice.

From a tactical point of view, little could be expected of the "political" members of the resistance or from draft evaders who had never in their lives held a weapon in their hands, except for those few who were veterans of the civil war in Spain.

Taking all of these considerations into account a basic question arises: what was accomplished by all of the "Fascist Saturdays," pre-military training, and various other military training programs to which the Italian populace was subjected for so many years to transform them into a warrior society?

For example, here is oral testimony relating to training with weapons:

> Then, when they handed me the submachine gun, I thought the bullets were supposed to come out of the holes [the vent holes in the cooling jacket of the Beretta MAB submachine gun]. Afterwards it didn't take much to learn about the weapon and how things were done.[1]

Savona in the days immediately following the liberation of Italy; the partisan in the center is holding a MAS 1938. *ISREC Savona*

A second observation regards the almost fanatical idolatry for the new weapon that had just recently been introduced: the submachine gun.

Fenoglio provides a vivid description of the impulses that motivated the partisans: "'...Geo said he couldn't resist the temptation to try firing on full automatic: didn't they understand? He had never fired a full auto burst!'" Tito then commented he would have to account to Mario for the missing rounds: "'And he readied the weapon,

Alba during the period of the "twenty-three days" of October 1944. The individual in shorts is "Maj. Mauri," with his ever-present Thompson slung over his shoulder. *Courtesy Don Angelo Siri*

but with a disdainful attitude – You have never fired a burst. Do you think you know how to control the burst the first time you try? You'll empty half a magazine before you realize it... - But in that moment Geo pulled the trigger, letting loose six or seven rounds at the intact tree trunks.'"[2]

Although not with the same compulsion, at least some idea of what was to be the distinctive hallmark of a commander is described in the first meeting between Duccio Galimberti and Giorgio Bocca:

We found ourselves in the midst of men dressed like shepherds from Abruzzi and we were amazed when we saw their armament. They all had rifles and the tallest one had

Giuseppe "Beppe" Fenoglio postwar. *Lorenza Balbo*

**Giuseppe Fenoglio** (March 1, 1922–February 18, 1963)—better known as Beppe Fenoglio—was a writer, partisan, and dramatist. He was an Anglophile with a command of the English language, enabling him to do translation work. In 1943, he was an officer cadet; following the September 8 armistice, he returned to the Langhe area and at first joined the Communist Garibaldi Brigades, but soon switched his allegiance to the "independent" or "Badoglio" 1st Alpine Division Group commanded by Enrico Martini ("Mauri"), ultimately serving in the "Belbo" Brigade 2nd Langhe Division under Piero Balbo. Thanks to his command of the English language, from January to April 1945, he was assigned as a liaison officer between the Allied forces and the partisan units led by Martini and Balbo. After the liberation of Italy he worked in a winery while also beginning to write articles and books, none of which met with much success. Suffering from bronchial cancer—he reportedly smoked up to sixty cigarettes a day—he died in February 1963. His most acclaimed novel, *Il partigiano Johnny* [Johnny the Partisan], in which he told the story of the Italian resistance movement in an innovative fashion that was neither moralistic nor ponderous, initially was not well received, but is now considered one of the leading voices of the resistance. It was published posthumously in 1968.

> a very strange weapon. He was the lawyer Galimberti. He answered our question with a laugh: "It's a MAS38, a French weapon, but I carry it to impress my friends, I have only twenty rounds in the magazine..."[4]

The "commoner" who has "never fired a burst" and wants to feel the thrill is thus contrasted to a cultured person who knows well what image he must project of himself and the power he wields.

Enrico Martini, better known as "Mauri" in the partisan movement. *Don Angelo Siri*

**Enrico Martini** (January 29, 1911–September 19, 1976) was known by the partisan pseudonym "Mauri." Martini attended the Italian Military Academy in Modena beginning in 1929, becoming an officer in the alpine corps. In 1936, while assigned to the 7th Alpine Regiment of the Pusteria Division, he participated in the Ethiopian campaign, fighting at the battle of Lake Ashangi, and was awarded the Cross for Military Valor. In April 1941, he was promoted to captain and was sent to North Africa, where he remained until 1943, by which time he had been promoted to major. He returned to Italy in spring 1943 and was assigned to the Italian Army Staff in Rome; following the September 8, 1943, armistice with the Allies, he joined a unit of Granatieri (Grenadiers) in an ill-fated attempt to defend Rome from German seizure. He then made his way to Piedmont, where he was captured by the Germans and imprisoned in Apuania; on the night of September 17 he escaped. His political orientation was supportive of the monarchy and he organized, founded, and commanded the partisan *1o Gruppo Divisioni Alpine* (1st Alpine Division Group), the largest and most effective independent partisan group of the Italian resistance movement. On April 25, 1945, it had nine partisan divisions with a total of some 10,000 men; during twenty months of fighting the Alpine Division Group participated in the liberation of Torino, Asti, Alessandria, Alba, Bra, Mondovì, Ceva, and Savona, and sustained some 900 killed and 1,000 wounded. In 1947, he retired from the Italian army as a lieutenant colonel and subsequently earned a law degree. Following the war, he changed his name to Enrico Martini Mauri. He died in a plane crash in Antalya, Turkey, on September 19, 1976. He was awarded many military decorations, including the Italian Gold Medal for Military Valor, the US Bronze Star, and the Polish Gold Cross. He was also awarded the title *Cavaliere di gran croce dell'Ordine al merito della Repubblica italiana* (Knight of the Great Cross of the Order of Merit of the Italian Republic) in 1963.

Witness to the fact the submachine gun had replaced the command baton can be found in a reference by Mauri—who was known for his partiality toward the Thompson—when one of his officers was treated badly by his men because "...he had the audacity to say that he is Bogliolo's chief of staff, .......but is armed with a carbine; if he was really a chief of staff he would be carrying at least a Sten."

> Mauri concludes:
> The partisan has a logic all his own; for him the hierarchy is a function of weaponry carried. It is partly for this reason that I continue to put up with the weight of the Thompson, which was a gift and remembrance of Maj. Temple.

From 1943 to 1945, use of the submachine gun was widespread by units of the Italian Social Republic and the partisans to the point it became the very

Maj. Neville Darewski, known by the alias "Maj. Temple" while working with the partisans. *Don Angelo Siri*

**Maj. Temple** was the pseudonym for Maj. Neville Lawrence Temple Darewski, 1st Special Force SOE. Darewski was born May 21, 1914, in London, the son of a well-known Russian-born conductor and composer, Herman Darewski, and Madge Temple. His mother's maiden name was used as an alias while in the SOE. Prior to his military service Darewski/Temple resided in Devonshire and was educated at Haileybury College, Hertfordshire. He became an officer in the Royal Army Ordnance Corps, but was later posted to the SOE. Darewski was one of the SOE's most experienced officers, having spent from August 1943 to March 1944 in the area of the Slovenian and Italian borderlands (Operation Livingstone II), during which time by his own estimate he covered some thousand miles on foot. Darewski was in the field in Italy since August 7, 1944, as part of Operation Flap, and was well known and liked by the partisans. On November 15, 1944, while directing evacuation of his mission under sustained enemy mortar fire, Darewski was accidentally crushed by a partisan truck in Marsaglia, in Val Ellero. The actual date of his death is somewhat unclear; although it appears the accident was on November 15, he did not succumb to his injuries until November 16. Darewski is buried in Staglieno Monumental Cemetery, Genoa; the cemetery has a separate section containing graves of British and Commonwealth servicemen from both world wars. Darewski was awarded the DSO.

Darewski's tombstone in Staglieno Cemetery, Genoa. *Sabina Usai*

military symbol of the civil war itself; if one looks at monuments to the resistance scattered throughout northern Italy, one will quickly notice all of the statues are carrying what came to be considered the icon of the movement: the Sten.

The insurgents particularly abhorred the various versions of the Model 1891 Carcano rifle and this determined the reaction of the resistance commands themselves, who were well aware that in an encounter between a man armed with a submachine gun and one armed with a rifle at a range of 300 meters [984 ft], the fate of the first was at the mercy of the second. This led the headquarters to deplore sovereign disrespect for the carbine and rifle and the cult that surrounded the submachine gun. Although recognizing this was certainly the ideal weapon for ambushes and close-in combat at less than 100 meters [328 ft.], the fact remained that in a mountain environment a reliable marksman armed with a carbine—or better yet an old Model 91 long rifle or a German Mauser—was worth more than a submachine gunner, making possible the dictum "one bullet for every enemy and one enemy for every bullet."

These instructions are contained in a circular dated January 25, 1945, in which the Piedmont Regional Military Headquarters requests subordinate units to adequately train personnel to avoid wasting ammunition often used in fruitless shooting because the targets were outside the range of the weapon.

Allied mission personnel—who were often career military personnel—shared the same outlook. For example, Roy Farran writes in his memoirs *Winged Dagger* concerning his experience in northern Italy: "They would fire with Stens at ranges of over two thousand yards, but if the Germans came any closer they would run away."[5]

If one considers the effective range of a Sten was between fifty and a hundred meters [164–328 ft], it can be easily understood how well-trained soldiers were dumbfounded at the absurd pretension of using it at a range exceeding 1,800 meters [5,905 ft]. Certainly the headquarters did not consider the fact it was not simple possession of a weapon, nor even a rapid-fire weapon such as the MG42 that could make a hero of a partisan.

On September 16, 1944, commander of the RSI "San Marco" Division Gen. Farina—billeted in western Liguria and with responsibility for the Langhe area as well—issued a circular addressed to all of his subordinates to rebut rumors being spread by partisans to put themselves in an impressive light.

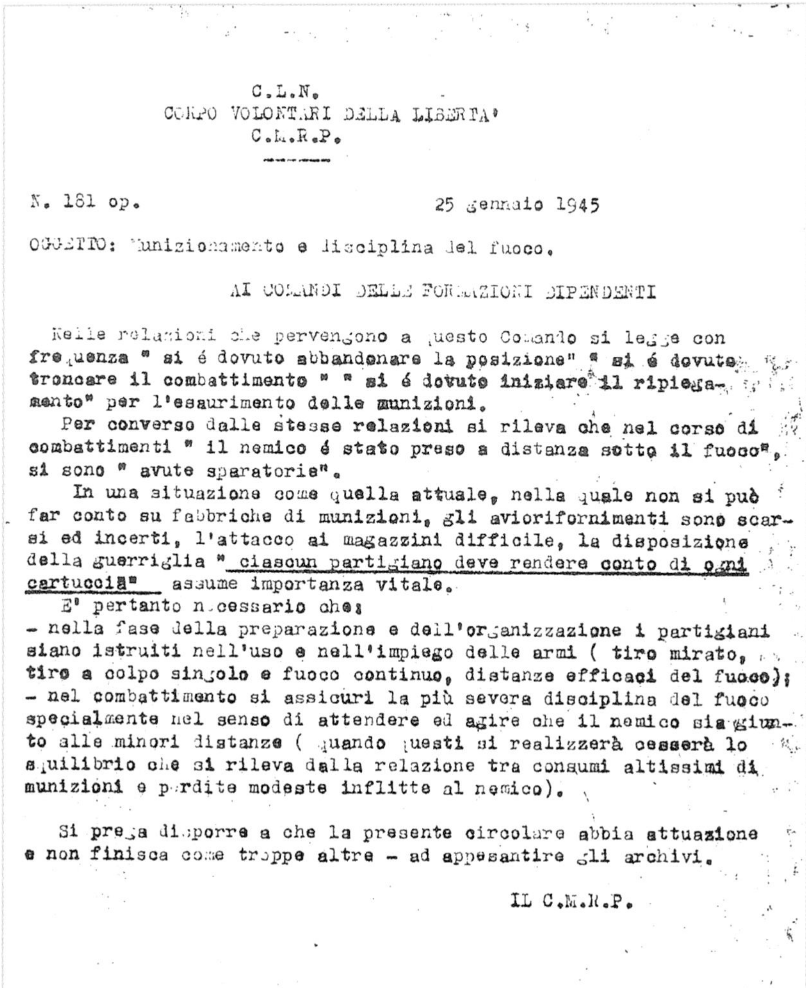

C.L.N.
CORPO VOLONTARI DELLA LIBERTA'
C.M.R.P.

N. 181 op. 25 gennaio 1945

OGGETTO: Munizionamento e disciplina del fuoco.

AI COMANDI DELLE FORMAZIONI DIPENDENTI

Nelle relazioni che pervengono a questo Comando si legge con frequenza " si é dovuto abbandonare la posizione" " si é dovuto troncare il combattimento " " si é dovuto iniziare il ripiegamento" per l'esaurimento delle munizioni.

Per converso dalle stesse relazioni si rileva che nel corso di combattimenti " il nemico é stato preso a distanza sotto il fuoco", si sono " avute sparatorie".

In una situazione come quella attuale, nella quale non si può far conto su fabbriche di munizioni, gli aviorifornimenti sono scarsi ed incerti, l'attacco ai magazzini difficile, la disposizione della guerriglia " ciascun partigiano deve rendere conto di ogni cartuccia" assume importanza vitale.

E' pertanto necessario che:
- nella fase della preparazione e dell'organizzazione i partigiani siano istruiti nell'uso e nell'impiego delle armi ( tiro mirato, tiro a colpo singolo e fuoco continuo, distanze efficaci del fuoco);
- nel combattimento si assicuri la più severa disciplina del fuoco specialmente nel senso di attendere ed agire che il nemico sia giunto alle minori distanze ( quando questi si realizzerà cesserà lo squilibrio che si rileva dalla relazione tra consumi altissimi di munizioni e perdite modeste inflitte al nemico).

Si prega disporre a che la presente circolare abbia attuazione e non finisca come troppe altre - ad appesantire gli archivi.

IL C.M.R.P.

One of the points he made related to the submachine gun:

> Regarding armament, you will hear the most astonishing claims that the partisan groups have cannons, mortars, machine guns, armored cars, and that every partisan has a submachine gun (Stens or Thompsons that have been air dropped). Speaking of the Sten, at 50 meters [164 ft] from the muzzle there is a 5-meter [16.4 ft] shot dispersion; there is a lot of noise but minimal effectiveness! The partisans suffer from a lack of ammunition; they end up paying 10 lire for each Sten cartridge.[6]

This opinion seems contrary to what Hermann Wygoda—commander of the “Gin Bevilacqua” Division operating in the Savona area—had to say with respect to this weapon:

C.L.N
VOLUNTEER CORPS FOR LIBERTY
C.M.R.P.

N. 181 op. 25 January 1945

SUBJECT: Ammunition and fire discipline.

FOR HEADQUARTERS OF SUBORDINATE UNITS

In reports received by this Headquarters it is frequently mentioned that "the position had to be abandoned", "the action had to be broken off", and "withdrawal had to be initiated" because ammunition ran out.

On the other hand the same reports reveal that during the combat engagements "the enemy was taken under fire at long range" and that "firing was exchanged".

In a situation such as we are presently in, in which we cannot count on ammunition supplies from factories, in which air drops are infrequent and uncertain, and attacks on storage facilities are difficult to carry out, the guerrilla maxim that "every partisan has to account for every cartridge" assumes a vital importance.

It is thus necessary that:

In the preparation and organization phase the partisans are instructed in the use and employment of weapons (aimed fire, single-shot and sustained fire, effective ranges);

In combat the most stringent fire discipline be ensured, especially in the sense of biding time and initiating action only when the enemy is within close range (when this is achieved the imbalance that is experienced between very high ammunition expenditure rates and modest losses inflicted on the enemy will cease).

Please see to it that this circular is acted upon and that it does not end up like too many others – that only serve to make the files heavier.

THE C.M.R.P.

> Later we acquired from the Allied command a great number of Sten guns. This British light submachine gun was the most efficient piece of automatic hardware we had on hand. These, along with somewhat less efficient German light submachine guns, were the best weapons for partisan use. With such a weapon, a man who was light on foot and had good agility, as well as a dose of courage, could perform miracles in the mountains, where topography was a partisan's best friend. For other types of battle, the rapid-firing German heavy machine gun was, we found, quite preferable to the slower, heavier British version.[7]

Another partisan leader named Giorgio Bocca did not allow himself to get caught up with this infatuation:

= COMITATO DI LIBERAZIONE NAZIONALE =
= CORPO VOLONTARIO DELLA LIBERTA' =
IV° BRIGATA D'ASSALTO "GARIBALDI" = D. MANIN =
Distaccamento SILVIO TORCELLO

lì 7 Novembre 1944

AL COMANDO DELLA IV° BRIGATA.

OGGETTO : Relazione dell'Ufficiale alle operazioni sull'azione compiuta.

Alle ore 0,30 di stamani gli uomini di una squadra si portavano - dopo aver ricevuto singole istruzioni - in posizioni adatte per attaccare una postazione tedesca.
8 uomini con una mitraglia stavano avvicinandosi al punto stabilito onde aprire il fuoco sulla sentinella e sul baraccamento che serve di alloggio al personale della postazione, quando il volontario SPEGNAFUOCO incaricato di eliminare col fuoco del semi-automatico il soldato di guardia, al solo vederlo distante circa 30 metri ha abbandonato l'arma dandosi a fuga precipitosa seguito da :
BEDINO = che abbandonava la canna di ricambio della M.G. 42 ;
TIGRE = che abbandonava la cassetta contenente le munizioni della mitragliatrice;
PARDO =
KIM =
Tale fatto ha pregiudicato irrimediabilmente il favorevole esito dell'azione, in quanto il fuggire scomposto dei suddetti volontari ha messo in allarme la sentinella ed ha lasciato il mitragliere con l'arma dotata di un nastro di soli 40 colpi.
Quanto sopra si fa presente per i provvedimenti del caso a carico dei sunnominati.

L'UFF. D'OPERAZIONI | I° C. SQ. | II° C. SQ.

IL COMMISS. POLIT. DI SQ.

The Model 1891 rifles and carbines are relatively plentiful. The British further furnish (and it almost seems to be a joke) rifles used in colonial wars at the turn of the century. Ammunition is in short supply, and a partisan usually carries about a dozen six-round clips in his knapsack. During the summer, about twenty out of a hundred partisans have an automatic weapon: submachine guns and *maschinenpistole*[8] captured from the enemy, but most of all Stens air dropped by the Allies. The

ITALIAN NATIONAL LIBERATION COMMITTEE
VOLUNTEER CORPS FOR LIBERTY
IV "GARIBALDI" ASSAULT BRIGADE "D. MANIN"
SILVIO TORCELLO Detachment

7 November 1944

TO HEADQUARTERS 1V BRIGADE
SUBJECT: Report of the Operations Officer relating to action completed.

At 0.30 hours this morning the men of a squad took up positions – after having received individual instructions – to attack a German post.

8 men with a machine gun were approaching the point established in order to open fire on the sentinel and against the barracks that served as housing for the personnel of the post when volunteer SPUTAFUOCO (SPITFIRE) who was charged with eliminating the soldier on guard with fire from the semi-automatic, upon being seen at a distance of about 30 meters dropped his weapon and ran off quickly, followed by: BEDINO = who abandoned the spare barrel of the MG42;
TIGRE (TIGER) = who jettisoned the chests containing the ammunition for the machine gun;
PARDO=
KIM=
This fact irremediably precluded the favorable outcome of the action, inasmuch as the flight of the above mentioned volunteers alerted the sentinel and left the machine gunner with a weapon with only 40 rounds in its belt.
The above information is provided for appropriate action by the above named addressees.

THE OPERATIONS OFFICER I SQUAD LEADER II SQUAD LEADER

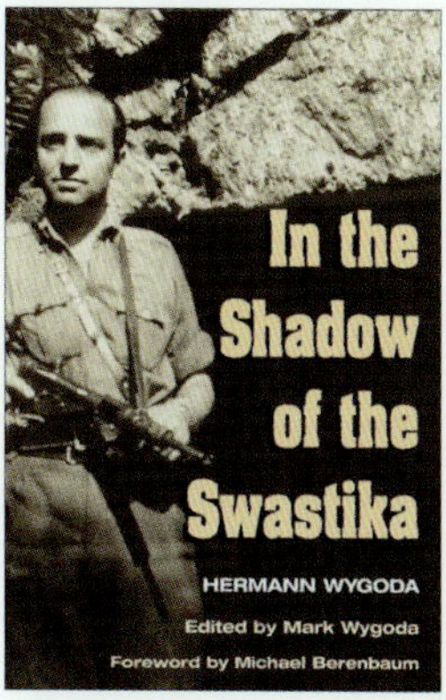


Hermann Wygoda, the Polish Jew who joined the partisan movement and became known as "Comandante Enrico." *ISREC Savona*

Hermann Wygoda was born in Germany in 1906, but around 1929, his family moved to Poland after his father died. In Poland, Wygoda earned a degree in civil engineering and became an officer in the Polish army. Wygoda, who was Jewish, spoke seven languages fluently and pretended to be an ethnic German to avoid the consequences of being a Jew. He eventually made his way to Italy as an employee of a German company, where in early 1944, he became a leader in the Italian partisan movement and was known as Comandante Enrico. In May 1944, he became the commander of the *20a Brigata d'Assalto Garibaldi* (20th Garibaldi Assault Brigade), which in August changed its name to *2a Brigata d'Assalto Garibaldi* (2nd Garibaldi Assault Brigade). In late summer 1944, Wygoda assumed command of the 4th Daniele Manin Brigade, and on February 1, 1945, he was appointed commander of the newly formed partisan *1a Divisione d'Assalto Garibaldi "Gin Bevilacqua"* (1st Garibaldi Assault Division "Gin Bevilacqua"). After the war he was awarded the US Bronze Star. He left Italy and moved to the United States, where he settled in Chattanooga, Tennessee, working at first as a ditch digger, but later becoming an independent home builder in the Chattanooga area. He died in 1982.

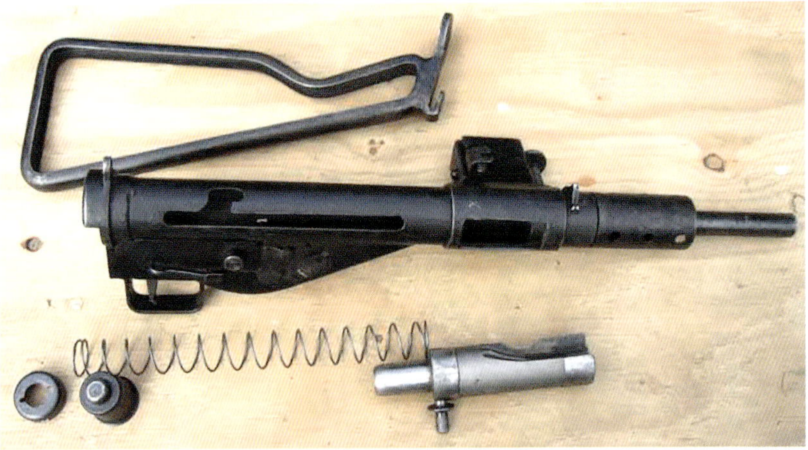

A disassembled Sten gun.

A recently discovered (2014) arms cache in Genoa. Whoever hid these weapons probably read the writings of Giorgio Bocca and realized the dream of having a Marlin UD M42 and an M1 carbine as a pair. *Gianluigi Usai files*

Sten is a short submachine gun that resembles a crude toy: a tube of blued metal covers the barrel and serves as a grip.

The weapon is easy to use, has a high rate of fire, and rarely jams, but it is made for use by commandos for short-range engagements; during sweeps in the mountains it is worthless, and at ranges of more than 60 meters [197ft] its fire is ineffective because of the large dispersal pattern and its poor sights. After initial bitter experiences there is among the partisans, if not refusal of the Sten, the desire to have some other

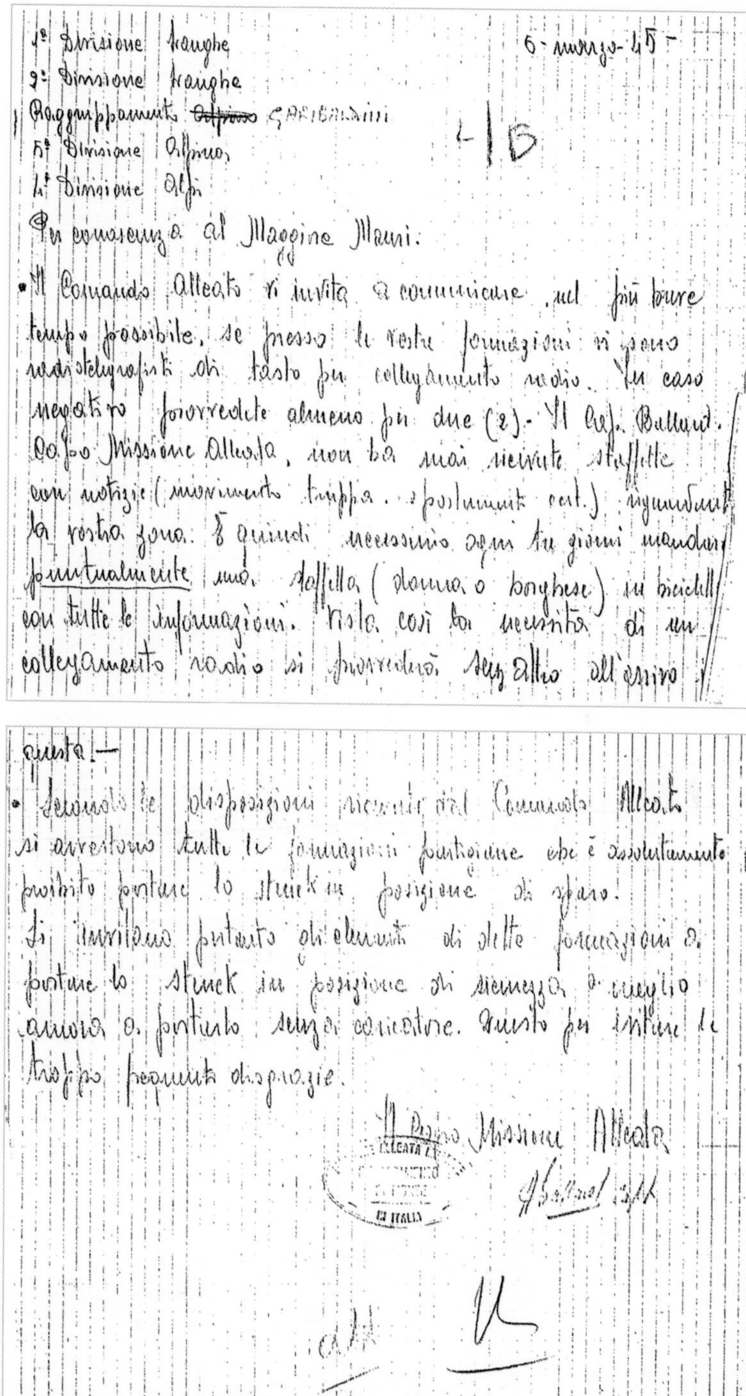

1ª Divisione Langhe — 6-marzo-45-
2ª Divisione Langhe
Raggruppamento ~~Alpino~~ GARIBALDINI
5ª Divisione Alpina
4ª Divisione Alpi

4 | B

Per conoscenza al Maggiore Mauri:

• Il Comando Alleato vi invita a comunicare nel più breve tempo possibile se presso le vostre formazioni vi sono radiotelegrafisti di tasto per collegamento radio. In caso negativo provvedete almeno per due (2). Il Cap. Ballard Capo Missione Alleata, non ha mai ricevute staffette con notizie (movimento truppa.. spostamenti ecc.) riguardanti la vostra zona. È quindi necessario ogni tre giorni mandare puntualmente una staffetta (donna o borghese) in bicicletta con tutte le informazioni. Vista così la necessità di un collegamento radio si provvederà senz'altro all'invio di questa!—

• Secondo le disposizioni ricevute dal Comando Alleato si avvertono tutte le formazioni partigiane che è assolutamente proibito portare lo sten in posizione di sparo.
Si invitano pertanto gli elementi di dette formazioni a portare lo sten in posizione di sicurezza o meglio ancora a portarlo senza caricatore. Questo per evitare le troppo frequenti disgrazie.

Il Capo Missione Alleata
A Ballard

Although this handwritten letter is signed by Maj. Ballard, it was in fact written by an Italian liaison officer, "Maestro" Pregliasco. *G. Toscani*

> type of weapon that is more powerful and more accurate. It is a rare occasion for a partisan to be happy with a Model 91 or a carbine. The absolute ideal—the dream combination—is a Marlin and an American carbine. The Marlin is a robust submachine gun with a long barrel, and the American carbine[9] is light and semi-automatic.[10]

The adoration for the new weapon also brought with it unintended consequences. Once again Fenoglio writes:

> In that instant in the inn there was the sound of a burst from the Skoda. [...] the partisans were pressed up against the walls and looked over to where three men were swaying, mortally wounded. The parabellum of the legionnaire was in its place on the round table, still pointing toward the three men, innocent and with Cheshire grins. The legionnaire who had laid it down [...] and René could not resist the temptation to

Maj. Hugh Ballard (right) with "Maestro" Pregliasco (left). *Don Angelo Siri*

Maj. Hugh Ballard, MC, was the son of a small farmer in Worcester. He joined the army in 1935, and was posted to the Royal Tank Regiment in India, achieving the rank of sergeant, after which he resigned and went to Southern Rhodesia, where he joined the British South African Police. At the outbreak of war, he resigned from the police and obtained a temporary commission in December 1942, posting to "F" Reinforcement Squadron Southern Rhodesia Armored Car Regiment. Ballard sailed with the regiment to Suez in January 1943, and was later posted to the South African Special Service Battalion Armoured Regiment in May 1943. That same month he was seconded to UK forces, specifically to the SOE. In July 1943, he was assessed as "an ideal commando type invaluable as a member of a sabotage party or as a commander of guerrillas..." (Alan Ogden, *A Spur Called Courage*) He remained in Cairo with Force 133 until October, when he was sent as a liaison officer to Dalmatia; in August 1944, he was posted to Bari with No. 1 Special Force as a temporary captain. His first assignment was to assume the responsibilities of Maj. Neville Darewski (alias Maj. Temple), who died on November 17 as a result of an accident. Ballard was infiltrated into the Langhe on November 18, 1944, along with Lt. Col. John Stevens. Ballard is credited with achieving a certain degree of cooperation between partisan units of differing outlooks and political ideologies and allegiances operating in Piedmont. On June 17, 1945, Ballard was appointed SO2 at AMG, then returned to South Africa by sea on December 22. He was awarded the Military Cross for his activities with the partisans; his military career ended on January 6, 1946, when he was demobilized.

1st Division Langhe 6 March 45
2nd Division Langhe
Garibaldini Groups
5th Division Alpina
4th Divison Alpi

For information of Major Mauri:

The Allied command invites you to communicate, as quickly as possible, if within your formations there are any radiotelegraph personnel who know Morse code for radio communications. If the answer is negative, take measures to provide two (2). Captain Ballard, Chief of the Allied Mission, has never received messengers with news (troop movements, displacements, etc.) regarding our zone. It is therefore necessary that every three days you send, on time, a messenger (a woman or a civilian) by bicycle with all of the information available. In view of the need for radio communication, appropriate measures should be taken as soon as possible upon receipt of this letter.

According to guidance received by Allied Headquarters all partisan formations are warned that it is absolutely forbidden to carry the stenck (sic) without the safety catch on.

Members of all units are therefore ordered to carry the stenck (sic) with the safety engaged or better yet to carry it without its magazine inserted. This is to avoid the all too frequent accidents.

Chief of the Allied Mission
H. Ballard Capt

A letter from Capt. Ballard, chief of the Allied mission in Piedmont, regarding the use of the "Stenck."

> admire it from up close and then to wield it with his proletarian hands, and the burst had cut loose as though divine.[11]

This is yet another example of how thoughtlessness and ignorance could lead to tragic consequences.

Aside from a few career military personnel, a large part of the partisans were completely in the dark regarding the use of weapons and, above all, were unaware of the precautions to take to avoid accidents.

One of the weapons considered to be most dangerous was the Sten itself, due to its ineffective safety.

As witness to how serious the problem was is a note from Maj. Ballard—at the time still a captain, but chief of one of the Allied missions to the partisans in Piedmont—dated March 6, 1945, with the oval stamp of the Allied Military Mission in Piedmont. The note calls for the need to move with the Sten with the safety always engaged and without a magazine when not on a mission to avoid tragic accidents.

This bare-bones note would be followed by numerous other missives confirming how serious the problem was. Here is a circular issued by headquarters of the "Gin Bevilacqua" Division operating in the Savona area:

COMITATO di LIBERAZIONE NAZIONALE
Corpo Volontari della Liberta

Comando
1 Divisione d'[illegible] Garibaldi
G. BE[illegible]

Prot. 30/178 Zona d'impiego, 7 marzo 1945

A TUTTI I COMANDI DIPENDENTI

Argomento ; Comunicazione

Dato il ripetersi di incidenti fra i Volontari per il maneggio degli Stens é necessario che i Comandi in-dirizzo provvedano ad avvertire i Volontari di maneggiare lo sten con molta attenzione e cautela.
Si fa notare che lo Sten presenta un particolare pericolo se lasciato battere col calcio a terra, perché può verificarsi in tal caso l'armamento automatico e di conseguenza la partenza imprevista di qualche colpo.
Questo incidente si verifica solo col carrello in posizione di riposo, mentre se il carrello é montato e in posizione di sicurezza questo non accade.

Il Commissario Politico Il Comandante M.

---

NATIONAL LIBERATION COMMITTEE
VOLUNTEER CORPS FOR LIBERTY

Headquarters
1 Garibaldi Assault Division
G. BEVILACQUA

File 30/178 Operational zone, 7 March 1945

TO ALL SUBORDINATE COMMANDS

Subject: Communication

Given the repeated incidents among Volunteers with respect to handling Stens it is necessary for the addressee Commands take steps to warn the Volunteers to handle the Sten with much attention and caution.
It should be pointed out that the Sten is particularly dangerous if its butt is allowed to slam on the ground, as in such a case the weapon may automatically be armed, leading to unexpected firing of several rounds.
This problem occurs only with the bolt in the armed position, but if the bolt is in the safe position this does not happen.

The Political Commissar The MilitaryCommander

To underscore how necessary this advice was, following is the report of a tragic accident in which a Sten was partially responsible:

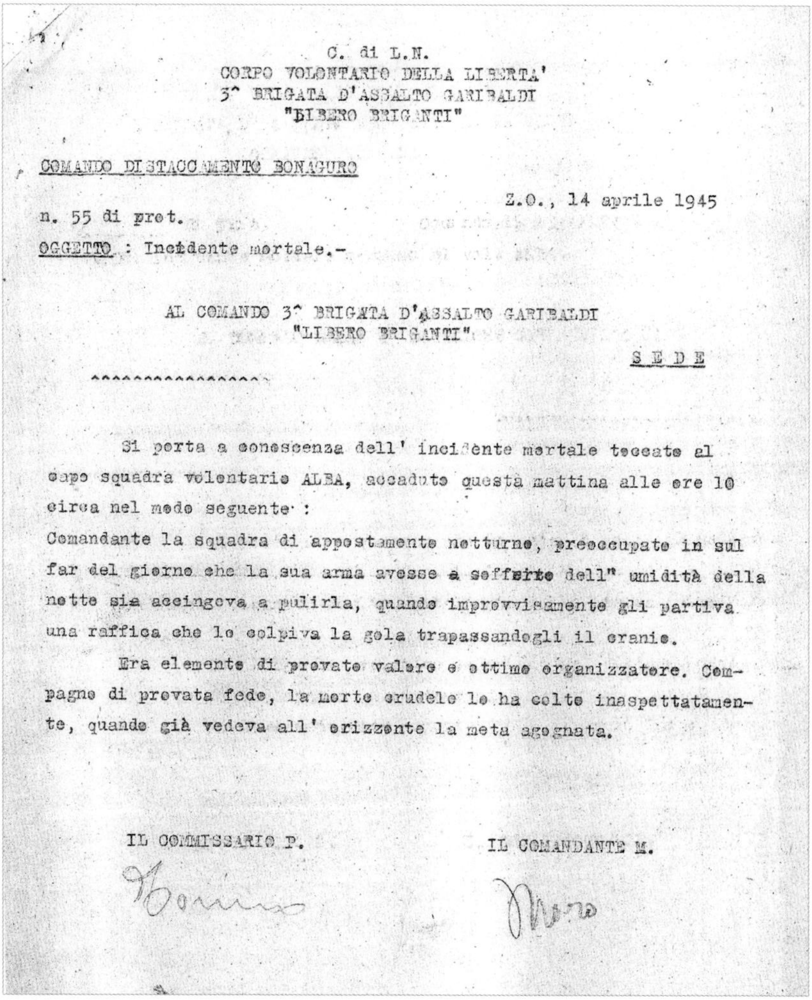

C. di L.N.
CORPO VOLONTARIO DELLA LIBERTA'
3^ BRIGATA D'ASSALTO GARIBALDI
"LIBERO BRIGANTI"

COMANDO DISTACCAMENTO BONAGURO

Z.O., 14 aprile 1945

n. 55 di prot.

OGGETTO : Incidente mortale.-

AL COMANDO 3^ BRIGATA D'ASSALTO GARIBALDI
"LIBERO BRIGANTI"

SEDE

^^^^^^^^^^^^^^^^

Si porta a conoscenza dell' incidente mortale toccato al capo squadra volontario ALBA, accaduto questa mattina alle ore 10 circa nel modo seguente :
Comandante la squadra di appostamento notturno, preoccupato in sul far del giorno che la sua arma avesse a sofferto dell'umidità della notte sia accingeva a pulirla, quando improvvisamente gli partiva una raffica che lo colpiva la gola trapassandogli il cranio.

Era elemento di provato valore e ottimo organizzatore. Compagno di provata fede, la morte crudele lo ha colto inaspettatamente, quando già vedeva all' orizzonte la meta agognata.

IL COMMISSARIO P.

IL COMANDANTE M.

N.L.C.
VOLUNTEER CORPS FOR LIBERTY
3RD GARIBALDI ASSAULT BRIGADE
"LIBERO BRIGANTI"

HEADQUARTERS BONAGURO DETACHMENT

Operations Zone, 14 April 1945

File no. 55

SUBJECT: Fatal accident

TO HEADQUARTERS 3RD GARIBALDI ASSAULT BRIGADE
"LIBERO BRIGANTI"
^^^^^^^^^^^^^^^^^^^^ HEADQUARTERS

This is to inform you of a fatal accident regarding the volunteer squad leader ALBA, which occurred this morning at around 10 o'clock in the following manner: Commander of the night shift detail, concerned that as daylight approached his weapon may have been affected by the damp night air, he began to clean it, when a burst unexpectedly fired which hit him in the throat and then passed through his head.

He was a person of proven valor and an excellent organizer. A comrade of proven loyalty, his cruel death took him unexpectedly, when he could see our long-awaited goal on the horizon.

THE POLITICAL COMMISSAR THE MILITARY COMMANDER

Yet another document with an even earlier date:

C. di L.N.
Volunteer Corps for Liberty
3rd Garibaldi Assault Brigade = L. Briganti

= S. Torcello Detachment =

File number. Headquarters, 1/1/1945.=

SUBJECT: Woundings. =

To Headquarters 3rd Brigade

Headquarters

"""""""""""""""""""""""""""""""""

This is to report that yesterday, due to an accident, volunteers Lince and Raffles were wounded by a burst of fire from a Sten. Volunter Lince sustained a chest wound at the seventh rib with the bullet exiting from his abdomen.
Volunteer Raffles was wounded in the right arm and forearm by a bullet that also exited.=
The doctor from Bardineto and the doctor from Toirano tended to the wounded individuals, the first of whom is convalescing at this camp and whose prognosis is guarded. =
Please take immediate steps to send a physician (preferably Dok) who can stay at this detachment for a few days xxxxxxxx as well as sending medical equipment

see page 41

C. di L. N.

Corpo volontario della libertà
3^Brigata d'assalto Garibaldi = L. Briganti
= Distaccamento S. Torcello =

N° / di prot. Comando, lì 1°/1/1945.=
OGGETTO: ferimento .=

Al Comando della 3^ Brigata

S e d e

""""""""""""""""""""""""""

Si comunica che ieri, causa un infortunio, sono rimasti feriti da una raf= fica di Sten i volontari Lince e Raffles.
Il vol. Lince ha riportato una ferita toracica alla settima intercostale con fuoruscita del proiettile al lato addominale.
Il Vol? Raffles e stato ferito al braccio ed all'a= vambraccio destro da un proiettile che pure esso ha attraversato fuoriuscendo.=
Il dottore di Bardineto e quello di Toirano hanno Visitato i feriti dei quali il primo é ricove= rato presso questo accampamento con prognosi riser vata.=
Pregasi voler provvedere immediatamente all'invio di un sanitario(possibilmente Dok) il quale possa sostare pre qualche giorno presso questo Distacca= mento ~~xxxxxx~~, nonché ad [illegible] iare materiale sanita=

Even though for some time improved Stens were available thanks to the addition of a more effective additional safety, nearly no trace of these improved models is to be found among those dropped to the resistance.

It is likewise odd that a brigade should feel the need to spell out the weapons should be cleaned and kept in working order:

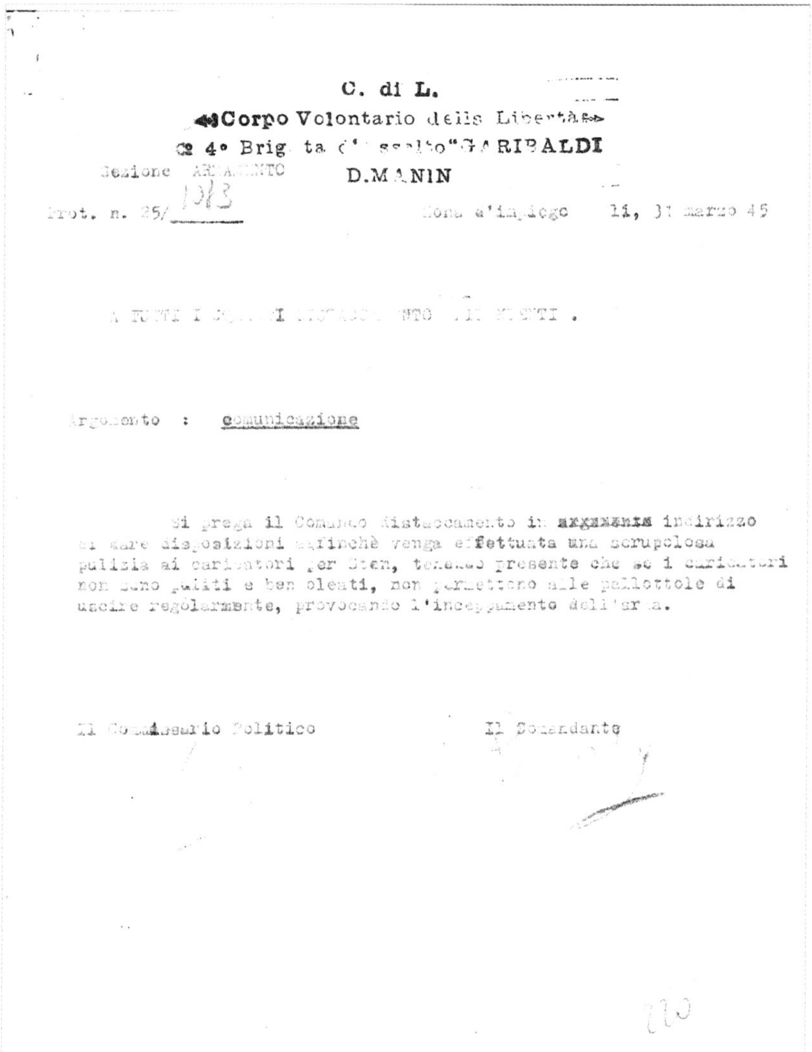

C. di L.

Corpo Volontario della Libertà

4° Brigata d'assalto "GARIBALDI"

D. MANIN

Sezione ARMAMENTO

Prot. n. 25/1013

Zona d'impiego li, 31 marzo 45

A TUTTI I [illegible] .

Argomento : comunicazione

Si prega il Comando distaccamento in xxxxxxxx indirizzo di dare disposizioni affinchè venga effettuata una scrupolosa pulizia ai caricatori per Sten, tenendo presente che se i caricatori non sono puliti e ben oleati, non permettono alle pallottole di uscire regolarmente, provocando l'inceppamento dell'arma.

Il Commissario Politico

Il Comandante

C. di L.
Volunteer Corps for Liberty
4th GARIBALDI Assault Brigade
D. MANIN

Weapons section

File number 25/1013 Operations zone 31 March 45

TO ALL SUBORDINATE DETACHMENT HEADQUARTERS.

Subject: Communication

All detachment headquarters addressed are requested to take measures to ensure that Sten magazines are very carefully cleaned, bearing in mind that if the magazines are not clean and well-oiled they do not allow the cartridges to feed properly, causing the weapon to jam.

The Political Commissar The Commander

Some attempts were made to teach the new recruits, even though it does not appear that whomever was assigned this task was among the best qualified; it is enough to ponder the recommendation to "put the points of the bullets toward the muzzle," as well as the admonition to not forget to take the magazines that are found in the pouch at the time of disarming the enemy to question the writer's qualifications.

COMITATO DI LIBERAZIONE NAZIONALE
Corpo Volontari della Libertà

ando Regionale
er la Liguria
EZIONE SABOTAGGI

Zona X, 16 Ottobre 1944

a TUTTE LE FORMAZIONI

OGGETTO: Istruzioni per l'uso delle più comuni armi tedesche

LA PISTOLA MASCHINE

La p.m. è un'arma automatica (simile come impiego al mitra), lunga circa mezzo metro, tutta in acciaio brunito, con impugnatore a pistola. L'avete vista certamentein mano a sotto'ufficiali tedeschi.

Sarebbe troppo lungo spiegarvi l'arma nei singoli pezzi, perciò vi spiegherò soltanto l'uso pratico di essa, quello che a voi specialmente serve.

Se venite in possesso di una p.m.; come fare per usarla?
Innanzi tutto non scordatevi di prendere anche i quattro caricatori che si trovano in una apposita fondina di tela appesa al cinturone del tedesco. Ogni caricatore ha 32 colpi. la p.m. è di calibro 9 lungo e le cartucce sono uguali a quelle che si usano per i mitra.

Impugnata la p.m.; con la mano destra ed un caricatore con la sinistra mettete il caricatore stesso (facendo attenzione a mettere le punte dei proiettili verso la canna) nell'apposito alveo che si trova nella parte inferiore della p.m.

E che si riconosce facilmente dai pini di invito. Poi col palmo della mano sinistra date un colpo secco alla parte inferiore del caricatore, dopo di che sentirete uno scatto. Il caricatore è a posto.

28

The complete Italian text of this document is presented in chapter 9.

NATIONAL LIBERATION COMMITTEE
Volunteer Corps for Liberty

Liguria Regional Headquarters Zone A, 16 October 1944

TO ALL FORMATIONS

SUBJECT: Instructions for use of the most common German weapons

THE MACHINE PISTOL

The MP is an automatic weapon (employed similarly as the submachine gun) about half a meter long, all in blued metal, with a pistol grip. You will certainly have seen it in the hands of German noncommissioned officers.

It would take too much time to explain each piece of the weapon, thus I will explain only its practical use, that which is of most use to you.

If you are able to acquire a MP, how do you use it?
Above all don't forget to take the four magazines that are found in a canvas carrying pouch that is hung from the German's belt. Each magazine holds 32 rounds. The MP is 9mm long caliber and the cartridges are the same as those used in the submachine gun.

Once you have picked up the MP with your right hand and a magazine with your left hand, insert the magazine itself (making sure to put the points of the bullets towards the muzzle) in the magazine well underneath the MP.

This is easily recognized by the flared opening. Then with the palm of the left hand give a sharp rap to the bottom of the magazine, after which you will hear a click. The magazine is now in place.

Meanwhile, in a brigade whose commander was a former career officer the situation was explained much more clearly:

ppena possibile).
Cura delle armi- Uno degli aspetti della disciplina e che caratterizza il uon combattente è la cura delle armi. L'arma deve essere sempre in condizione i funzionare. I Comandanti militari devono controllare la manutensione delle rmi. I Capi Nucleo saranno responsabili personalmente davanti ai Comandanti sul a manutensione delle armi (dei suoi uomini). Bisogna curare che le armi siano scariche nel momen o della pulitura e quando il volontario non è di servizio. Le armi devono esse- e caricate e poste in posizione di sparo prima del riposo e poste alla porta a di mano di ogni singolo volontario per l'uso immediato in caso di necessità. gni leggerezza, nell'uso delle armi, deve essere repressa e i responsabili defe iti al Tribunale del Distaccamento. Non deve avvenire che si perda o colpi per disattenzione ed ancor peggio autolesionarsi o colpire altri olontari. Contro tali leggerezze bisogna prendere le misure più draconiane.

<u>Care of weapons</u> – One of the aspects of discipline that characterizes the good combat soldier is care of weapons. The weapon should always be ready to use. Military commanders must check the maintenance of weapons. Squad leaders are personally responsible to the Commanders for the state of maintenance of the weapons of his men. Care must be taken to ensure that the weapons are unloaded while cleaning and when the volunteer is not on duty. Weapons must be loaded and ready to fire before being set aside and should be placed within easy reach of each volunteer for immediate use in case it is necessary. All cases of improper use of weapons should be repressed and the guilty parties should be remanded to the Court of the detachment. There must be no stray rounds fired because of lack of attention nor, even worse, should there be any self-inflicted wounds or wounding of other volunteers. The most draconian measures must be taken against such improper use of weapons.

Perhaps this other document gives proof of the fact that someone well understood the substantial difference between a Sten and a long-range rifle, while others still had to learn that to entrust one's life to a weapon required the greatest care and respect:

C. di L. N.
Corpo Volontario della Libertà
3^Brigata d'Assalto Garibaldi-LIBriganti
Distaccamento S. Torcello

N°/____/ di prot. Comando, lì 28/2/45
OGGETTO: armá: stato di conservazione.=

Al Comando della 3^Brigata
s e d e

""""""""""""""

Si fa presente a codesto Comando Brigata che, aderendo alle richieste del vol. Montenero, questo Distaccamento ha creduto opportuno effettuare il cambio di uno Sten con un semiautomatico tedesco. Ciò in considerazione che, data la stagione e la zona scoperta il semiautomatico é di gran lunga più efficace dello Sten, sia per l'attacco che per la difesa in montagna.=

Permutata l'arma habbiamo dovuto riscontrare che il semiautomatico era in condizioni di manutenzione deplorevoli. Tutte le parti metalliche dell'arma erano saturë di ossidazioni; la parte della canna in cui scorre il pistoncino per il rinculo del carrello ed il movimento semiautomatico era segnata in modo che il movimento del pistoncino non potefa essere effettuato ed il fucile non si ricaricava automaticamente; le alette metalliche indipendenti del càrrello, indebilite nelle loro parti, sparando un colpo di prova, saltarono, rendendo completamente inefficiente l'arma.

Si porta quanto sopra a conoscenza di codesto superiore comando in modo che prenda, se lo ritiene necessario, provvedimenti affinche le armi di quei partigiani che non fanno vita di reparto e quindi non hanno bisogno di essere armati, vengano ritirate ed affidate a chi di competenza perché siano curate e messe al sicuro.

Il Commissario Pol  Il Comandate

173

C. di L.N.
Volunteer Corps for Liberty
3rd Garibaldi Assault Brigade – L. Briganti
S. Torcello Detachment

File no./_____/ Headquarters, 28/2/45
SUBJECT: weapons: state of maintenance

To Headquarters 3rd Brigade
branch

“”””””””””””””

This is to inform the Brigade Headquarters that, in accordance with the request of volunteer Montenero, this Detachment felt it appropriate to swap a Sten for a German semiautomatic. This was in consideration of the fact that, given the season and the open nature of the area the semi-auto is far more effective than the Sten, both in the attack as well as for use in the mountains.=

Having exchanged the weapons we observed that the semi-auto was in a deplorable state of maintenance. All of the metal parts of the weapon were full of rust ; the part of the barrel in which the bolt recoil piston rides was so bad that the piston could not move and the rifle would not reload automatically; the metal lugs independent of the bolt were weakened to the point that when a test round was fired it rendered the weapon completely unusable.

The above information is brought to the attention of this higher headquarters so that it may take any measures it may deem necessary so that weapons of those partisans who are not assigned to operational units, and who thus have no need to be armed, be collected and entrusted to the appropriately qualified personnel so that they may be properly maintained and stored safely.

The Political Commissar The Commander

Maj. Hope's tombstone in the British section of Staglieno Cemetery, Genoa, Italy. *Sabina Usai*

Because every medal has two sides, the accidental death of Maj. Hope—an SOE officer—at Cisterna d'Asti on April 15, 1945, came at the hands of a carabinieri NCO, in this instance probably due to too much familiarity with weapons. In fact, comments ex-partisan Chiaffredo Bellero, a technician of the "Cisterna d'Asti" Brigade: "One does not go to a meeting with the weapon cocked for firing. When not in action, the magazine should be removed so there is no chance of introducing bullets into the barrel." The killing of Hope did not happen because of "[..] malice, but there were several elements of serious fault, that is to say imprudence and negligence."[12]

The ex-partisan Bellero also disproves blaming the Sten for this death:

> The weapon with which the partisan accidentally killed Maj. Adrian Hope had been captured by him from a GNR unit. The gun was a submachine gun of Italian manufacture with nice lines, of a type I had never seen before [...]. The partisan carried it proudly, but evidently had not examined it well. [...] if the bolt was not completely cocked it was held by the magazine safety [20- or 40-round magazines identical to those of the Beretta 1938 SMG]. By touching this catch the bolt was freed and driven by its spring, stripping off a round and causing it to fire. This safety catch, if used properly, acted as a second safety. [...] gave me the weapon so I could examine it. Despite my young age I was the group's weapons technician. No one had done so before me and no one had ever noticed this was not a Sten.[13]

If the partisans made a mistake by misunderstanding the different uses and capabilities of each type of weapon, going overboard in their desire for relatively

Maj. Adrian Hope. *G. Toscani*

**Maj. Adrian Hope**, MA, BCL, SC(V) (November 19, 1897–April 17, 1945) was from Johannesburg, Transvaal, South Africa. He was the son of Charles D. and Alice Hope, and was married to Morag E. Hope. Hope was somewhat older than the average SOE field operative; his parent unit was the South African Staff Corps, but he was also a veteran of Indian army service. He was seconded to British forces in 1944, and was posted to No. 1 Special Force SOE, then assigned to the Chariton Mission in Italy. Hope was extremely well liked by the partisans for a number of reasons: he was apparently quite successful arranging for weapons and supplies to be airdropped to the partisans, and was the source of some amusement for the partisans because of his precise, clipped British diction that carried over in his attempts to speak Italian. On April 17, 1945, Hope was the victim of a bizarre but tragic accident involving a TZ45 submachine gun, which was notorious for its penchant for accidentally firing; at the close of a party celebrating a successful supply drop one of the partisans—a *carabiniere* named Pasquale Bolle—went to shake Hope's hand, but in doing so, his submachine gun slipped from his shoulder and landed on the floor in a manner causing it to fire a single bullet that struck Hope in the liver and kidney, killing him instantly. Bolle and the other partisans were devastated by Hope's death; in recognition of his effort to aid the partisans, after his death the *6a Divisione Alpina "Asti – magg. Hope"* (6th Alpine Division "Asti – Maj. Hope) was named after him. He is buried in the British section of Staglieno Cemetery in Genoa, Italy.

A TZ45 submachine gun. *G. Toscani*

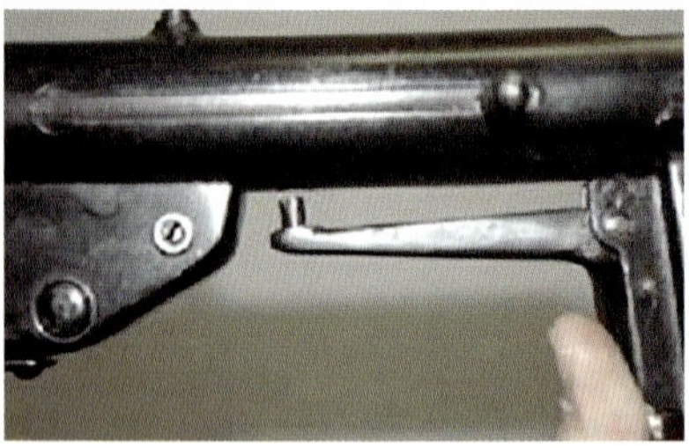

Detail of the grip safety of the TZ45. *G. Toscani*

useless weapons such as the submachine gun and refusing to use rifles that were more effective for long-range, such as the Italian 91 series or the German Mauser, one can easily imagine their disappointment when they found drop containers were filled with weapons like Vetterli-Vitali[14] rifles that were already obsolete by the time of WWI.

With respect to these particular weapons Gildo Milano relates an anecdote:

> The night before there was an air drop and Augusto had complained loudly about the quality of the goods that rained down from the sky: Makallè [single-shot rifles used during the previous century in Africa by the Italian army during the earliest colonial wars] and cans of beans. Ballard responded that even that was too much for disgusting colonial people such as us. I got an idea. "Return to Ballard" I said to Augusto, "play the part of a humble and repentant servant and tell him I want to invite him to a dinner with the entire mission to honor and thank him for all that he does for us—he's stupid and arrogant enough that he'll fall for it."
>
> "But what do you plan on doing?"
>
> "Don't give it a thought; do as I tell you, invite him for noontime on Sunday and come yourself, and you'll see how he gets repaid for all his unpleasantness and haughtiness." I sent a truck to Bogliolo with a note asking him to send me around a hundred Makallè to play a joke

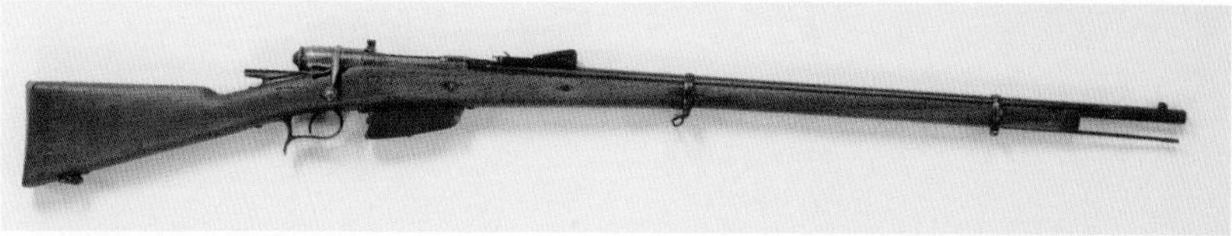

A Vetterli-Vitali 1870/87/16, presumably the type of rifle referred to as the "Makallè" by the partisans. *Ralph Riccio Collection*

> on the English. Bogliolo quickly sent me a hundred of those rifles, adding that he would have willingly taken part in the joke but couldn't do it for obvious reasons, but he gave me his approval anyway. Atti had the old blunderbusses polished to perfection, to the point that after half a day's work they seemed to be priceless antiques made of mahogany and brass. Precisely at noon the unsuspecting bumpkin arrived, followed by the obsequious crowd of his "court," and stiffly reviewed the company, which presented arms with the long Makallès. He did not notice, or feigned that he did not notice the joke, even while at the dinner table, at least not until the third course. In the large room festooned with flags and with the fireplace blazing away in the best English tradition, a number of cooks with hats and white aprons served us an antipasto of beans, bean soup, and a main dish of beans. It was only at that point that Ballard got up indignantly, followed by his retinue of bootlickers, and left to the salute of "present arms" by the company that awaited him in the courtyard. This time the muzzles of the Makallès had been topped with empty English bean cans.[15]

Confirming the delivery of these weapons, Lazagna writes: "Half of the weapons dropped consisted of very old and very long weterling [sic] rifles that probably had been issued to the army of the Negus of Ethiopia."[16]

Partisan Firmino Rota, a colleague of Fenoglio, was of a completely different opinion. Writing about a combat engagement on April 19, 1945, at Montemagno he stated: "...to keep them [the Germans] at a distance, the Macallè rifles that had been dropped by the British who had taken them from the Italians in Africa were excellent."

Thus, at least one partisan appreciated these long rifles that were effective at longer ranges than the normal Model '91 rifles.[17]

# CHAPTER III
# EXAMINING THE DOCUMENTS

The resistance was a group effort that demonstrated a will to cooperate and help one another, but there were many instances of egoism: although it is true the Allies provided obsolete weapons to the partisans that the Allies no longer used, it is likewise evident that when a partisan unit obtained a better weapon it willingly handed over its oldest or least reliable weapons to other units, putting a good face to the myth of cooperation (for example, when Bren guns were obtained from the British, Breda 30 light machine guns were ceded to the "poor cousins," or defective weapons or weapons whose ammunition was hard to find were handed over).

C. DI L.N.
VOLUNTEER CORPS FOR LIBERTY
IV GARIBALDI ASSAULT BRIGADE
D. MANIN

HEADQUARTERS BONAGURO DETACHMENT

FILE: 5/45 21 / 10 / 44

To Headquarters IV GARIBALDI Assault Brigade

Subject: Sckoda (sic) automatic rifle

This is to inform the above Headquarters that the Sckoda automatic rifle sent to us by REBAGLIATI at the time that this Detachment was organized does not function; even at the time that it was issued to the REBAGLIATI it did not work; when we obtained it we thought that it had been repaired. We tested it a number of times but were never able to make it function.

We ask your Headquarters to make a determination if we should send the weapon to you or if we should keep it here while we wait for you to pick it up.

The Political Commissar The Commander

The Armorer

see page 51

C. DI L. N.

CORPO VOLONTARIO DELLA LIBERTA'

IV BRIGATA D'ASSALTO GARIBALDI

D. MANIN

COMANDO DISTACCAMENTO B O N A G U R O

PROT: 5 / 45 21 / IO / 44

Al Comando IVa Brigata d'assalto GARIBALDI

Argomento: fucile mitragliatore Sokoda

Si comunica a Codesto Comando che il fucile mitragliatore Sokoda inviatoci dal REBAGLIATI al momento della costituzione di questo Distaccamento, non funziona; già quando era in dotazione al REBAGLIATI esso non funzionava; noi quando l'avemmo, credemmo che fosse stato riparato. L'abbiamo più volte provato ma non siamo mai riusciti a farlo funzionare.

Lo mettiamo a disposizione di Codesto Comando al quale chiediamo se doverlo inviare oppure tenerlo qua in attesa che venga da voi ritirato.

Il Comm.P.l. Il Comandante

L'armiere

The following is another example of an attitude that is not exactly the most cooperative:

C. di L. N.
Corpo Volontario d. Libertà
Cª 3 Brigata d'As Garibaldi
"LIBERO BRIGANTI"

Prot.n.3/ 25 novembre 1944

Al Comando della 4^ Brigata
" Daniele MANIN "

ARGOMENTO: Mitragliatrice del Melogno.

Riscontro V/s. 25/482 corr.23 allo stesso argomento.

Questo Comando Brigata, non ha soddisfatto la richiesta del Distacc. REBAGLIATI perchè in quei giorni, come ancora oggi, giornalmente serve perchè i S.Marco continuano puntate al Melogno. La mitraglia poi è stata data in prestito al BRUZZONE che attualmente controlla la predetta zona.

Poi l'arma era stata data in dotazione a questa Brigata da codesta e non troviamo ne logico ne cameratesco il togliercela, perchè è l'unica arma pesante che questa Brigata possiede, e perchè se al Rebagliati sono state portate via due armi, chi deve rimetterci si crede non dover essere proprio noi.

Con ciò, attendiamo risposta in merito e se l'arma dovrà ritornare, sarà ritornata.

IL COMMISSARIO P. IL COMANDANTE

C. di L.N.
Volunteer Corps for Liberty
Hq. 3 Garibaldi Assault Brigade\
"LIBERO BRIGANTI"

File no. 3/359 25 November 1944

To Headquarters of the 4th Brigade
"Daniele MANIN"

SUBJECT: Melogno Machine gun

Reply to your 25/482 of 23 this month same subject.

This Brigade Headquarters did not satisfy the request of the REBAGLIATI Detachment because in those days, as is still the case, there is a daily need because the S. Marco continues forays aimed at Melogno. The machine gun was then loaned out to BRUZZONE (detachment) which currently controls the aforementioned area.

Because the weapon was issued to that Brigade by this Hq. and we find it neither logical nor comradely to take it away from them, because it is the only heavy weapon that this Brigade has, and because two weapons were taken away from the Rebagliati (detachment), we don't believe that we should be the ones to have to take the loss.

That said, we await a reply with regard to the issue, and if the weapon has to be returned, it will be returned.

THE POLITICAL COMISSAR THE COMMANDER

Between nearby units and those with shared political sentiments the exchange of various types of equipment was fairly common.

In correspondence between detachments of the same division we were able to find many examples of exchange of material and offer a few samples.

C. di L. N.

CORPO VOLONTARIO DELLA LIBERTA'

COMANDO DIVISIONE S.A.P.
ANTONIO GRAMSCI

Zona d'impiego, 2/3/1945

Al Comando Brigata S.A.P. "CLELIA CORRADINI "

Siamo lieti di comunicarvi che la IV^ Brigata D.MANIN ha assegnato alla nostra Divisione S.A.P. altri dieci STEN corredati del necessario.

E' probabile che ci assegnino anche un certo quantitativo di SIPE e di plastico. Vi invitiamo pertanto a inviare un congruo numero di uomini al Comando della IV^ Brig.per il ritiro di detto materiale,e Vi autorizziamo a chiedere uomini alla"BERTOLA" e alla "PES" per effettuare il trasporto. Il materiale va ripartito nel modo seguente:

N° 3 STEN li lascierete alla "PES" dando disposizioni perchè uno venga dalla "PES" mandato alla "PEROTTI"

N° 2 STEN saranno da voi trattenuti.

N° 5 STEN saranno passati alla"BERTOLA" Dando disposizioni che la BERTOLA ne trattenga due per sè,e consegni gli altri tre alle Brigate di Savena.

E' ovvio che il munizionamento,le SIPE,e plastico eventuale saranno ripartiti proporzionalmente come gli STEN,dandoci conto della ripartizione avvenuta.

Vi alleghiamo lettera di accompagnamento.

SAluti garibaldini.

VIVA L'ITALIA LIBERA !! MORTE AI NAZIFASCISTI !!

IL COMANDO DIVISIONE

C. di L.N.
VOLUNTEER CORPS FOR LIBERTY

S.A.P. DIVISION HEADQUARTERS
ANTONIO GRAMSCI

Operations area. 2/3/1945

To Headquarters S.A.P.Brigade 'CLELIA CORRADINI'

We are happy to inform you that the IV Brigade D. MANIN has assigned our S.A.P. Division another ten Sten guns with necessary equipment.

It is probable that a certain quantity of SIPE and plastique can also be supplied. We thus request that you send an adequate number of men to the Headquarters of the IV Brigade to pick up said material, and we authorize you to ask for men from the "BERTOLA" and from the "PES" to carry the material. The material is to be apportioned as follows:

3 STEN guns you will leave with the "PES" with instructions for the "PES" provide one to the "PEROTTI" (detachment)

2 STEN guns will be retained by you,

5 STEN guns will be given to the 'BERTOLA" with instructions that BERTOLA retain two for its use and delivers the other three to the Savona Brigades.

It is obvious that the ammunition, the SIPE, and the plastique should be split up proportionally as for the STENs, providing us with an accounting of how these items were apportioned.

Attached is an accompanying letter.

Garibaldian regards,

LONG LIVE FREE ITALY ! DEATH TO THE NAZI-FASCISTS !!

THE DIVISION COMMANDER

The Belgian automatic rifle mentioned in the following communication is probably the same weapon mentioned several times as the Obel in various lists and reports issued by the same brigade: it is likely a Browning automatic rifle produced by FN in Belgium for the Belgian or Polish army.[18]

C. di L. NAZIONALE
Corpo Volontario della Libertà

Comando
Divisione d'Assalto GARIBALDI
"GIN BEVILACQUA
Sez. ARMAMENTO .

Prot. n. 30/______ li,,21 marzo 45

Al Comando V^ Brigata d'Assalto " BALTERA " .

Argomento: richiesta arma

Questa Sez. Armamento, richiede il fucile-mitragliatore ( Belga) da riparare, come d'accordi presi in precedenza con il Com. SAM ed Ernesto. Al fine di poter riparare il predetto mitragliatore, cotesto Comando è pregato allegare un caricatore, con alcuni colpi ( originali ).

Potrete servirvi a tale scopo del Volontario latore della presente .

Saluti garibaldini

Il Responsabile Sez. Armamento :

C. di L. NAZIONALE
Volunteer Corps for Liberty

Headquarters
GARIBALDI assault Division
GIN BEVILACQUA
Section: ARMAMENT.

File no. 30/______ 21 March 45

To Headquarters V Assault Brigade "BALTERA" .

Subject: request for weapon

This Armaments Section requests the (Belgian) automatic rifle to be repaired, as per previous agreement with Commander SAM and Ernesto. In order to repair the aforementioned automatic rifle, your Headquarters is kindly requested to supply a magazine, with some (original) rounds.

For this purpose you can provide the item to the Volunteer who is the bearer of this message.

Garibaldian regards

Chief of the Armaments Section:

Exchange of equipment assumed a bureaucratic character that seems excessive for the time; this is another example relating to a weapon that presented difficulties supplying ammunition and spare parts, the MAS 38.

VOLUNTEER CORPS FOR LIBERTY
Subordinate to the C. di L.N.
4th Garibaldi Assault Brigade
D. Manin
From the Calcagno Detachment Headquarters

File 11.157 20.11.1944

To the Guazzotti Detachment Headquarters

Subject: MAS magazine

The Headquarters of the "C. Corradini" Brigade needs a magazine for the "Mas" cal. 7.65 long automatic weapon to be used as a model to fabricate other such magazines. Said magazine shall be immediately returned as soon as possible.

The Pol. Commissar The Commander

see page 58

CORPO VOLONTARIO DELLA LIBERTA'
Aderente al C. di L.N.
4ª Brigata d'Assalto Garibaldi
D. Manin
Dal Comando Distaccamento Calcagno

Prot. 11.157 20.11.1944

Al Comando Distaccamento Guazzotti.

Oggetto:Caricatore MAS.

Al Comando della Brigata "C.Corradini" occorre un caricatore dell'arma automatica "Mas" cal. 7,65 lungo che serve per modello per la costruzione di altri.

Il detto caricatore sarà immediatamente restituito appena possibile.

Il Commissario P. Il Comandante P.

The speed of the postal service is astonishing, as it was posted only four days later.

C. di L.N.
Volunteer Corps for Liberty
Hq. 4th GARIBALDI Assault Brigade
D. MANIN

File 25.494 24.11.44

Headquarters "CORRADINI" SAP Brigade

Subject: MAS Magazine

In reply to your letter, same subject, we inform you that it is impossible to send you the magazine for the MAS-type machine pistol as we have two weapons of that type with only one magazine.

We will query the 5th Brigade to see if they might be able to satisfy your request.

The Political Commissar The Commander

C. di L.N

Corpo Volontario della Libertà

Cdo 4° Brigata d'Assalto "GARIBALDI"

D.MANIN

Prot.25.4961                24.11.44

Comando Brigata SAP " CORRADINI"

Argomento : Caricatore per M A S

In risposta alla Vs. allo stesso argomento vi comunichiamo che ci é impossibile inviarvi il caricatore per pistola mitragliatrice tipo M A S dato che possediamo due armi di tali tipo con un solo caricatore.

Cercheremo alla 5^ Brigata se eventualmente può soddisfare alla Vs.richiesta.

Il Commissario P.                Il Comandante

Yet another demonstration that some weapons proved difficult to supply with ammunition because of uncommon caliber:

TO HEADQUARTERS GARIBALDI ASSAULT DIVISION
GIN BEVILACQUA

Subject: Request for ammunition

Having come in possession of a TOMPSON (sic) type automatic weapon, and being completely without ammunition for it, we kindly request, if it is within your ability, to send us some as quickly as possible as well as possibly a magazine that will serve us as a sample for fabricating others.

LONG LIVE FREE ITALY
Best wishes from the SAP

The Political Commissar                The Commander

see page 60

AL COMANDO DIVISIONE D'. ASSALTO GARIBALDI
G I N   B E V I L A C Q U A

Oggetto: Richiesta munizioni

Vunuti in possesso di un'arma automatica tipo TOMPSON ,ed essendo completamente spro= sisti di munizioni, vi preghiamo, se cio é in vostra possibilita di inviarcene quanto prima e possibilmente con un caricatore che ci servi = rà come campione per la costruzione di altri .

W L'ITALIA LIBERA
Saluti Sapisti

Il Commissario P.    Il Comandnante

Note the somewhat tongue-in-cheek tone of this note following a request that was evidently unwelcome:

-.-.-.-.-.-.-

E poi ancora, la 6^ Brigata ha avuto un lancio. La suddivisione delle armi era troppo chiederla, ma uno Sten, uno solo avrebbe pur potuto inviarlo, se non altro per vedere come era fatto.

-.-.-.-.-.-.-

41

./..

======

On top of that, the 6th Brigade received an air drop. The distribution of the weapons was too much to expect, but at least one Sten, a single one, they certainly could have sent us, at least so we could see how it was made.

======

At times requests reflected a certain naivetè on the part of the writer: in this case perhaps the writer did not take into account the fact that if seven or eight rounds were not enough to hit the target he would have had no better results with thirteen bullets (nor fifteen as hypothesized).

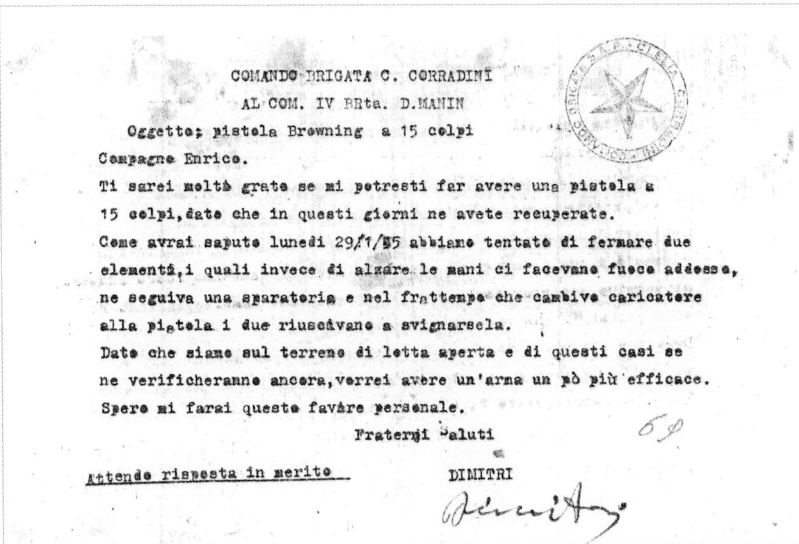

COMANDO BRIGATA C. CORRADINI
AL COM. IV BRta. D.MANIN

Oggetto; pistola Browning a 15 colpi

Compagno Enrico.

Ti sarei moltò grato se mi potresti far avere una pistola a 15 colpi, dato che in questi giorni ne avete recuperato.
Come avrai saputo lunedì 29/1/45 abbiamo tentato di fermare due elementi, i quali invece di alzare le mani ci facevano fuoco addosso, ne seguiva una sparatoria e nel frattempo che cambivo caricatore alla pistola i due riuscivano a svignarsela.
Dato che siamo sul terreno di lotta aperta e di questi casi se ne verificheranno ancora, vorrei avere un'arma un pò più efficace.
Spero mi farai questo favòre personale.

Fraterni Saluti

Attendo risposta in merito

DIMITRI

HEADQUARTERS C. CORRADINI BRIGADE
TO HQ IV BDE. D. MANIN

Subject: 15-round Browning pistol

Comrade Enrico,

I would be very grateful if you could let me have a 15-round pistol, inasmuch as you have recently recovered some.
As you will have known on Monday 29/1/45 we attempted to stop two individuals, who instead of raising their hands began to open fire on us, a shootout followed and in the meantime as I was changing my pistol's magazine the pair managed to break off and run.
As we are in open terrain and incidents of this sort will happen again, I would like to have a weapon that is a bit more effective. I hope you will do this as a personal favor.

Brotherly wishes,

I await a reply concerning this request

DIMITRI

Then there is the case of this request for a supply of automatic weapons dreading a hypothetical assault by enemy forces:

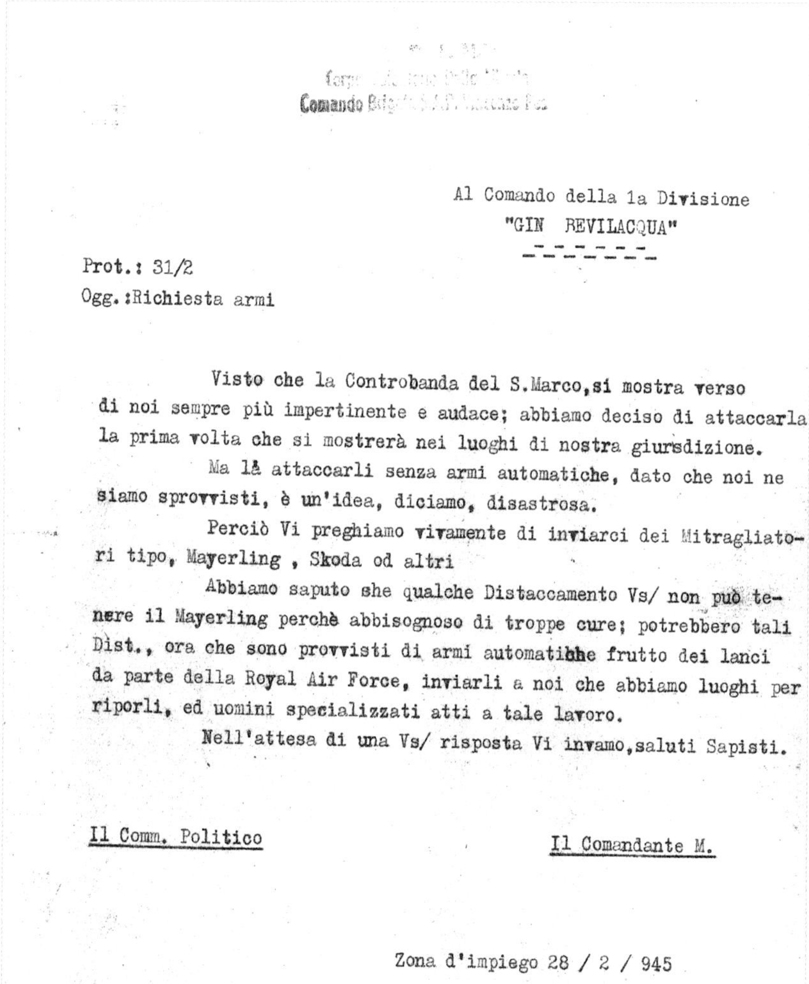

Al Comando della 1a Divisione
"GIN BEVILACQUA"

Prot.: 31/2
Ogg.: Richiesta armi

Visto che la Controbanda del S.Marco, si mostra verso di noi sempre più impertinente e audace; abbiamo deciso di attaccarla la prima volta che si mostrerà nei luoghi di nostra giursdizione.

Ma lå attaccarli senza armi automatiche, dato che noi ne siamo sprovvisti, è un'idea, diciamo, disastrosa.

Perciò Vi preghiamo vivamente di inviarci dei Mitragliatori tipo, Mayerling , Skoda od altri

Abbiamo saputo she qualche Distaccamento Vs/ non può tenere il Mayerling perchè abbisognoso di troppe cure; potrebbero tali Dist., ora che sono provvisti di armi automatibhe frutto dei lanci da parte della Royal Air Force, inviarli a noi che abbiamo luoghi per riporli, ed uomini specializzati atti a tale lavoro.

Nell'attesa di una Vs/ risposta Vi invamo, saluti Sapisti.

Il Comm. Politico

Il Comandante M.

Zona d'impiego 28 / 2 / 945

C. di L.N.
Volunteer Corps for Liberty
Headquarters S.A.P. Brigade Vincenzo Pes

To Headquarters of the Division
"GIN BEVILACQUA"
- - - - - - - - - -

File: 31/2
Subj: Request for weapons

In view of the fact that the anti-partisan unit of the S. Marco is showing itself to be increasingly aggressive and bold towards us; we have decided to attack it the first time that it shows itself in places under our jurisdiction.

But to attack them without automatic weapons, given that we have none, is an idea that is, shall we say, disastrous.

We therefore request urgently that you send us machine guns of the Mayerling, Skoda or other types.

We have been informed that some of your Detachments cannot keep the Mayerling because it requires too much maintenance; could these Detachments, which are now equipped with automatic weapons as a result of air drops by the Royal Air Force, send them to us as we have places to store them and men who are specialists in their maintenance.

Awaiting your reply, we send you S.AP. regards

The Political Commissar | The Military Commander

Operations zone 28/ 2/ 945

A good example of why the Allies may have had some misgivings about placing any faith in the capabilities of the partisans can be found in the following two documents, especially considering a partisan brigade numbered 250–300 men and a division 750–900:

COMIT. di LIBER. NAZ.
Corpo Volont. della Libertá
Com. Brg. D'assalto
"NINO BIXIO"
ADERENTE AL COMANDO REGIONALE DI GENOVA

PROT. N° 6b/ Zona liguria, IO/IO/44

AL COMANDO OPERATIVO DI SOTTOZONA SV/

OGGETTO: formazione della zona d'influenza-armamenti

In risposta alla vs/ del 7 u.s. si comunica che la zona d'influenza di questa Brigata è:
GIUSVALLA - PONTINVREA - MIOGLIA - GIOVO - SANTA GIUSTINA-CORONA - STEKLE - SASSELLO - FERRANIA - MONTENOTTE INF. E SUP. fino al Rivo VOLTA.
Da rivo VOLTA ad ALTARE - BRAGNO - DEGO -CARCARE vi è la Brg/ MMv Savona che opererà in uno con questa Brigata
Per le munizioni e l'armamento questa Brg/ ha bisogno delle seguenti:
N° IOO "stain" con 5 caricatori a 40 colpi
" 50 mitragliatori tipo "Skoda" con 5.000 colpi per arma.
" IOO mitra o simili; es.thompson - mass.
" I5 mitragliatrici leggere tipo Breda o Fiat 35
" 3000 colpi per mitra Berretta e relativi caricatori, possibilmente da 32 (urgentissimo)
" 2000 colpi cal.I2 per tompson
" 2000 " " " " [illegible] prolungato.

IL COMMISSARIO P. IL COMANDANTE MIL

CMTE for NATL. LIBER.
Volunteer Corps for Liberty
Hq Assault Bde.
"NINO BIXIO"
SUBORDINATE TO THE GENOVA REGIONAL COMMAND

FILE No 6b/ Liguria Zone, 10/10/44

TO THE SV SUBZONE OPERATIONAL COMMAND

SUBJECT: formation of the zone of influence – armaments

In response to your letter of the 7th of last month this is to inform you that the area of influence of this Brigade is:
GIUSVALLA – PONTINVREA – MIOGLIA – GIOVO – SANTA GIUSTINA – CORONA – STELLE – SASSELLO – FERRANIA – MONTENOTTE INF. E SUP. As far as Rivo VOLTA.
From rivo VOLTA to ALTARE – BRAGNO – DEGO – CARCARE it is the Savona Bde that operates as one with this Brigade.

This Bde has need of the following ammunition and weapons:
100 "stain" (Sten) guns with 5 40-round magazines.
50 "Skoda" type machine guns with 500 rounds per weapon.
100 submachine guns or similar weapons; for example thompson – mass (sic)
15 light machine guns such as the Breda or Fiat 35
3000 rounds for Beretta submachine gun and accompanying magazines, of 32 rounds if possible (very urgent)
2000 12 caliber (.45 ACP) rounds for the thompson
2000 9mm long rounds

THE POLITICAL COMMISSAR THE MILITARY COMMANDER

Note the letter contains a number of confusing items: the Sten magazine holds 32 rounds, not 40; while the Beretta magazine holds 40 rounds rather than 32. For some reason the request for 100 Stens has been separated from the generic request for 100 other submachine guns; similarly, there are separate requests for 3,000 rounds for the Beretta and 2,000 rounds of 9 mm "long" ammunition, which are the same round.

If the request for 265 automatic weapons for a unit theoretically consisting of 250–300 men might seem excessive, what should one think of the following request asking for a drop of 3,000 automatic weapons for some 750–900 men, bragging about having 1,500? There were also complaints of a lack of credibility on the part of the Allies.

PER LE BRIGATE:

NINO BIXIO
BALTERA
DANIELE MANIN

BRIGATA proveniente da Giustizia e Libertà.
Tutte agli ordini del Comando Regionale per la Liguria.

Campo di lancio di Cairo Montenotte: long.4°=3'=53 ''
lat.44°=23'=48''
altezza del campo mt.328

C.CARBAZZO.............706 lat. mt. 725
CASCINAZZA.............799 " " 925
M.S.GIORGIO...........840 " " 2850

RICHIESTA: 3000=armi automatiche con munizioni
mitragliatrici pesanti e leggere c/munizioni
Mortai da 81 e munizioni
Ordigni esplosivi ed incendiari, bombe a mano.
Cannoni di 47 m/m e munizioni
Scarpe ( 27=28=29)Coperte=vestiario

MESSAGGI SPECIALI : IL CAVALLO SCALPITA
I SONAGLI SQUILLANO

Brigate dislocate in...................forti di 1500 uomini agguerriti. Hanno fatto deragliare treni, saltare ponti e sostenuto vittoriosi combattimenti contro forze numericamente assai superiori di fascisti e tedeschi.

Sono in corso di mobilitazione altri 4000 uomini che andranno ad aumentare gli effettivi di queste brigate.

FOR THE BRIGADES:

NINO BIXIO
BALTERA
DANIELE MANIN

BRIGADE belonging to Justice and Liberty
All under command of the Regional Command for Liguria

Cairo Montenotte drop zone: long 4°=3'=53"
Lat.44°=23'=48"
height of drop zone 328 meters

C. CARBAZZO……706 alt. meters 725
CASCINAZZA…….799 " " 925
M.S. GIORGIO…….840 " " 2850

REQUEST: 3000=automatic weapons with ammunition
heavy and light machine guns with ammunition
81mm mortars and ammunition
Explosive and incendiary devices, hand grenades
47mm guns and ammunition
Shoes (sizes 27=28=29) Blankets and clothing

SPECIAL MESSAGES: THE HORSE IS GRAZING
THE BELLS ARE PEALING

Brigade deployed in ………………..with a strength of 1500 battle-proven men. They have derailed trains, blown up bridges, and carried out victorious engagements against numerically larger Fascist and German forces.

Another 4000 men are being mobilized who will be added to the effective strength of this brigade.

We cannot understand the reason for choosing the Sten as the icon of the resistance movement. In our opinion, if one wishes to truly show courage one has to carry a weapon that one has torn from the hands of the enemy, rather than a weapon reluctantly supplied by a doubting ally.

Strangely, in contrast to other European resistance organizations, there is no evidence that any weapons were clandestinely produced, aside from the elusive Variara.[19] If we examine the history of various movements we see that in several countries (Poland for example) there was a proliferation of secret workshops producing an unending stream of copies. Undoubtedly, the most well known was a derivative of the Sten (the Blyscavica), but at least four or five other Polish types are known (Choroszmanow, Samorobka, Bechowiec…), and many other types were produced in Norway and Denmark, while in Italy there was nothing of the sort. We would not say the Italian partisans were less capable of producing weapons than other Europeans, so what could the answer be?

A Polish partisan armed with a Błyskawica (Polish for "lightning"), a modified copy of a Sten; the most notable improvement was the introduction of a folding stock.

## CHAPTER IV

# THE CONTROVERSY INVOLVING THE ACQUISITION OF WEAPONS

Among the weapons issued to this RSI unit are several Stens, in all probability obtained by intercepting an Allied air drop to the partisans. *E. Scarone*

Without taking exception to Fenoglio, in whose writings we often find attempts to save his own weapons or to grab those of competing units,[20] we can point out the habit of lighting fires as soon as an aircraft was heard approaching in the hope that the pilot could be tricked into dropping supplies, especially weapons.

Sometimes members of Allied missions were also victims of these ploys and saw supplies "forked over" to units that did not expect them.[21] On several occasions Allied missions dropped supplies to partisan formations that had lit beacon fires but were not supposed to be the actual recipients of the supplies—a rather common trick. Once this ruse was discovered, the Allied missions supplied radios to the partisan formations they sponsored and supported so the identity of the receiving unit could be verified; if proper identification was not provided Allied aircraft strafed the beacon fires and the adjoining area.

Lighting fires was also used by units of the RSI, as attested by the fact we can find many photos of Republican units armed completely with Stens or Brens.

An RSI formation marching in a northern Italian city; two soldiers in the front row are armed with Stens. *E. Scarone*

The weapons, their distribution, and their possession were the source of many jealousies and vendettas, with unending discussions even among units subordinate to the same command; note the griping directed by a detachment to the brigade it belonged to. Also note the improper use of Bremm and Stein, which were never properly assimilated.

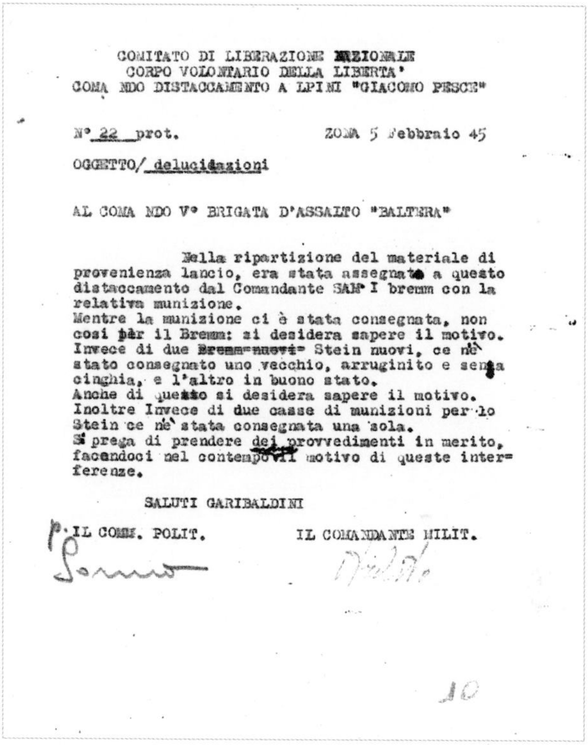

COMITATO DI LIBERAZIONE NAZIONALE
CORPO VOLONTARIO DELLA LIBERTA'
COMANDO DISTACCAMENTO ALPINI "GIACOMO PESCE"

N° 22 prot. ZONA 5 Febbraio 45

OGGETTO/ delucidazioni

AL COMANDO V° BRIGATA D'ASSALTO "BALTERA"

Nella ripartizione del materiale di provenienza lancio, era stata assegnata a questo distaccamento dal Comandante SAM I bremm con la relativa munizione.
Mentre la munizione ci è stata consegnata, non così per il Bremm: si desidera sapere il motivo.
Invece di due Stein nuovi, ce n'è stato consegnato uno vecchio, arruginito e senza cinghia, e l'altro in buono stato.
Anche di questo si desidera sapere il motivo.
Inoltre Invece di due casse di munizioni per lo Stein ce n'è stata consegnata una sola.
Si prega di prendere dei provvedimenti in merito, facendoci nel contempo il motivo di queste interferenze.

SALUTI GARIBALDINI

P. IL COMM. POLIT. IL COMANDANTE MILIT.

10

COMMITTEE OF NATIONAL LIBERATION
VOLUNTEER CORPS FOR LIBERTY
HEADQUARTERS "GIACOMO PESCE" ALPINE DETACHMENT

File No. 22 ZONE 5 February 45

SUBJECT/clarification

TO HEADQUARTERS V ASSAULT BRIGADE "BALTERA"

In apportioning the material obtained from the air drop, Commander SAM had assigned 1 bremm (sic) with relative ammunition to this detachment.
While the ammunition was handed over to us, the Bremm was not; we would like to know the reason. Instead of two new Stein (sic) guns, were given one old and rusty gun without a sling, and another in good condition.
We would also like to know the reason for this.
In addition, instead of two cases of ammunition for the Stein we were given only a single case.
We ask that you take appropriate measures, in the meantime apprising us of the reasons for these problems.

GARIBALDIAN REGARDS

THE POLITICAL COMMISSAR THE MILITARY COMMANDER

Indicative of the continuous diatribes over ownership of weapons are the letters that follow; the impression is the life of a partisan was worth less than that of the weapon he possessed.

COMITATO DI LIBERAZIONE NAZIONALE
CORPO VOLONTARI DELLA LIBERTA'

Comando
.GATA D'ASSALTO GARIBALDI
"BALTERA"

Zona, 2 Marzo 1945

N. 205

OGGETTO: Invio pistola e restituzione mitra.-

AL COMANDO DELLA 3^ BRIGATA D'ASSALTO GARIBALDI "I. BRIGANTI"

- - - - - - - -

Con riferimento al foglio di Codesto Comando in data 28/2/c.a. di prot. 321, si comunica che la pistola richiesta è stata immediatamente ritirata e pertanto si invia, a mezzo dello stesso corriere, in restituzione all'Ufficiale alle Operazioni di Codesta Brigata, RENE'.

Con l'occasione, questo Comando spera che con la medesima celerità, sia restituito il mitra Beretta che era in consegna all'ex volontario Invisibile di questa Brigata e giustiziato dal Distaccamento "Bonagura'

Unitamente al mitra, pregasi restituire anche i relativi caricatori.-

Saluti garibaldini.

IL COMM. POLITICO

IL COMANDANTE MILIT.

14

COMMITTEE OF NATIONAL LIBERATION
VOLUNTEER CORPS FOR LIBERTY

Headquarters
GARIBALDI ASSAULT BRIGADE
"BALTERA" Zone, 2 March 1945

No. 0205

SUBJECT: Forwarding pistol and return of submachine gun. –

TO HEADQUARTERS OF THE 3RD GARIBALDI ASSAULT BRIGADE "I. BRIGANTI"

\- ----

Reference letter of your Headquarters 28/2/this year, file 321, we inform you that the requested pistol was immediately pulled from service and is thus forwarded, by this same courier, in return to the Operations Officer of your Brigade, RENE'.

On this occasion, this Headquarters hopes that the Beretta submachine gun that was issued to ex-volunteer Invisibile from this Brigade and who was executed by the "Bonagura" Detachment, will be returned to us just as quickly.

Along with the submachine gun, please return its magazines.

Garibaldian regards.

THE POLITICAL COMMISSAR THE MILITARY COMMANDER

COMMITTEE OF NATIONAL LIBERATION
VOLUNTEER CORPS FOR LIBERTY
V GARIBALDI ASSAULT BRIGADE "BALTERA"
HEADQUARTERS

File no. 0277 Blt. Zone, 14 March 1945

SUBJECT: Delivery of weapons

TO HEADQUARTERS OF DETACHMENTS MORONI/REVETRIA AND PESCE/

The Headquarters of the Detachments as addressees should take measures to use the quickest means possible to deliver to this Brigade Headquarters the following weapons belonging to the Mauriane units, weapons which must be later returned to the units to which they were issued:

| | |
|---|---|
| Moroni Detachment: | 1 officer's belt with shoulder harness, belonging to the deceased Marzola. |
| "Revetria" " | 1 American rifle – 1 Italian carbine – 1 Stens |
| "Pesce" " | 1 Beretta submachine gun with two magazines, belonging to the deceased Marzola. 3 hand grenades. |

In the event that the detachments as addressees have other weapons belonging to mauriani who came to Calizzano,- they are obliged to send all of them to this Headquarters, as it is necessary to effect complete return of all material that does not belong to our Brigade.

THE POLITICAL COMMISSAR THE MILITARY COMMANDER

198
15-3-45

see page 72

COMITATO DI LIBERAZIONE NAZIONALE
CORPO VOLONTARI DELLA LIBERTA'
V^ BRIGATA D'ASSALTO GARIBALDI "BALTERA"
C O M A N D O

N° 127 di prot. Blt. Zona, 14 Marzo 1945

OGGETTO: Invio di armi.-

AI COMANDI DEI DISTACCAMENTI MORONI/REVETRIA E PESCE/

- - - - - - -

I Comandi dei Distaccamenti in indirizzo provvedano col mezzo più celere, a far giungere a questo Comando Brigata le seguenti armi di appartenenza alle formazioni Mauriane, armi che debbono essere successivamente restituite ai reparti di appartenenza:

Distaccamento Moroni: 1 Cinturone da ufficiale con spallaccio, del defunto Marzola.
" "Revetria": 1 fucile americano - 1 moschetto italiano - 1 Stens -
" "Pesce": 1 mitra Beretta con due caricatori, del defunto Marzola.
3 Bombe a mano.

Nella eventualità che i distaccamenti in indirizzo, posseggano ancora altre armi sempre di appartenenza dei mauriani venuti in Calizzano,- sono tenuti ad inviarle tutte a questo Comando, poiché è necessario eseguire una completa restituzione di quanto non appartiene alla nostra Brigata.-

IL COMM. POLITICO IL COMANDANTE MILIT.

198
15-3-45

This is the final response to a series of complaints concerning the apportionment of weapons acquired by annihilating a republican unit:

COMITATO DI LIBERAZIONE NAZIONALE
CORPO VOLONTARI DELLA LIBERTA'
V^ BRIGATA D'ASSALTO GARIBALDI "BALTERA"
C O M A N D O

N° 0309 di prot.Blt. Zona, 20 Marzo 1945

OGGETTO: Richiesta mitra Beretta.

AL COMANDO DELLA 3^ BRIGATA D'ASSALTO GARIBALDI "L.BRIGANTI"

e, per conoscenza:

AL COMANDO DELLA I^ DIVISIONE D'ASSALTO GARIBALDI "G.BEVILACQUA"

\- - - - - - - - -

In risposta al foglio di Codesto Comando, in data 7 c.m. di prot.333, allo stesso oggetto, si specifica quanto segue:

1°) - La mitragliatrice Ocis (imprestata al Distaccamento Bruzzone) è stata occultata nei pressi del forte Tortagnà, dopo che fu resa inservibile dall'esplosione di una bomba nemica.

2°) - Il Comandante ARDITO, non è in possesso di alcun mitra né appartenente al Distaccamento "Ines Negri" né ad altri. Si è presentato a Calizzano armato di uno Stens acquistato da un ex volontario di Mauri.

3°) - Alla squadra di otto volontari che collaborò alla cattura degli alpini in Calizzano, venne consegnata una parte equa del bottino e precisamente: n° 8 moschetti con relative giberne e munizioni e n° 1 mitragliatrice pesante "Breda".
Il Comandante della squadra stessa, vol. Tempesta, si era dichiarato più che soddisfatto della parte ricevuta, in quanto egli stesso sapeva bene a qual punto aveva trovato lo svolgersi della azione, al momento del suo arrivo a Calizzano.

Da parte nostra ci stupisce non poco il fatto che si insista tanto sulla ripartizione del bottino quando si è sicuri che la squadra partecipò all'azione per puro spirito combattivo, come il "Revetria" è venuto spesso in aiuto, anche non richiesto, di Codesta Brigata sia al Melogno, come anche a Bardineto, senza mai chiedere alcuna ricompenza dai bottini di armi, perchè conscio di adempiere unicamente al proprio dovere.

Il mitra Beretta da noi più volte richiesto, apparteneva di diritto ad un nostro volontario. Dalla voce pubblica soltanto, si venne a conoscenza che quest'ultimo era stato giustiziato dal Distaccamento Bonagura, che si impossessò dell'arma che il volontario Liggo Gallea aveva al momento della cattura. Questo Comando non crede di essere oltremodo esigente se si fa rimarcare che sarebbe stato un elementare atto di cortesia, l'informare il Comando della Brigata alla quale il volontario Gallea (Invisibile), apparteneva, circa l'avvenuto arresto e i motivi che determinarono la sua

./. 12

COMMITTEE OF NATIONAL LIBERATION
VOLUNTEER CORPS FOR LIBERTY
V GARIBALDI ASSAULT BRIGADE "BALTERA"
HEADQUARTERS

File no. 0309 Blt. Zone, 20March 1945

SUBJECT; Request for Beretta submachine gun

TO HEADUARTERS OF THE 3RD GARIBALDI ASSAULT BRIGADE "L. BRIGANTI"

and, for information

TO HEADQUARTERS OF THE 1ST GARBALDI ASSAULT DIVISION "G. BEVILACQUA"

– – – –

In response to the letter of Your Headquarters, dated 7 this mont, file no. 333, same subject, the following is provided:

1). – The Ocis (sic) machine gun (lent to the Bruzzone Detachment) was hidden near Fort Tortagna, after it had been rendered unserviceable by the explosion of an enemy bomb.

2). - Commander ARDITO is not in possession of any submachine gun belonging either to the "Ines Negri" Detachment nor to any other detachment. He showed up in Calizzano armed with a Sten acquired from an ex-volunteer from Mauri.

3). – The squad of eight volunteers that collaborated in the capture of the alpine in Calizzano was given an equal share of the booty, specifically: 8 carbines with their ammo pouches and ammunition and 1 "Breda" heavy machine gun.
The Commander of the squad, vol. Tempesta, had declared himself more than satisfied with the part received, and in this he himself knew very well at what point the action had reached at the time of his arrival in Calizzano.

On our part we are more than a little amazed by the fact that there is much insistence on the sharing of the booty when there is no doubt that the squad participated in the action out of a pure fighting spirit, as the "Revetria" often lent its help, even when not requested, to Your Brigade both at Melogno as well as at Bardineto, without ever asking for any share of the booty of weapons, because it was conscious of carrying out its proper duty.

The Beretta submachine gun, requested by us numerous times, by rights belonged to one of our volunteers. It was only by public knowledge that we became aware that he had been executed by the Bonagura Detachment, which then took possession of the weapon that volunteer Pippo Gallea had at the time of his capture. This Headquarters does not believe out of order it makes the observation that it would have been a basic act of courtesy to have informed the Brigade to which volunteer Gallea (Invisibile) belonged, of his arrest and the reasons that determined his execution.

## CHAPTER V

# TURNING IN WEAPONS

**PROVINCIAL NOTICE No. 1**

**TO ALL PARTISANS**

The handing in of arms by Partisans will be carried out as a Military operation under orders issued by the Provincial Military Commission.

These arms will then be handed over to Allied Military Authorities through normal Military channels.

All Divisional and Brigade Commanders of Partisan formations have been advised of the method of procedure.

W. TURNER-COLES

**AVVISO PROVINCIALE N. 1**

**A TUTTI I PARTIGIANI**

La consegna delle armi da parte dei partigiani verrà effettuata come una operazione militare: gli ordini verranno impartiti dalla Commissione Militare Provinciale.

Tali armi saranno consegnate alle Autorità Militari Alleate tramite organi militari.

Tutte le divisioni ed i comandi di Brigata dei partigiani sono già stati avvisati del metodo da seguire.

W. TURNER-COLES

A notice in English and Italian providing instructions concerning handing over arms held by the partisans to Allied military authorities. *G. Gonnella*

As called for by the Rome agreements between the CLNAI and the Allies shortly after the liberation of Italy, a weapons turn-in program was to be instituted and all partisan formations were to be completely disarmed. In many cases there were parades and large public displays:

A mass turn-in of weapons by partisans. The presence of a Soviet flag and the prevalence of red neckerchiefs indicates the partisans belonged to communist dominated units. The photo was taken in the old Roman colosseum known as "the Arena" in Verona. *Anonymous*

An impressive amount of weapons turned in. *Anonymous*

In other places the procedure was much more bureaucratic, with annotated records of the type of weapon and the serial numbers.

Based on an examination of documentation from the "Fumagalli" partisan division operating in Valbormida, we were able to pull some interesting notations concerning the weapons the unit had on hand that it gradually turned in during May and June 1945.

Setting aside the great number of Italian and German rifles and carbines—long and short and designated in various ways—the exam led to a number of doubts, inasmuch as:

- Certain types of weapons are completely absent from the lists, such as handguns: semi-automatic pistols and revolvers;
- Individual automatic weapons of all types are absent except for a dozen or so Stens, although there were only a few spare magazines and almost no ammunition;
- Many automatic rifles of varying types were listed, the Bren being among the most common, but with few spare magazines; this was surpassed by the "Skoda" (probably the Czech ZB26) and a few other models, such as Hotchkiss, St. Etienne, Breda, and "machine gewehr," accompanied by ammunition chests and magazines, and almost always followed by the notation they were unserviceable.

MILITARY HEADQUARTERS<br>Of the Presidio of ALBISSOLA<br>"E. FUMAGALLI" DIVISION<br>"G. GARIBALDI" BRIGADE

The Patriots listed hereunder turn over their personal weapons

| | | | |
|---|---|---|---|
| 1 Condemi Giuseppe | moschetto 38 | Serial no. | 4681 |
| 2 Malpede " | " | " | 3753 |
| 3 Reitano " | carbine U.S. PROPERTY | " | QC 2461 |
| 4 Pipitone Giacomo | ΕΛΛΗΝΙΚΟΣ ΣΤΡΑΤΟΣ ΑΡΙΘ 1940 | | |
| 5 Riggio Carmelo | moschetto 38 | " | 8422 |
| 6 Rossetti Aurelio | " | " | 8684 |
| 7 DeFranco Vittorio | " | " | VQ1330 |
| 8 Rimondi Elvio | " | " | 1291 |
| 9 Sclaro Franco | " | " | C8564 |

Patriots Finucci Vittorio and Massorani Armando, civilian delegate, handed in their weapons to my company headquarters.

Albissola 1-6-45

THE COMPANY COMMANDER

The presence of a Greek Hotchkiss 1926 is a bit curious:

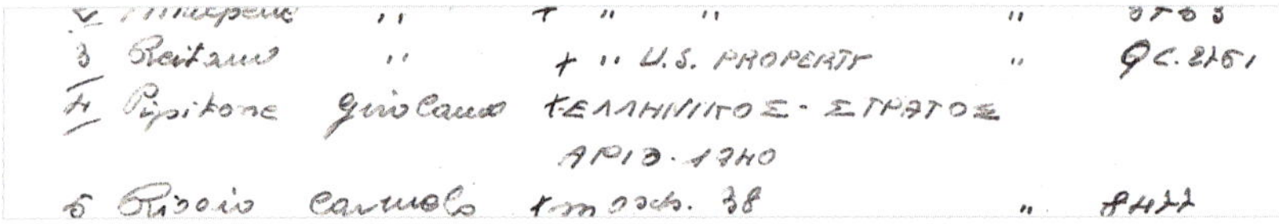

| | | | |
|---|---|---|---|
| 3 Reitano " | carbine U.S. PROPERTY | " | QC 2461 |
| 4 Pipitone Giacomo | ΕΛΛΗΝΙΚΟΣ ΣΤΡΑΤΟΣ<br>ΑΡΙΘ 1940 | | |
| 5 Riggio Carmelo | moschetto 38 | " | 8422 |

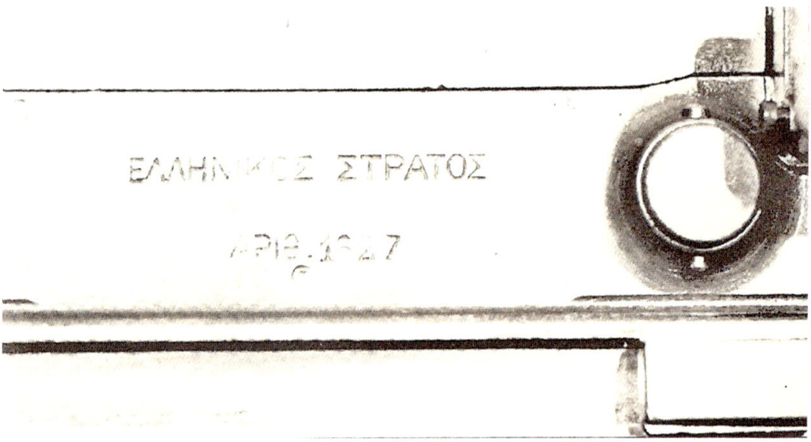


Markings on the receiver of a Model 1926 Greek Hotchkiss light machine gun. *Diana Armi magazine*

It is also interesting to note the presence of various US weapons, although it is somewhat difficult to understand precisely which weapons are referred to: in the document shown a carbine marked "US PROPERTY" is mentioned, but the serial number (QC 2461) cannot refer to a carbine; instead it may correspond to a rifle, probably an Enfield produced in the United States by Savage Arms Company. Enfields produced by Savage were marked "US PROPERTY" and the 1941–1942 serial number blocks consisted of four digits with an OC prefix, so it is likely the O was mistakenly copied as a Q in the document. Another document mentions two English Remington rifles—attributing rifles produced in America to the United Kingdom—while another document lists two US carbines with seven- and six-digit numbers, thus possibly M1s.

Less understandable is the presence of a "brevetto america 24440M."

Various heavy machine guns were turned in, including the Breda 37, Fiat 35, Saint Etienne, and Okhis, and all invariably unserviceable (but then again, in the case of the Hotchkiss, how could it be expected to function properly when it was missing so many of the letters of its name that it became the Okhis?).

Among puzzles to be solved are those of a "machine gun 8 mm Browning," an 8 mm British machine gun, and a Maxim.

Among the decidedly less common weapons were a British PIAT grenade launcher with three rounds, a "55 mm English mortar" with thirty rounds, and a "Panzer-Waust."

Examining a group of photos of various detachments of the division—some of which are shown in this book—it is possible to determine and confirm the presence of some of these weapons, as well as the rather strange absence of others.

We thus see in several groups of the "Fumagalli" Division the presence of more Stens than appear to have been delivered, as well as a Browning 1919 (probably the "machine gun 8 mm Browning") and an MG42, as well as a plethora of Beretta MABs—both the 38A and the 38/42—various MP40, and a pair of Thompsons, of which there is no mention in the lists.

A group of partisans from the Fumagalli Division with a seeming abundance of light and medium automatic weapons. *G. Toscani*

Who knows if the PIAT seen in the photo is the same one mentioned as having been delivered and if the Enfield is not the same one mentioned as being a British Remington.[22] Several German "semi-automatics" are also described as delivered, presumably such as this Gew 41.

Another well-armed Fumagalli Division team; note especially the PIAT anti-tank grenade launcher. *G. Toscani*

Nevertheless, even early on doubts began to surface concerning the effectiveness of the weapons turn-in process. Although the Allies' doubts may be understandable—they had already begun to worry about it earlier and had held back on some deliveries—it is somewhat strange that as early as May 13, 1945, some partisan formations had also begun to entertain suspicion.

DIVISIONE FUMAGALLI
1A; Brigata Giovanni Chiarlone
COMANDO 4a. Compagnia

SEGRETO = RISERVATO

Il Comandante di questa Compagnia dopo attente osservazioni ed informazioni assunte fa presente al Comando di Brigata, per gli opportunità che crede, quanto segue :

Da molto tempo le formazioni Garibaldine dislocate nella Zona di Giusvalla, Forte dei Giovi,- Pareto - Pontinvrea - Mioglia -quantunque procedano al disarmo dei propri uomini, le armi non vengono se non in minima parte ( e sono armi pressoché inutilizzabili) consegnate al Comando di Liberazione Nazionale, o ai Sindaci dei Paesi. Alcuni Comandanti o Commissari Politici di cui questo Comando é in stretta relazione, ma ha fatto presente che le armi vengono nascoste non tanto per non essere consegnate agli alleati, ma bensì per un'eventuale imposizione del Partito da loro rappresentato anche con l'impiego delle forze. Questo é quanto devo comunicare al Comando di Brigata per opportuna conoscenza.

li, 13/5/1943

IL COMANDANTE DELLA COMPAGNIA
firmato (Male)

per copia conforme all'originale
Dinamico ( Carlo Drommi ) Capo di S.M. della Div. Fumagalli
XXXXXXXXXXXXXXXXXXXXXXXXXXXXXXXXXXXXXXXXXXXXXXXXXXXXXXXXXXXXXX
V. MASTRANGELO XXXXXXXXXXXX

FUMAGALLI DIVISION
1ST Brigade Giovanni Chiarlone

HEADQUARTERS 4th Company

SECRET = CONFIDENTIAL

The Commander of this Company, based on careful observations and information obtained, informs the Brigade Headquarters that he believes as follows:

For some time the Garibaldi units located in the area of Giusvalla, Forte dei Giovi, - Pareto – Pontinvrea – Mioglia- whenever the proceed to disarm their men, except for a very small number of weapons (and these are weapons that are practically unusable) the weapons are not turned over to the National Liberation Headquarters or to the mayors of the towns. Some Commanders or Political Commissars with whom this Headquarters is in close contact have made it known that these weapons are being hidden not so much as to not turn them over to the Allies, but for an eventual imposition of the Party they represent, even with the use of force. This is what I have to report to the Brigade Headquarters for appropriate action.

13/5/1943

THE COMPANY COMMANDER
signed (Male)

Copy conforming to the original signed by
Dinamico (Carlo Dromi) Chief of Staff of the Fumagalli division
XXXXXXXXXXXXXXXXXXXXXXXXXXXXXXXXXXXXXXX
V. MASTRANGELO XXXXXXXXXXXX

Orders were issued to once again specify all weapons were to be turned in; evidently there were some partisans who felt they would like to take a souvenir home with them.

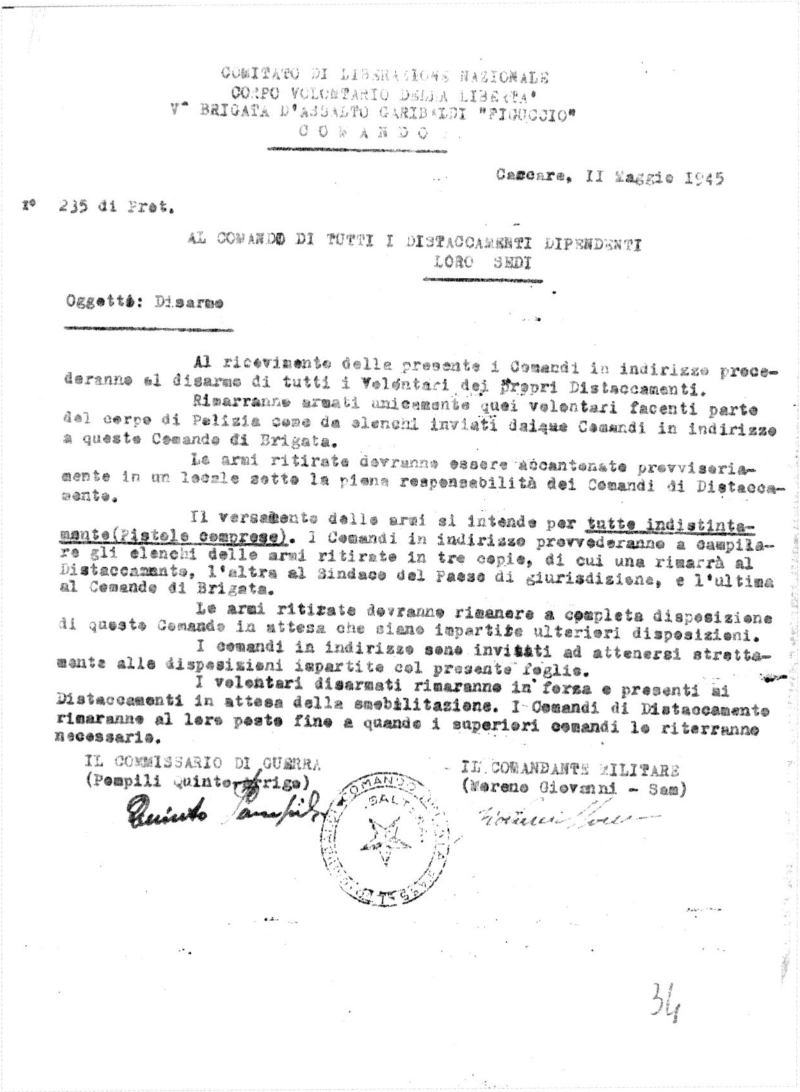

COMITATO DI LIBERAZIONE NAZIONALE
CORPO VOLONTARIO DELLA LIBERTA'
V^ BRIGATA D'ASSALTO GARIBALDI "FIGUCCIO"
C O M A N D O

Carcare, II Maggio 1945

N° 235 di Prot.

AL COMANDO DI TUTTI I DISTACCAMENTI DIPENDENTI
LORO SEDI

Oggetto: Disarmo

Al ricevimento della presente i Comandi in indirizzo procederanno al disarmo di tutti i Volontari dei propri Distaccamenti.

Rimarranno armati unicamente quei volontari facenti parte del corpo di Polizia come da elenchi inviati daique Comandi in indirizzo a questo Comando di Brigata.

Le armi ritirate dovranno essere accantonate provvisoriamente in un locale sotto la piena responsabilità dei Comandi di Distaccamento.

Il versamento delle armi si intende per tutte indistintamente(Pistole comprese). I Comandi in indirizzo provvederanno a compilare gli elenchi delle armi ritirate in tre copie, di cui una rimarrà al Distaccamento, l'altra al Sindaco del Paese di giurisdizione, e l'ultima al Comando di Brigata.

Le armi ritirate dovranno rimanere a completa disposizione di questo Comando in attesa che siano impartite ulteriori disposizioni.

I comandi in indirizzo sono invitati ad attenersi strettamente alle disposizioni impartite col presente foglio.

I volontari disarmati rimaranno in forza e presenti ai Distaccamenti in attesa della smobilitazione. I Comandi di Distaccamento rimaranno al loro posto fino a quando i superiori comandi lo riterranno necessario.

IL COMMISSARIO DI GUERRA
(Pompili Quinto-Frigo)
Quinto Pompili

IL COMANDANTE MILITARE
(Moreno Giovanni - Sem)

34

COMMITTEE OF NATIONAL LIBERATION
VOLUNTEER CORPS FOR LIBERTY
7TH GARIBALDI ASSAULT BRIGADE "FIGUCCIO"
HEADQUARTERS

Carcare, 11 May 1945

File no. 235

TO HEADQUARTERS OF ALL SUBORDINATE COMMANDS
RESPECTIVE BRANCHES

Subject: Disarmament

Upon receipt of this letter all receiving Headquarters will proceed to disarm all Volunteers in their respective Detachments.

Only those Volunteers who are part of the Police corps will remain under arms, as on lists sent by the addressee Headquarters to this Brigade Headquarters.

The weapons which are turned in must be temporarily stored in a location under the complete responsibility of the Detachment Headquarters.

The weapons hand-over is meant to apply to all types of weapons (Pistols included). The Headquarters as addressees will take measures to compile a list of weapons handed over in three copies, one of which will remain at the Detachment, another with the Mayor of the town of jurisdiction, and the final copy to the Brigade Headquarters.

The weapons collected must remain at the complete disposition of this Headquarters while awaiting for further instructions to be given.

The headquarters addressed are invited to adhere strictly to the dispositions given by the present letter.

The disarmed volunteers will remain in force and present in the Detachments while awaiting demobilization. The Detachment Headquarters will remain in place until such time as higher headquarters may deem necessary.

THE COMMISSAR OF WAR
(Pompili Quinto - Arrigo)

THE MILITARY COMMANDER
(Moreno Giovanni – Sam)

Confirming that many weapons had not been turned in, an order was given to the police to provide a monthly report of the number of weapons found (a page of an outline is transcribed).

Although for some months the reports were negative, they were often quite full, with discoveries of cannons, mortars, and heavy machine guns. It is difficult to believe certain of these categories represented mere souvenirs.

SAVONA POLICE HEADQUARTERS
POLITICAL SQUAD
Subject: Discovery of weapons
Savona, 3 November 1952
TO THE CHIEF OF POLICE

It is hereby communicated that during the past month of October the following weapons were found by this squad:

British "Bren" light machine guns.........3
Replacement barrels for the aforementioned guns.........1
British "Sten" submachine guns.........9
Mod. 91 "moschetti".........12
German "Mauser" rifles.........4
Beretta 38/A "long" submachine guns.........2
8 mm Belgian type heavy machine guns.........2
Revolvers.........2
German P38 pistol.........1
Magazines for P38.........2
Magazines for Sten.........39
Magazines for Bren light machine gun.........24
British Mod. 26 hand grenades.........14
Italian hand grenades.........6
German anti-tank hand grenades.........2
German hand grenades.........4
Complete machine gun ammunition belts.........6
Detonators contained in a box.........100
Electric detonators.........2
Detonators for mines.........20
Stock for "moschetto".........1
Bolt for "moschetto".........1
Ammunition chargers for light machine gun.........65
Ammunition pouches.........1 pair
Fuse cord.........8 coils
Barrels for German Mauser rifles.........1
Stripper clips for Mauser rifles.........1
Magazines for Beretta 38/A.........3
Projectiles for German Bazuska (sic).........2
TNT blocks.........3
Tube with 200 grams of TNT.........1
Explosive tubes.........20
Various cartridges.........5772

The Police Sergeant[23]

The police continued to monitor the situation, and in May 1951, arranged for a series of inspections to be carried out by the principal industries in the Savona area, ordering:

> ... a careful technical inspection, based on original blueprints..., providing for the demolition of all suspect wall construction that may have been carried out without the knowledge of the management... The above is ordered in order to find possible clandestine caches of weapons and explosives; recent repeated discoveries have shown these incidents to be not uncommon in industrial establishments.

This prodding evidently had little effect, as on October 11, 1952, the *questura* (police headquarters) noted in its morning report:

> Last night, functionaries and agents of the local questura, in conjunction with soldiers of the arm of the carabinieri, carried out a sweep at the local Scarpa and Magnano factory, during which numerous weapons and ammunition were found in perfect working order and well oiled.[25]

Even more than seventy years later, such caches continue to be discovered. An example is the large cache shown, containing more than a hundred Italian and German rifles, several machine guns, and mortar grenades found in the Savona area in 2002, thanks to the confession of a repentant partisan who reported it to the newspapers and to an author from Valbormida who inserted the photo and the accompanying letter in a book he wrote.[26]

A partisan arms cache found in a cave near Savona in 2002. *F. Sasso*

We can see another example in the photograph that accompanies Profile 63, showing several machine guns found in the Finale area in 2010.

Two of the weapons carried by Beppe Fenoglio; the M1 carbine is a "hybrid" that has the adjustable rear sight, but lacks the bayonet stud. *Courtesy Bruno Murialdo, Archivio Centro Studi Beppe Fenoglio Alba*

As late as October 2013, the weapons "forgotten" by Beppe Fenoglio[27] were found in a closet in his home.

Most of the weapons confiscated were turned over to the appropriate Italian artillery headquarters, while the best examples were kept by the reporting agency for service needs; thus was the state of equipment issued to police forces 1945–1950.

## CHAPTER VI

# WEAPONS AND CORRESPONDING AMMUNITION

As can be seen in the following table, obtaining ammunition must have been a real nightmare for the partisan supply officer; ammunition resupply problems caused many of the less common types of weapons to be retired from use following the early days of the resistance.

### Pistol/Submachine Gun Ammunition

| | |
|---|---|
| 6.35 Browning, 6.35 × 16 | All pocket pistols used by higher officers and by many civilians |
| 7.62 Tokarev, 7.62 × 25 | TT30 and TT33, PPSH41 and other Russian weapons |
| 7.62 Nagant, 7.62 × 28 | Mod. 1895 revolver |
| 7.63 × 25 | Mauser C96 |
| 7.65 Browning, 7.65 × 17 | Beretta 1915/17, Mod. 1922, Mod 1932, Mod. 1935, Sauer & Sohn 38H, CZ 27, FN 1922, Ruby |
| 7.65 longue, 7.65 × 19.5 | SACM 1935A and 1935S, MAS 1938 |
| 9 corto, 9 short, 9 kurz, 9 × 17 | Beretta 1934, CZ38, FN1922, FeG37, Astra 300 |
| 9 Glisenti, 9 × 19 | Glisenti 1919, Beretta 1915, Beretta 1923, Beretta 18/30 |
| 9 parabellum, 9 × 19 | P08, Mauser C96 and derivatives, Radom VIS, FN HP35, German Steyr 1912, Sten, MP40, MP 34 (o), MP35, MP18, MP28, MP41, Suomi M31, UD M42, M3 (9 mm), Astra 600 |
| 9M38, 9 × 19 | Beretta 38A and 38/42, FNAB43, TZ45 |
| 9 largo, 9 × 23 | Astra 400 |
| 9 Steyr, 9 × 23 | Austrian Steyr 1912, Austrian MP34(o) |
| .38/200 (approximately 9 mm) | Enfield, Webley, Smith & Wesson revolvers |

| | |
|---|---|
| .38 special (approximately 9 mm) | Smith & Wesson, Colt revolvers |
| 10,35, 10.35 × 22 | Model 1889 revolver |
| .45 ACP, 11.43 × 23 | Colt 1911A1 and various derivatives, various model Thompsons, M3 (.45), Smith & Wesson and colt revolvers |
| .455 | Webley revolvers |

## Rifle/Machine Gun Ammunition

| | |
|---|---|
| 6.5 × 52 | All Model 1891 weapons, Colt 1895, Breda 30, Fiat 1914, Vetterli/Vitali 70/87/16 |
| 6.5 × 54 | Greek Hotchkiss 1926, Greek Mannlicher |
| 7.35 × 51 | Model 91/38 weapons |
| 7.5 × 54 | Model 1924m29 |
| .30M1, 7.62 × 33 | M1 carbine |
| .30-06, 7.62 × 63 | Mod 1903A3, M1 Garand, BAR, Browning 1919A4 |
| 7.62 × 54R | Mosin Nagant 1891, DP28 |
| 7.65 × 53 | Belgian Mauser, Belgian BAR |
| .303, 7.7 × 56 | Enfield, Bren, Vickers, Breda-Safat |
| 7.92 Kurz, 7.92 × 33 | StG44 |
| 7.92 × 57 | German and foreign Mausers, MG34, MG42, FG42, Gew 41, Gew 43, ZB26 and ZB30 |
| 8 Mannlicher, 8 × 50 | Schwarzlose, M1895 rifles and carbines |
| 8 Lebel, 8 × 50 | Hotchkiss 19194, Saint Etienne 1907 |
| 8 Breda, 8 × 59 | Fiat 1914/35, Breda 37 |
| 10.4 Vetterli, 10,4 × 48 | Vetterli 70 and Vetterli-Vitali 70/87 |
| 12,7 × 81 | Breda Safat |
| .50, 12.7 × 99 | Browning M2HB |

The document that follows gives some idea of the difficulties encountered and helps explain what some of these weapons might be.

We are provided confirmation the "Skoda" was 7.92 mm, even though there seems to be no reason to separate that request from that for ammunition for all of the other German weapons of the same caliber.

It is likewise curious there is a request for 6.5 mm ammunition for the Breda 30 light machine gun and no such request for Mod. 91 weapons that were surely on hand. It is possible the understood but not specifically stated request was for rounds to be supplied along with the charger trays needed for the Breda 30.

There were also many accidents caused by the use of inappropriate cartridges, i.e., accidents caused by the use of similar but not equal ammunition, such as the Italian 9M38 submachine gun round used in the Glisenti Model 1910 pistol designed and built to use the 9 mm Glisenti round, which was a much less powerful round than the 9M38.

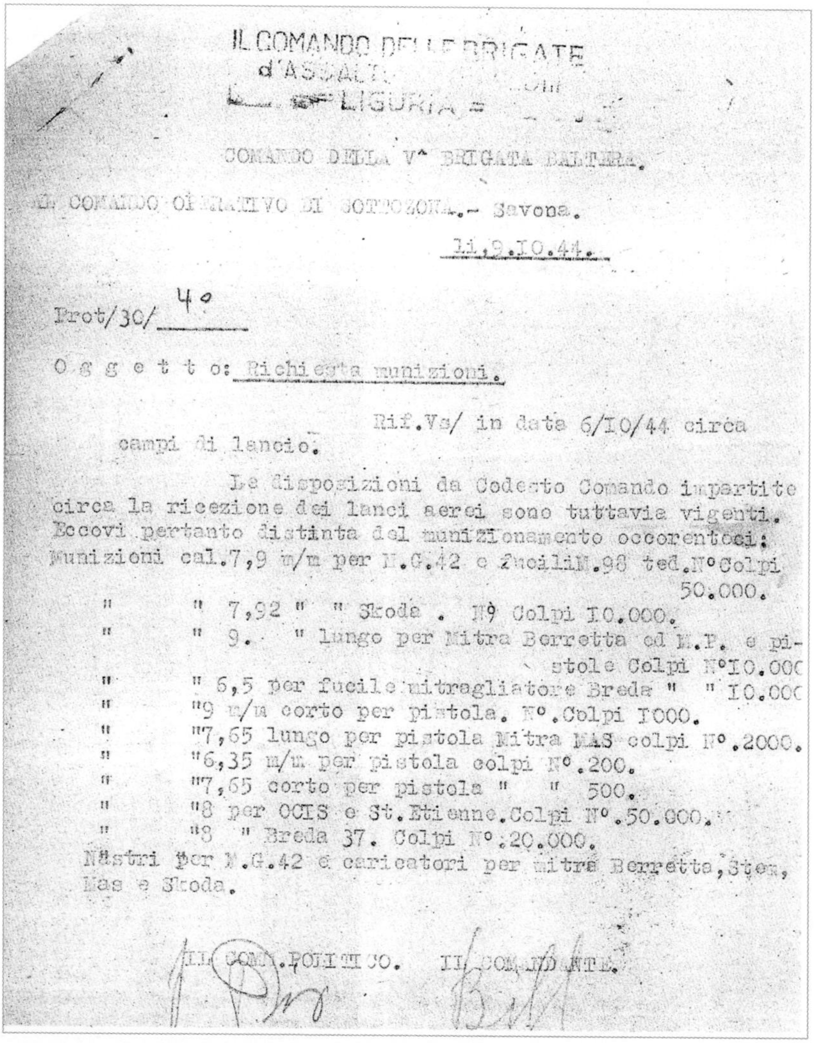

IL COMANDO DELLE BRIGATE
d'ASSALTO
LIGURIA

COMANDO DELLA V^ BRIGATA BALTERA.

AL COMANDO OPERATIVO DI SOTTOZONA.- Savona.

li, 9.10.44.

Prot/30/ 40

Oggetto: Richiesta munizioni.

Rif.Vs/ in data 6/10/44 circa campi di lancio.

Le disposizioni da Codesto Comando impartite circa la ricezione dei lanci aerei sono tuttavia vigenti. Eccovi pertanto distinta del munizionamento occorrentoci:

Munizioni cal.7,9 m/m per M.G.42 e fucili M.98 ted. N° Colpi 50.000.
" " 7,92 " " Skoda . N° Colpi 10.000.
" " 9. " lungo per Mitra Berretta ed M.P. e pistole Colpi N°10.000
" " 6,5 per fucile mitragliatore Breda " " 10.000
" "9 m/m corto per pistola. N°.Colpi 1000.
" "7,65 lungo per pistola Mitra MAS colpi N°.2000.
" "6,35 m/m per pistola colpi N°.200.
" "7,65 corto per pistola " " 500.
" "8 per OCIS e St.Etienne.Colpi N°.50.000.
" "8 " Breda 37. Colpi N°.20.000.

Nastri per M.G.42 e caricatori per mitra Berretta, Sten, Mas e Skoda.

IL COM. POLITICO. IL COMANDANTE.

HEADQUARTERS GARIBALDI
ASSAULT BRIGADES
LIGURIA

HEADQUARTERS V BALTERA BFRIGADE

TO THE SUB-ZONE OPERATIONAL COMMAND. – Savona.

9.10.44

File/30/40

Subject: Request for ammunition

Ref Your/dated 6/10/44 regarding drop zones.

The dispositions from this Headquarters issued with respect to air drops are still in effect. Here then is a list of ammunition we need:

Ammunition cal. 7.92 m/m for M.G.42 and German M.98 rifles No. rounds 50,000
" " 7.92 " " Skoda No. rounds 10,000
" " 9. " long for Beretta submachine guns and M.P. and pistols No. rounds 10,000
" " 6.5 for Breda light machine gun No. rounds 10,000
" " 9m/m short for pistol No. rounds 1,000
" " 7.65 long for MAS machine pistol No. rounds 2,000
" " 8 for OCIS or St. Etienne No. rounds 50,000
" " 8 " Breda 37. No. Rounds 20,000

Belts for M.G.42 and magazines for Beretta, Sten, Mas and Skoda weapons.

THE POLITICAL COMMISSAR THE COMMANDER

Martini-Mauri, Report to Headquarters on 25.12.45 AIRSP B45 b stated: "Instances are cited of machine guns that are not utilized because of the explosion of ammunition not suitable for a particular type of weapon."

Some weapons were subjected to odd modifications to more common calibers: there are stories of Steyr 1912 pistols in 9 mm Steyr that had field modifications to their chambers so they could chamber the 9 mm parabellum.

In correspondence between partisan formations several examples of modifications can be found, such as this proposal relating to a Belgian Model 1930 automatic rifle—a copy of the Browning BAR—to convert the caliber from 7.65 × 53 to 7.5 × 54.[28]

COMITATO DI LIBERAZIONE NAZIONALE
CORPO VOLONTARI DELLA LIBERTA'
V^ BRIGATA D'ASSALTO GARIBALDI "BALTERA"
C O M A N D O

N° 0141 di prot.BLT. Zona 16 Febbraio 1945

OGGETTO: Richiesta di un alesatore.-

AL COMANDO DELLA I^ DIVISIONE D'ASSALTO GARIB
" A. BEVILACQUA "

- - - - - -

Codesto Comando è pregato di richiedere al competente organo, un alesatore per approfondire la camera di scoppio di un fucile mitragliatore Obel. A tal'uopo si allegano due cartucce sulle quali dovrà essere costruito l'alesatore richiesto.

La richiesta è fatta in quanto il Distaccamento "Revetria" che ha in dotazione il fucile mitragliatore menzionato, non ha munizioni per il medesimo,mentre invece dispone di un gran numero e di ogni specie di munizioni per fucile mitragliatore Saint Etienne, le quali differiscono di minimissima misura da quelle dell'Obel.

Il lavoro dell'approfondimento della camera di scoppio, sarà eseguito da questa Brigata.-

Dalla figura annessa si può rilevare chiaramente quale deve essere la parte tagliente dell'attrezzo richiesto.-

IL COMM.POLITICO IL COMANDANTE MILIT.

101

COMMITTEE OF NATIONAL LIBERATION
VOLUNTEER CORPS FOR LIBERTY
V GARIBALDI ASSAULT BRIGADE "BALTERA"
HEADQUARTERS

File No. 0141BLT. Zone 16 February 1945

SUBJECT: Request for reamer.-

TO HEADQUARTERS OF THE IST GARIBALDI ASSAULT DIVISION
"A. BEVILACQUA"

------

Your Headquarters is kindly requested to request from the appropriate source a reamer to enlarge the firing chamber of an Obel light machine gun. To this end two cartridges are attached for which the required reamer can be produced.

This request is being made because the "Revetria" Detachment, which has the aforementioned light machine gun on hand, has no ammunition for it, while it has a large stock of all types of ammunition for the Saint Etienne light machine gun, whose specifications differ only minimally from those of the Obel.

The work of reaming out the chamber will be performed by this Brigade.

The enclosed drawing clearly shows where the cutting edge of the requested tool should be.

THE POLITICAL COMMISSAR THE MILITARY COMMANDER

Although during the early days of cooperation the Allies provided relatively few weapons—partially because weapons could be obtained by taking them from the enemy—it was insufficient ammunition drops that influenced the ability to carry out guerrilla warfare, not only with respect to combat activity, but also hindering the training of new recruits.

Having only a limited number of cartridges available, it was only with difficulty that partisans could engage in protracted combat against Anglo-American forces in the event of a hypothetical rebellion against them.

COMITATO DI LIBERAZIONE NAZIONALE
CORPO VOLONTARI DELLA LIBERTA'

Comando
BRIGATA D'ASSALTO GARIBALDI
" BALTERA "

Zona, 2 Marzo 1945.

N. 0201 di prot. Pdk

OGGETTO: Tiri di prova d'armi.-

AL COMANDO DEI DISTACCAMENTI BORI/BRUZZONE/MORONI/PESCE/REVERTIA/

Si è constatato che in questi giorni, sotto la forma di prova d'armi o esercitazioni di tiro, quasi tutti i distaccamenti in indirizzo, fanno un grandissimo spreco di munizioni di ogni genere.

Si ordina pertanto, che, ad evitare :

1°) - di compromettere la segretessa sulla dislocazione degli accampamenti;

2°) - di generare falsi allarmi od errate interpretazioni degli spari;

3°) - l'inutile spreco di munizioni mai sufficenti per il nostro fabbisogno,

vengano immediatamente sospesi tiri di qualsiasi genere.

Nella eventualità di una necessaria ed indispensabile prova di una qualsiasi arma, sia preventivamente avvisato questo Comando Brigata, indicando l'arma, il giorno, il luog. e l'ora della prova.

Per l'effettuaziòne della prova dovrà essere atteso il nulla osta di questo Comando.

E' da ricordare pertanto che, le migliori e più utili esercitazioni di tiro, sono quelle eseguite durante le azioni di attacco ai nostri nemici.-

IL COMM. POLITICO

IL COMANDANTE MILIT.

157
2-3-45

12

COMMITTEE OF NATIONAL LIBERATION
VOLUNTEER CORPS FOR LIBERTY

Headquarters
GARIBALDI ASSAULT BRIGADE
"BALTERA" Zone, 2 March 1945

SUBJECT: Test firing of weapons.-

TO HEADQUARTERS OF THE BORI/BRUZZONE/MORONI/PESCE/REVETRIA DETACHMENTS

---------

It has been noticed that in recent days, under the guise of test firing or weapons training, almost all of the detachments noted as addressees, are wasting a very large amount of ammunition of all types.

It is therefore ordered that, in order to avoid:

1st) - compromising the secrecy of the locations of encampments;

2nd) – generating false alarms or mistaken interpretation of the firing;

3rd) – useless waste of ammunition that is never enough for our needs,

that all firing of any type be suspended immediately.

In the event that it is necessary and indispensable to test fire any weapon, this Brigade Headquarters be advised beforehand, indicating the weapon, the day, the place and the hour of the test.

Clearance by this Headquarters must be received before carrying out any test firing.

It should also be remembered that the best and most useful firing practice are those that are carried out during attacks against our enemies. –

THE POLITICAL COMMISSAR THE MILITARY COMMANDER

Nonetheless, in addition to those captured from the enemy or brought along by deserters, during the later phases of the war large quantities were air dropped, generally 6.5 mm Italian, 9 mm for submachine guns, and 7.7 mm (.303) for the Bren gun; these types of ammunition were considered the most useful.

At times requests by the partisans were difficult to fulfill. In one case a request was made for ammunition for German rifles and machine guns that had fallen into the hands of the rebels and the reply was: "We're sorry that we don't have any, you are closer to the German ammunition dumps, go get some yourselves."[29]

Shortages of ammunition greatly influenced operational activity of the partisans and forced them into odd barter arrangements among themselves.

Following are several examples found in the documents of units operating in the Savona area.

C. di L.N

Corpo Volontario della Libertà

4° Brigata d'assalto "GARIBALDI

D.MANIN

ProT. 25/339 — 4 Novembre 44

Comando distaccamento Calcagno

Argomento : Munizioni

Il Comando della 5^ Brigata Baltera ci comunica di avere disponibili 5000 colpi per S.Etienne leggera. Dato che il comando della Baltera non può utilizzare detta munizione per il semplice motivo che non ha in dotazione tale genere di arma, ha proposto un adeguato cambio di munizioni di altro calibro e tipo, quali; ad esempio, munizioni per moschetto 6,5 , 7,35, 7,9 .=

Restiamo in attesa di un vs.cenno di risposta.

Il Commissario P. — Il Comandante

---

C. di L.N.

Volunteer Corps for Liberty

4th "GARIBALDI" assault Brigade

D. MANIN

File 25/339 — 4 November 44

Headquarters Calcagno Detachment

Subject: Ammuntion

Headquaters 5th Baltera Brigade informs us that they have available 5,000 rounds for the light St. Etienne. Given that the Baltera can no longer use the aforementioned ammunition for the simple reason that it no longer has that type of weapon on hand, we propose an appropriate exchange of ammunition of another type and caliber, such as for example, ammunition for 6.5, 7.35. 7.9 rifles. =

We await your reply.

The Political Commissar — The Commander

The light St. Etienne was the Chatellerault M1924 M29 automatic rifle in 7.5 × 54; great efforts were made to use this ammunition.

Considering the following document, doubt arises whether by swapping the rare French 7.65L ammunition with equally hard-to-find US .45 ammunition was tantamount to jumping from the frying pan into the fire.

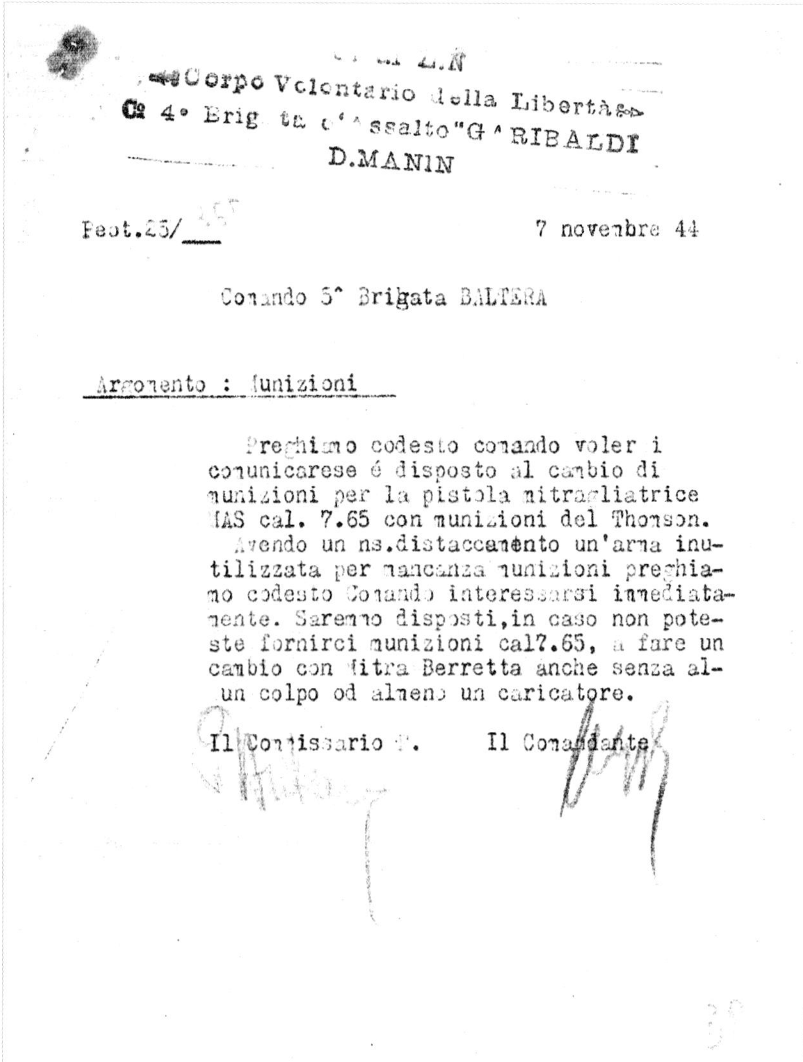
C.V.L.
Corpo Volontario della Libertà
Cª 4ª Brig. ta d'Assalto "GARIBALDI"
D.MANIN

Prot.25/ 7 novembre 44

Comando 5^ Brigata BALTERA

Argomento : Munizioni

Preghiamo codesto comando voler i comunicarese é disposto al cambio di munizioni per la pistola mitragliatrice MAS cal. 7.65 con munizioni del Thomson.

Avendo un ns.distaccamento un'arma inutilizzata per mancanza munizioni preghiamo codesto Comando interessarsi immediatamente. Saremmo disposti,in caso non poteste fornirci munizioni cal7.65, a fare un cambio con Mitra Berretta anche senza alcun colpo od almeno un caricatore.

Il Commissario P. Il Comandante

C. di L.N.
Volunteer Corps for Liberty
4th "GARIBALDI" assault Brigade
D. MANIN

File 25/358 7 November 44

Headquarters 5th BALTERA Brigade

Subject: Ammunition

We kindly request that your headquarters inform us it is willing to exchange ammunition for the 7.65 MAS machine pistol for ammunition for the Thompson.

As our detachment has a weapon that is unusable because of lack of ammunition we kindly request your Headquarters to address this immediately. We would be willing, in case you are not able to supply us with 7.65 caliber ammunition, to accept a Beretta submachine gun with either no ammunition or at least one full magazine.

The Political Commissar The Commander

In fact, the search for ammunition and spare parts for the Thompson was frenetic:

COMMITTEE OF NATIONAL LIBERATION
Volunteer Corps for Liberty

Headquarters
1 Garibaldi Assault Division
G. BEVILACQUA

File 30/265 Operational zone, 17 March 45

To headquarters SAP Brigade "Clelia Corradini"

Subject: Request for ammunition

Reference your letter our same subject we advise you that we are not able to fulfill your request for ammunition for the Thompson submachine gun as there is only one such weapon issued to our Brigades and ammunition is scarce.

We are sorry that we cannot help you, Garibaldian regards.

The Political Commissar The Military Commander

see page 98

COMITATO di LIBERAZIONE NAZIONALE
Corpo Volontari della Libertà

Comando
1 Divisione d'assalto Garibaldi
G. BEVILACQUA

Prt. 30/265 Zona d'impiego, 17 marzo 45

Al Comando Brigata SAP " Clelia Corradini"

Oggetto : Richiesta munizioni

In riferimento al vs.foglio allo stesso nostro argomento comunichiamo che non siamo nella possibilità di esaudire la vostra richiesta di munizioni per pistola automatica Tompson dato che in dotazione alle nostre Brigate é una sola di tali armi e il munizionamento é scarso.
Spiacenti di non potervi accontentare, saluti garibaldini.

Il Commissario Politico Il Comandante Militare

This not-so-subtle criticism of ammunition wastage is somewhat unusual:

To Headquarters SAP Detachment "Faggi"

Subject: Ammunition report

From your report of 4/1/45 on ammunition we show that you have 1500 Cal. 6.5 moschetto rounds. A report dated 12/3/45 shows only 180 rounds. You are kindly requested to clarify the reason for this discrepancy as soon as possible.

The Political Commissar The Military Commander

see page 99

Al Comando Distaccamento S A P "Faggi3

Oggetto: Relazioná sul munizionamento

Dalla vostra relazione sull' armamento del 4/1/945, ci risultano N° I500 colpi da moschetto Cal.6,5 . Mentre dalla relazione in data I2/3/45, ne risultano solamente N° I80, Pertanto siete pregati a chiarire al più presto possibkle il suddetto equivoco.

Il Commissario P.          Il Ceamndante

## CHAPTER VII

# GLOSSARY

Provided is a small sample of nicknames adopted to designate various weapons, often somewhat fancifully and, in some cases, still today incomprehensible.

Many of the terms are in the Italian dialect of the region or are local corruptions of foreign designations that were only barely understood. The same weapon could be given different nicknames, even in areas not far removed from each other. For example, the US UD M42 submachine gun produced by the Marlin Firearms Company and air dropped along with British SOE missions assumes widely varied designations that are understandable enough, such as Marilyn, Mariline, Marlen…

Piero Balbo, the partisan commander known by the pseudonym "Poli." *Lorenza Balbo*

**Piero Balbo** used the *nom de guerre* Poli, was also known as "comandante Nord," and was also referred to simply as Piero in partisan correspondence. Born on June 12, 1916, Poli had a law degree, became a reserve officer in the Italian Navy, and served with the 12th Flottiglia MAS in Leros until the September 8, 1943, armistice, when he was transferred to Pola and was captured by the Germans. He escaped, making his way by bicycle from Pola to the area of Asti, where he joined one of the early partisan bands whose loyalty was to the Kingdom of the South and which did not always maintain cordial relations with communist-led partisan groups. He was an officer in the *1o Gruppo Divisioni Alpine* (1st Alpine Division Group) commanded by Enrico Martini ("Mauro"); Poli assumed command of the 2nd "Langhe" Division. Piero Balbo's father "Pinin" was one of the 178 dead partisans of the division and was awarded the Italian Gold Medal for Military Valor. Poli likewise was awarded the Gold Medal for Military Valor. Balbo died on March 19, 2003, and is buried in the family cemetery plot in Cossano Belbo.

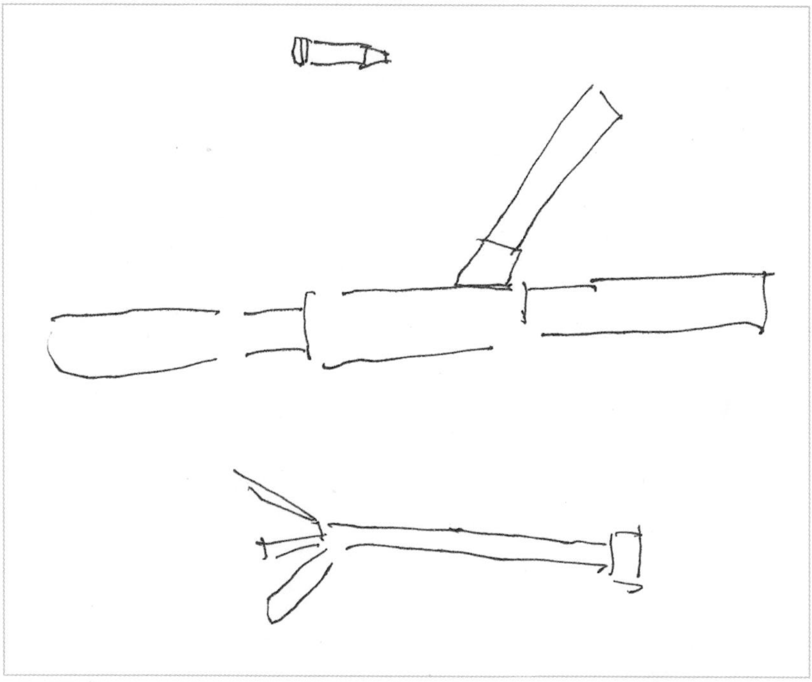

Sketch of a Steyr-Solothurn MP34 carried by Poli; the sketch was made by one of Piero Balbo's relatives.

N. Revelli's *La guerra dei poveri* shows he began the war with two "parabellum" and a "machinepistole" that were souvenirs of the war in Russia,[30]....... and in another book we read: "Piero had pulled out the Czech parabellum that had been taken in Crete in 1942 and brought home in a trunk with around a thousand cartridges as far as Cossano..."[31]

From research and testimony the weapon turned out to be an Austro-Swiss Steyr-Solothurn: we thus are faced with a double error of attribution (Czech) and designation (parabellum) which we have previously seen in Fenoglio at page 36.[32]

**Brend, Brent, Brem, Brehm** – corruptions of the simpler word Bren.

**Buffalo** – Browning machine gun, a term frequently used by Fenoglio.

**Fislinger** – possibly the FG42.

**Loebel** – unknown type of light machine gun, but probably the Saint Etienne mod. 1924–29, which fired the Lebel 7.5 × 54 round

**Macinino, macinacaffè** – translated as "coffee grinder" or "coffee mill"; probably a reference to the US M3 submachine gun because of its prominent cocking handle.

**Makallè** – presumably a Vetterli-Vitali 1870/87/16 bolt-action rifle.

**Marlen, Marylin, Marilena** – the US UD M42 submachine gun produced by Marlin.

**Mashine pistol, machine pistol, mascin pistol…** – corruption of the German "Maschinen pistole"—a generic term for machine pistols but mainly used in reference to the MP40.

**Mayerling** – some believe this refers to the MG42, others to the Gew 41, and still others to the MP44; there is no definitive answer.

**Obel** – unknown type of light machine gun, but probably an FN Browning produced in Belgium for the Polish army.

**Otcis, Occis, Okhis, and similar** – Hotchkiss machine gun or light machine gun.

**Parabello, Parabellum** – generally referring to the Russian PPSh41 submachine gun, although earlier it referred to the German P08 or Luger.

**Saint Etienne** – probably the French Mod. 1924–29 light machine gun.

**Sciù-scià, Suchard** – somewhat rhyming variants of Chauchat.

**Skoda, Skodak, Skodas** – Zb26 or Zb30 light machine gun, but also refers to an unknown type of light machine gun probably of Czech manufacture; in some areas it also refers to the Austrian MP34 submachine gun.

**Smith** – US M3 submachine gun; probably a corruption of the English abbreviation SMG (submachine gun).

**Stein, Steier, Steyer, Stenk**… – all corruptions of the simple Sten.

**Wetterlin, Wetterling** – see Makallè.

## CHAPTER VIII

# ABBREVIATIONS AND ACRONYMS

| | |
|---|---|
| CLN | *Comitato di Liberazione Nazionale* (Committee of National Liberation) |
| CZ | *Ceska Zbrojovka*, Czech arms factory |
| FM | *Fucile mitragliatore* (automatic rifle or light machine gun) |
| FG | *Fallschirmjägergewehr* (paratrooper's rifle) |
| GNR | *Guardia Nazionale Repubblicana* (Republican National Guard) |
| Gew. | *Gewehr*; German for "rifle" |
| GIL | *Gioventù italiana del Littorio* (Italian Littorio Youth) |
| Le.MG | *Leicht Maschinengewehr*; German for "light machine gun" |
| M | US acronym for Model |
| MAB | *Moschetto automatic Beretta* (Beretta SMG) |
| MAC | *Manufacture d'armes de Chatellerault* |
| MAS | *Manufacture d'armes de Saint Etienne* |
| MAT | *Manufacture d'armes de Tulle* |
| Ml | *Mitragliatrice leggera* (light machine gun; automatic rifle) |
| MG | *Maschinen Gewehr*; German for "machine gun" |
| Mp | *Mitragliatrice pesante* (heavy machine gun) |
| Mk | Mark; British acronym for model |
| Mk | *Maschinen Karabiner*; German for "automatic rifle" |
| MP | *Maschinen Pistole*; German for "machine pistol" |
| OSS | Office of Strategic Services, the US unconventional warfare organization |
| PM | *Pistola mitragliatrice* (machine pistol) |
| PIAT | Projector Infantry Antitank; British anti-tank grenade launcher |

| | |
|---|---|
| SAP | *Squadre di Azione Patriottica* (Patriotic Action Squads); these were partisan groups in cities that operated in support of partisan groups in the mountains, providing information, supplies, and weapons and, in extreme cases, shelter. |
| SAS | Special Air Service; British commando forces |
| SMG | US acronym for submachine gun |
| SOE | Special Operations Executive; British sabotage organization |
| S/a | *Semiautomatica* (semi-automatic) |
| Sch MG | *Schwere Maschinengewehr*; German for "heavy machine gun" |
| StGew | *Sturmgewehr*; German for assault rifle |
| Vz | Abbreviation of *vzor*, the Czech word for Model |
| WaA | *WaffenAmt*; German proof and acceptance agency |
| Wz | Abbreviation of wzor, the Polish word for Model |

# CHAPTER IX
# PROFILES

Before beginning to look at individual profiles of the major weapons used by the Italian resistance movement, it should be noted that the weapons shown and described represent only a small part of the various weapons in circulation and use during the period. With respect to handguns, the twenty or so models shown are just a small sample of what could be found in partisan hands. During WWI Italy, as was true of many other nations, found it could not produce enough of its own weapons to meet requirements and imported a significant quantity of handguns—pistols and revolvers—from Spain. In addition, there were many revolvers of Belgian and Spanish manufacture in circulation, almost always inexpensive copies of much more highly pedigreed American or English models.

During the earliest days of the resistance movement, every type of weapon available was pulled out of chests and drawers to be used until they ran out of required ammunition or could be replaced by more "military" weapons. The situation actually became even more complicated once partisans began to arm themselves with weapons taken from German officers; at that point weapons originating from all over Europe could be encountered (Poland, Norway, Belgium, Czechoslovakia); all nations seem to have been represented, not only by proper military weapons, but also with anything that even vaguely resembled a pistol.

When examining photographs from the period, keep in mind it is not always easy to distinguish one weapon from another and often common design origin further complicates the issue; on page 106 we can see a Browning-designed pistol that could be a Colt 1911A1, a Llama, a Norwegian Kongberg M1914, or a Ballester-Molina.

On pages 108–109, members of the gentler sex are carrying weapons that are not easily identifiable.

At other times there is a strange mix of web gear and weapons of varying provenance; page 110 shows an example of a partisan from Genoa standing alongside a US Army major. A holster for a British revolver holds what appears to be a Beretta Model 32 pistol accompanied by a US ammunition pouch. An American M1 carbine is slung over his shoulder.

A partisan of the "Fumagalli" Division in the immediate postwar; the semi-automatic pistol in the open holster is probably a Browning 1900 produced by FN in Belgium that made its way to Italy while being worn by a German officer. *G. Toscani*

Detail of the Browning-designed large-frame pistol. *ILSREC Genova*

This staged photo appears to be somewhat lighthearted, although the sign above the squatting individual reads *La fine dei traditori* ("The end of traitors"). *ILSREC Genova*

**Leslie J. Vanoncini** was born on August 22, 1917, in Humboldt County, California; some sources spell the surname as Vannoncini, but official records reflect Vanoncini. The surname Vanoncini is closely associated with the region of Lombardy; presumably Vanoncini spoke the Lombard dialect. Vanoncini enlisted at the Presidio of Monterey on February 21, 1942, as US Army private 39090148, was later commissioned as an officer in the OSS, and served with Inter-Allied Mission Helen in France in 1944 and Mission "Peedee" in Italy in 1945. On January 18, 1945, sixteen Italo-American agents under command of Capt. Leslie Vanoncini ("Captain Van") were sent to Monte Antola, in the province of Genova. The aim of this mission was to save partisan brigades surrounded by a German sweep operation code-named Aachen, and later to train the partisans to prevent Germans from employing a scorched earth policy. Vanoncini died on January 27, 1996, in California. He was awarded the Legion of Merit with V device and the Air Medal with Oak Leaf cluster.

This female may be an ammunition bearer for a machine gun team, or the belted ammunition with which she is festooned may be purely to enhance the effect of the photo. *ILSREC Genova*

This female partisan is carrying an unidentified semi-auto pistol in a cloth web holster. *ILSREC Genova*

The US officer (right) is Maj. Leslie Vanoncini, an Italian-American from California who led an OSS team supporting the partisans. *ILSREC Genova*

# Semi-Automatic Pistols and Revolvers

## Profile 1 — *Italy*

## Bodeo Model 1889 Revolver

Following the Lefaucheux Mod. 1858 and Chamelot-Delvigne Mod. 1874, in 1889, this revolver was introduced and would for many years remain issued to the Italian armed forces and Italian police agencies. Up until as late as the 1930s, the *Guardia di Finanza* (Finance Guard) continued to acquire this weapon, which would remain in service until the immediate postwar period, when it was replaced by semi-automatic pistols.

In addition to Bodeo revolvers produced in Italy, during the resistance many similar revolvers produced in Spain over the course of WWI were used, including the "Tettoni" (named after their importer); these were unlicensed copies of the Smith & Wesson and the later Baston-Bodeo whose only common feature was their caliber.

**Years of manufacture:** 1889–1931
**Caliber:** 10.40 × 22
**Magazine/capacity:** Cylinder, six rounds
**Length:** 232 mm (9.13 in.)
**Barrel length:** 115 mm (4.53 in.)
**Weight:** 0.95 kg (2.09 lb.)

A 10.4 mm Model 1889 Bodeo "Type A" revolver. *Gianluigi Usai*

A well-dressed young partisan holding a "Type A" Bodeo postwar. *B. Chionetti*

## Profile 2 *Italy*

# Glisenti Model 1910 Semi-Automatic Pistol

Following introduction of the Mauser Mod. 1899 by the Italian Navy, the army began studies aimed at acquiring a semi-automatic pistol that—after several models were considered—resulted in adoption of the Glisenti Model 1910. Due to a vague resemblance to the German P08 Luger, the Glisenti was sometimes described as "the poor man's Luger," but that characterization does not render proper justice to this small mechanical masterpiece.

The negative point of the Glisenti is the cartridge it is chambered for, which is quite similar to the 9 mm Parabellum but is lower powered, which led to accidents during the resistance caused by using inappropriate ammunition. By using cartridges more powerful than the pistol was designed for led to jamming, if not to actual explosion of the weapon.

There were three cartridges of similar dimensions but with progressively more powerful loadings: 9 mm Glisenti, 9 mm Parabellum (with a 15% greater powder charge), and the Italian 9 mm 9M38 (with an additional 15% greater powder charge); each could lead easily to confusion among personnel who were not well trained or versed in the cartridges' differences.

**Years of manufacture:** 1910–1920
**Caliber:** 9 mm Glisenti
**Magazine/capacity:** Detachable magazine, seven rounds
**Length:** 220 mm (8.66 in.)
**Barrel length:** 95 mm (3.7 in.)
**Weight:** 0.82 kg (1.8 lb.)

A Glisenti Model 1910 pistol. *Courtesy Leonardo M. Antaris, MD*

Members of the "Biondino" mobile team; the partisan on the right has a Glisenti on his belt. *G. Toscani*

Detail of the Glisenti. *G. Toscani*

## Profile 3 — *Italy*

# Beretta Brev. 1915 and Beretta Brev. 1915 Mod. 17 Semi-Automatic Pistols

During WWI, the Italian army adopted the first semi-automatic pistol produced by Beretta, establishing a long series of pistols that are still in use today with the Model 92.

The 1915 was adopted in two models in different calibers: the 9 mm Glisenti and the 7.65 mm Browning, designated the Brevetto 1915 and Brevetto 1915 Mod. 17, respectively. There are a number of production differences between the two models (such as the "Glisenti" type safety and the buffer present on the larger caliber version) as well as dimensional differences. In the years following WWI, there were further developments of these weapons that culminated in the design of the Mod. 34.

| | **Brev 1915** | **Brev.1915 Mod. 17** |
|---|---|---|
| **Years of manufacture:** | 1915–1918 | 1917–1921 |
| **Caliber:** | 9 mm Glisenti | 7.65 Browning |
| **Magazine/capacity:** | Magazine, 7 rounds | Magazine, 8 rounds |
| **Length:** | 170 mm (6.69 in.) | 150 mm (5.9 in.) |
| **Barrel length:** | 94 mm (3.7 in.) | 85 mm (3.34 in.) |
| **Weight:** | 0.85 kg (1.87 lb.) | 0.57 kg (1.25 lb.) |

A 9 mm Glisenti Beretta Model 1915 pistol. *Courtesy Leonardo M. Antaris, MD*

A 7.65 mm Beretta Model 1915/17 pistol. *Gianluigi Usai*

Profile 4 *Italy*

## Beretta Model 34 and Model 35 Semi-Automatic Pistols

These are considered among the best semi-automatic pistols of WWII. Even with their caliber limitations— which many, especially Americans, consider marginally adequate for a military weapon—their simplicity, ruggedness, and small size have gained a cult following. The story is told that almost every Allied soldier who served in Italy had one in his knapsack to take home as a souvenir.

These pistols were also highly appreciated by the Germans, who continued their production after the September 8, 1943, armistice. Even though the exterior finish of the pistols declined to a very low level, the functionality and reliability of the pistols remained high thanks to its inherently good design. Its ability to be easily concealed, simplicity, and ease of maintenance were also well appreciated by the partisans.

| | **Mod. 1934** | **Mod. 1935** |
|---|---|---|
| **Years of manufacture:** | 1934–1991 | 1935–1967 |
| **Caliber:** | 9 × 17 | 7.65 × 17 |
| **Magazine/capacity:** | Magazine, 7 rounds | Magazine, 8 rounds |
| **Length:** | 146 mm (5.75 in.) | 146 mm (5.75 in.) |
| **Barrel length:** | 86.5 mm (3.4 in.) | 86.5 mm (3.4 in.) |
| **Weight:** | 0.672 kg (1.48 lb.) | 0.650 kg (1.43 lb.) |

A 9 mm corto (.380 ACP) Beretta Model 1934 pistol. *Ralph Riccio*

A 7.65 mm (.32 Browning) Beretta Model 1935 pistol. *Ralph Riccio*

Not even priests were averse to carrying a Beretta pistol; note the "open cage" holster. *G. Toscani*

## Profile 5 *Germany*

# P08 Luger Semi-Automatic Pistol

The Luger is one of the most iconic pistols in the world and has a devoted following. Possessing one of these pistols is often considered proof of courage, and we often see them being worn by partisan leaders. The weapon was introduced shortly before WWI, and production continued until 1942, despite the introduction of the P38, which could be produced more quickly and less expensively. Initially produced by DWM (Deutsche Waffen und Munitionsfabriken), it was also produced by other manufacturers, including Mauser, Krieghoff, and the Erfurt Arsenal. The pistol did require attention to maintenance, as dirt could accumulate and easily cause jamming, and partisan life did not lend itself to thorough cleaning procedures.

**Years of manufacture:** 1908–1942
**Caliber:** 9 × 19 Parabellum
**Magazine/capacity:** Detachable magazine, eight rounds
**Length:** 223 mm (8.78 in.)
**Barrel length:** 102 mm (4.02 in.)
**Weight:** 0.85 kg (1.87 lb.)

A 9 mm German P08 Luger. *Ralph Riccio*

Although this Luger was not actually used by the partisans, it did pass through partisan hands, as related in the written description accompanying the pistol. The inscription reads: "Luger pistol, cal, 9 mm parabellum, belonging to General Gunther Meinhold, commander of German armed forces in the Meinhold sector, handed over by the German officer to Professor Carmine Romanzi, delegate of the CLN in Liguria, at the time of negotiations for the surrender of German troops to the Committee of National Liberation." *ILSREC Genova*

Profile 6 *Germany*

## Walther P38 Semi-Automatic Pistol

Designed to replace the P08, which suffered from problems and shortcomings with complexity, production, and maintenance requirements, the P38 proved to be an excellent weapon, so much so that production continued under various designations until the mid-1980s. It was less expensive, easier to produce, more robust, and stood up better under battlefield conditions than the Luger. Walther was the initial producer, followed by Mauser and Spreewerke, although many components were subcontracted to other firms.

Troops of the Italian RSI divisions trained in Germany were initially issued the P38, so it was relatively common to find them in partisan hands not only as captured items, but also because they were brought by deserters.

**Years of manufacture:** 1938–1986
**Caliber:** 9 × 19 Parabellum
**Magazine/capacity:** Detachable magazine, eight rounds
**Length:** 213 mm (8.39 in.)
**Barrel length:** 127 mm (5.0 in.)
**Weight:** 0.84 kg (1.85 lb.)

A P38 pistol. *Ralph Riccio*

Capt. (later Maj.) Ballard examining a P38; who knows what may have happened to it? *Don Angelo Siri*

## Profile 7 *Austria*

# Steyr M1912 Semi-Automatic Pistol

This pistol dates to WWI, when it was issued to Austro-Hungarian forces. Many of these pistols made their way to Italy as souvenirs picked up by Italian soldiers, and many were stored by the Italian army in depots as war booty.

When Germany annexed Austria in 1938, it found many of these weapons in storage; to standardize its caliber with pistols already in German service, they took steps to re-chamber them in 9 × 19 (9 mm Parabellum), while also applying German acceptance marks. As a consequence, it is possible to find these pistols in Italian partisan use in the original 9 mm Steyr caliber and modified examples, depending on how and where they were acquired. Two different calibers caused more than a few problems.

**Years of manufacture:** 1911–1918
**Caliber:** 9 × 23 Steyr; 9 × 19 Parabellum
**Magazine/capacity:** Stripper clips, eight rounds
**Length:** 216 mm (8.5 in.)
**Barrel length:** 128 mm (5.0 in.)
**Weight:** 0.99 kg (2.18 lb.)

A 9 mm Steyr 1912 pistol. *Al Gerth*

A partisan using a Steyr to execute a prisoner. This is a well-known photo that has appeared in numerous Italian magazines.

Profile 8 — *Belgium*

## Browning FN HP 35 (Hi Power) Semi-Automatic Pistol

Stemming from the fertile mind of inventor John M. Browning, this pistol was produced by the Belgian Fabrique Nationale works beginning in 1935. When the Germans invaded Belgium in 1940, they seized a large quantity of weapons and arranged for production to continue, adding German acceptance marks to Belgian-produced weapons, so it is quite easy to encounter the HP 35 with German markings.

When Belgium was invaded, a number of Belgian FN technicians fled first to England and thence to Canada, where production of the FN 35 was resumed at the Inglis factory on behalf of the British. It was possible to find almost identical weapons on both sides of the fighting, differing only in their markings, and they could also be found arming the various "missionaries" sent by the Allies. The weapon was very much appreciated by users for many of its qualities, but especially for its thirteen-round magazine, which was almost twice the capacity of its more common contemporaries.

**Years of manufacture:** 1935–1945
**Caliber:** 9 × 19 Parabellum
**Magazine/capacity:** Detachable magazine, 13 rounds
**Length:** 203 mm (7.9 in.)
**Barrel length:** 120 mm (4.7 in.)
**Weight:** 0.86 kg (1.9 lb.)

A Belgian FN Browning HP 35 Hi Power pistol. *Al Gerth*

A partisan brandishing a Hi Power taken in a photography studio in Savona. *B. Chionetti*

Profile 9 *Poland*

## Radom wz/35 Vis Semi-Automatic Pistol

Another weapon captured in a country occupied by Germany, this Polish pistol also exhibits similarities to John Browning's designs, incorporating many Browning characteristics.

The pistol was produced in the Polish Radom factory, and there is a noticeable difference between pistols manufactured prior to the German occupation and those made afterward, including the elimination of the slide stop and its finish quality, which became progressively worse. During the latter stages of the war production of this pistol was also carried out by Steyr in Austria.

**Years of manufacture:** 1935–1945
**Caliber:** 9 × 19 Parabellum
**Magazine/capacity:** Detachable magazine, eight rounds
**Length:** 211 mm (8.3 in.)
**Barrel length:** 115 mm (4.5 in.)
**Weight:** 1.05 kg (2.31 lb.)

A 9 mm Radom wz/35 Vis pistol. *Pat Egan*

Here is a September 1944 inventory of weapons held by a partisan detachment in the Savona area in which fully three "Polish type pistols" are listed.

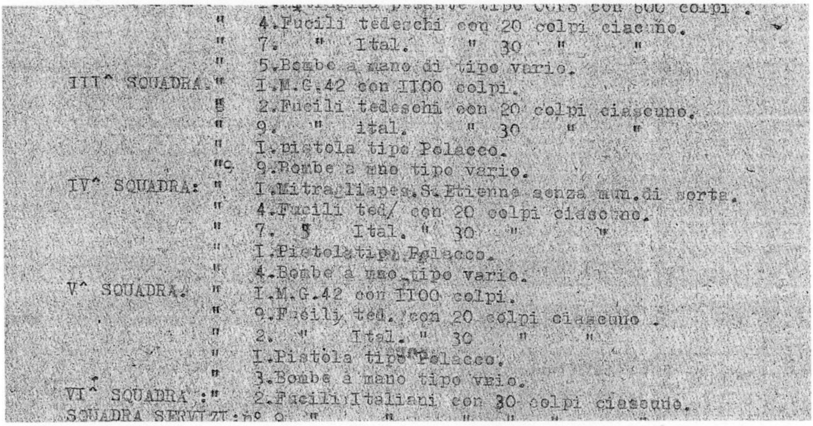

" 4.Fucili tedeschi con 20 colpi ciascuno.
" 7. " Ital. " 30 " "
" 5.Bombe a mano di tipo vario.
III^ SQUADRA." I.M.G.42 con II00 colpi.
" 2.Fucili tedeschi con 20 colpi ciascuno.
" 9. " ital. " 30 " "
" I.pistola tipo Polacco.
" 9.Bombe a mno tipo vario.
IV^ SQUADRA: " I.Mitragliatr.S.Etienne senza mun.di sorta.
" 4.Fucili ted/ con 20 colpi ciascuno.
" 7. " Ital. " 30 " "
" I.Pistola tipo Polacco.
" 4.Bombe a mno tipo vario.
V^ SQUADRA: " I.M.G.42 con II00 colpi.
" 9.Fucili ted. con 20 colpi ciascuno .
" 2. " Ital. " 30 " "
" I.Pistola tipo Polacco.
" 3.Bombe a mano tipo vrio.
VI^ SQUADRA :" 2.Fucili Italiani con 30 colpi ciascuno.

" 4 German rifles with 20 rounds each
" 7 Italian " " 30 " "
" 5 hand grenades of various types
III^rd squad " 1 M.G. 42 with 1100 rounds
" 2 German rifles with 20 rounds each
" 9 Italian " " 30 " "
" 1 Polish type pistol
" 9 hand grenades of various types
IV^th squad " 1 S. Etienne machine gun with no ammunition
" 4 German rifles with 20 rounds each
" 7 Italian " " 30 " "
" 1 Polish type pistol
" 4 hand grenades of various types
V^th squad " 1 M.G. 42 with 1100 rounds
" 9 German rifles with 20 rounds each
" 2 Italian " " 30 " "
" 1 Polish type pistol
" 3 hand grenades of various types
VI^th squad " 2 Italian rifles with 30 rounds each
SERVICE SQUAD

Extract of a letter in which the Radom pistol is clearly mentioned.

poi farcelo pervenire per effettuare un controllo dell'ammanco verifi=
catosi durante la giacenza nella nostra zona.
Con l'occasione vi preghiamo di farci ritornare lo sten con relative
munizioni e la pistola Radom in possesso di Alba.
Intanto vi comunichiamo che lo sten di Bill è in nostre mani, mancano
no però i caricatori quello stesso che devono essere stati ritirati la
sera di S.Giuseppe da un vostro volontario.
Vi preghiamo ancora di dare ordine al neo volontario Alvaro, giunti
costi 3 giorni addietro proveniente dalla S.A.P. di Pietra Ligure, di ri
tornarci con sollecitudine la pistola a tamburo americana in suo posses=

We ask that you take this opportunity to return the sten with its relative ammunition and the Radom pistol in Alba's possession.

In the meantime we would like to inform you that Bill's sten is in our hands, however the magazines for it are missing which should have been picked up the night of San Giuseppe by one of your volunteers.

We ask you once again to give orders to your new volunteer Alvaro, who arrived here 3 days ago, coming from the S.A.P. of Pietra Ligure, to return the American revolver to us.

Profile 10 — *Norway*

## M/1914 Kongsberg Semi-Automatic Pistol

This pistol is one of the many types attributable to John Browning. Shortly before WWI, Norway decided it needed a new side arm, so it turned to the United States and acquired production rights for the 1911 from Colt. The Kongsberg Colt was identical to the Colt M1911, except for different checkering on the hammer and a modified slide stop. Production proceeded at a slow pace until WWII, and was still under way at the time of the German invasion of Norway. The Germans continued production of the weapon, applying their usual acceptance markings.

**Years of manufacture:** 1914–1945
**Caliber:** .45 ACP
**Magazine/capacity:** Detachable magazine, seven rounds
**Length:** 216 mm (8.5 in.)
**Barrel length:** 127 mm (5.0 in.)
**Weight:** 1.12 kg (2.47 lb.)

A .45 ACP Norwegian Model 1914 pistol. *Al Gerth*

Profile 11 *Germany*

## Mauser C96 Semi-Automatic Pistol and Derivatives

This weapon was produced in a seemingly infinite number of variants and by a great number of different manufacturers, including makers in Spain and China, with innumerable modifications: aesthetics, mechanical, and caliber. Introduced in 1896, the C96 was initially adopted as a military weapon by the Italian Navy while it enjoyed considerable commercial success. It was originally chambered for the 7.63 mm Mauser round, but during WWI, was produced in 9 × 19. Production was time-consuming and costly, and because the pistol was made like a fine watch it was not very forgiving of mud in the trenches or ice on certain fronts. Under pressure from competition by Spanish producers, in 1932, Mauser was forced to unveil fully automatic versions.

**Years of manufacture:** 1896–1945
**Caliber:** 7.63 Mauser; 9 × 19 Parabellum
**Magazine/capacity:** Internal magazine, 6, 10, or 20-round stripper clips
**Length:** 312 mm (12.3 in.)
**Barrel length:** 139 mm (5.5 in.)
**Weight:** 1.25 kg (2.76 lb.)

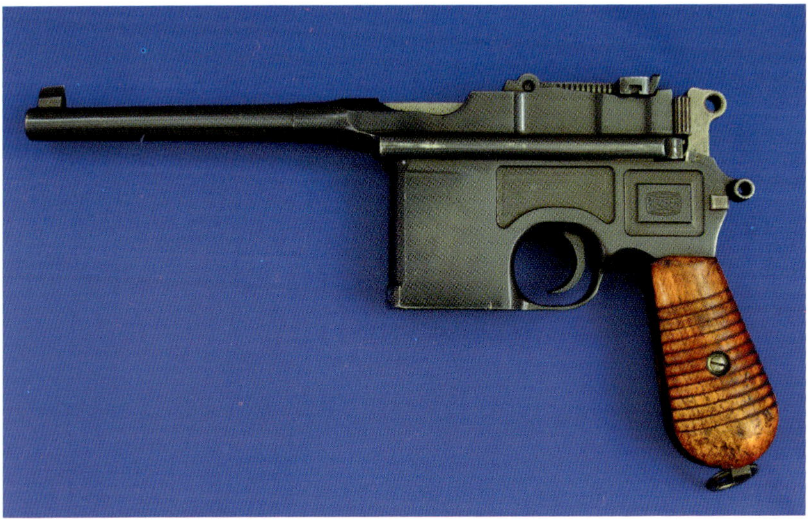

A Mauser C96 with its characteristic "broom handle." *Colin Doane*

Torino aprile 1945, partigiani della brigata Matteotti. Bruno Selis e Marco Trombini.

Two partisans from the Matteotti Brigade in Torino in April 1945; in addition to the Beretta MAB38s, the partisan on the right has a Mauser C96 hanging from his belt. *E. Scarone*

Profile 12 *Spain*

## Astra Semi-Automatic Pistol, Various Models

In addition to capitalizing on arms production in all of their occupied territories, the need for weapons forced Germany to use production from countries not under their reign, such as Spain. One of the firms that Germany turned to was Astra, from which various models in differing numbers were acquired:

| |
|---|
| Approximately 85,000 Model 300 in .380 caliber and 7.65 mm Browning (.32 ACP) |
| 6,000 Model 400 in 9 mm Largo caliber |
| Approximately 10,000 Model 600 in 9 × 19 Parabellum caliber |
| Various other models. |

Many Astra pistols were marked with German acceptance stamps.

| | **M300** | **M400** | **M600** |
|---|---|---|---|
| **Years of manufacture:** | 1921–1945 | 1921–1945 | 1943–1950s |
| **Caliber:** | 9 × 17 (.380) | 9 × 23 Largo | 9 × 19 Parabellum |
| **Magazine/ capacity:** | 9 rounds | 8 rounds | 8 rounds |
| **Length:** | 254 mm (10 in.) | 225 mm (8.9 in.) | 205 mm (8.1 in.) |
| **Barrel length:** | 152 mm (6 in.) | 150 mm (5.9 in.) | 135 mm (5.3 in.) |
| **Weight:** | 1.14 kg (2.5 lb.) | 1.08 kg (2.4 lb.) | |

An Astra M300 pistol chambered for the 9 mm kurz (.380 ACP) round. *Courtesy Leonardo M. Antaris, MD*

Astra M400 pistol chambered for the 9 mm largo round. *Courtesy Leonardo M. Antaris, MD*

An Astra M600 chambered for the 9 × 19 Parabellum round. *Courtesy Leonardo M. Antaris, MD*

An RSI follower about to be executed with an Astra pistol, Milan, late April 1945. *E. Palma*

## Profile 13 *Spain*

# Llama and Star Semi-Automatic Pistols

Spain took advantage of its neutrality, selling weapons to all of the warring nations, so it is not surprising to find these pistols in the hands of German and British soldiers. The British acquired sizeable quantities in the early years of the war, when they were in desperate need of weapons. As the availability of weapons improved, the British found it useful to turn these pistols over to various resistance movements whose needs they judged less critical.

As these pistols were copies of the US Colt 1911 designed by Browning, neither the Germans nor the British encountered any problems with their use, and the 9 × 19 caliber ammunition rendered them compatible with most of the submachine guns and pistols then in use. The first weapons of this type had arrived in Italy prior to the beginning of the war as souvenirs with returning Italian veterans who served in the Spanish Civil War.

Data refers to the Star Model B pistol:
**Years of manufacture:** 1924-1944
**Caliber:** 9 × 19 Parabellum
**Magazine/capacity:** Detachable magazine, eight rounds
**Length:** 202 mm (7.9 in.)
**Barrel length:** 127 mm (5.0 in.)
**Weight:** 0.96 kg (2.12 lb.)

A Llama pistol manufactured by Gabilondo y Cia., Elgoibar, Spain. *Courtesy Leonardo M. Antaris, MD*

A 9 × 19 Parabellum Spanish Star pistol produced by Continuadora de B. Echeverria, Eibar. *Courtesy Leonardo M. Antaris, MD*

## Profile 14 *USSR*

# Nagant Model 1895 Revolver

When the USSR was attacked in June 1941, the Germans captured more than a million Soviet soldiers along with their weapons, among which were many Nagant revolvers whose design dated to the end of the previous century. The Nagant was an unusual weapon of Belgian design in which cocking the hammer also moved the cylinder forward, so it closed the gap between the cylinder and the barrel, thus eliminating the loss of gas normally associated with revolvers.

These and other Russian weapons were subsequently used to arm German divisions composed of Soviet soldiers of various ethnic groups, many of whom were sent to the Italian front. Desertions from their ranks—as well as disarming these troops, who lacked motivation to fight for the Germans—led to partisan acquisition and use of pistols, rifles, and submachine guns originating far from Italy.

**Years of manufacture:** 1895–1945 (?)
**Caliber:** 7.62 × 38 Nagant
**Magazine/capacity:** Cylinder, seven rounds
**Length:** 229 mm (9.0 in.)
**Barrel length:** 110 mm (4.3 in.)
**Weight:** 0.79 kg (1.74 lb.)

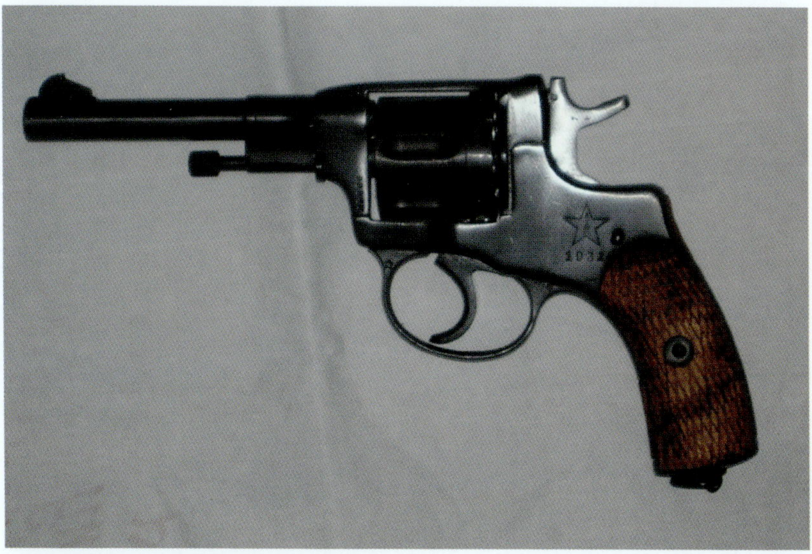

A Nagant Model 1895 revolver. *Jon Cohen*

Profile 15 USSR

# Tokarev Model TT30 and TT33 Semi-Automatic Pistols

This pistol—a simplified version of the 1903 Browning and Colt 1911 with some variations—was developed by Russian weapons designer Fedor Tokarev and was introduced in 1930. It was further modified in 1933, becoming the T33.

As with the Nagant 1895, large numbers were captured when Germany invaded the Soviet Union and were then issued to Russian divisions organized by the Germans.

**Years of manufacture:** 1930–1945
**Caliber:** 7.62 × 25
**Magazine/capacity:** Detachable magazine, eight rounds
**Length:** 193 mm (7.6 in.)
**Barrel length:** 116 mm (4.6 in.)
**Weight:** 0.83 kg (1.83 lb.)

A 7.62 mm Russian Tokarev TT33 pistol. *Gianluigi Usai*

## Profile 16 — USA

# Colt 1911A1 Semi-Automatic Pistol

The Colt M1911 is the forefather of a long line of pistols designed by US arms designer John Moses Browning. The M1911 and improved M1911A1 were in service with US forces from 1911 until 1990, when it was replaced by the Beretta 92 (designated M9 in US military service). There are still many in the American military who long for the weapon, mainly because of its powerful cartridge.

This type of pistol was not supplied directly to the Italian partisans, except in cases of individual weapons carried by Allied representatives or partisan units that fought along the Gothic Line who were able to obtain them because they frequently crossed over into Allied lines.

**Years of manufacture:** 1911–1990
**Caliber:** .45 ACP
**Magazine/capacity:** Detachable magazine, seven rounds
**Length:** 220 mm (8.7 in.)
**Barrel length:** 127 mm (5.0 in.)
**Weight:** 1.12 kg (2.47 lb.)

The iconic .45-caliber Colt Model 1911A1 pistol. *Colin Doane*

Profile 17 *Argentina*

## Ballester Molina Semi-Automatic Pistol

The Ballester Molina is yet another copy of the Browning-Colt design produced under license. Many examples were supplied to Britain during the early stages of the war, when Britain sought weapons wherever it could; the weapons furnished to Britain had B-prefix serial numbers. Once the British arms situation was resolved, these pistols were used to arm partisans of various countries occupied by Germany, not the least of which was Italy.

**Years of manufacture:** 1927–1945
**Caliber:** .45 ACP
**Magazine/capacity:** Detachable magazine, seven rounds
**Length:** 215 mm (8.5 in.)
**Barrel length:** 127 mm (5.0 in.)
**Weight:** 1.02 kg (2.25 lb.)

The .45 ACP Ballester Molina pistol. *Al Gerth*

Commander "Poli" showing off the Ballester Molina given to him by Canadian Capt. "Buck" MacDonald of the 2nd SAS, who in turn received a Beretta 34 from "Poli."
*Lorenza Balbo*

## Profile 18 — USA

# Colt and Smith & Wesson Revolvers

When the United States entered WWI, they found their forces short of sidearms and turned to two major arms producers—Colt and Smith & Wesson—acquiring over 300,000 commercially available revolvers. They were converted to the standard .45 ACP caliber and used half-moon clips that allowed rapid reloading and extraction of spent rounds.

These revolvers continued in service well beyond WWI, being issued to personnel who were not expected to have to use them in combat situations. As an example, many of these revolvers were issued to aviation personnel. It is unclear how some of these weapons made their way into the hands of Italian partisans, although their use is documented; one can speculate they were turned over by American pilots or air crew who were rescued by partisans after forced landings.

**Years of manufacture:** 1917–1918
**Caliber:** .45 ACP
**Magazine/capacity:** Cylinder, six rounds
**Length:** 272–274 mm (10.7-10.8 in.)
**Barrel length:** 140 mm (5.5 in.)
**Weight:** 1.02–1.135 kg (2.25–2.98 lb.)

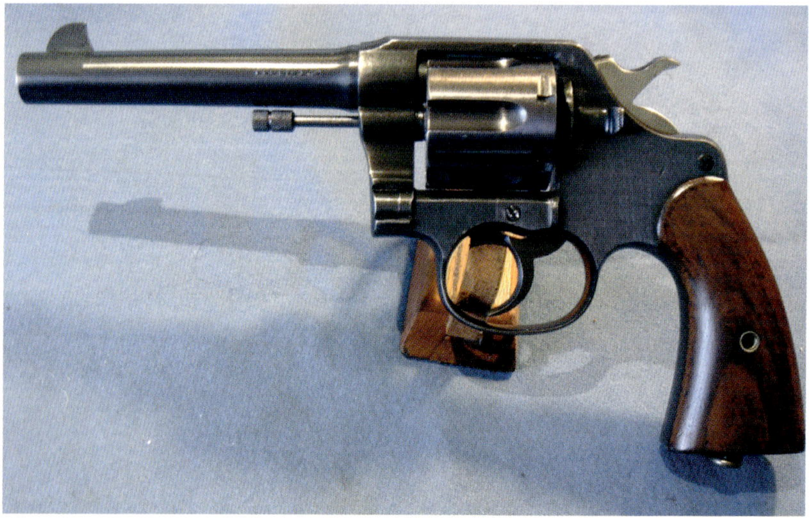

A .45 ACP Colt Model 1917 revolver. *Scott Benedict*

The two revolvers are both probably Smith & Wesson .38-200s, as described in the following profile. *ILSREC Genova*

## Profile 19 — Great Britain

# Webley and Enfield Revolvers

Following WWI, British analysts concluded the caliber then in use (.455) was obsolete and decided to adopt a new caliber with better performance characteristics (.38-200). After much legal wrangling between Webley and Enfield who accused each other of copying designs, it was decided to adopt both revolvers, from which several models (Marks) subsequently derived. Some examples were also acquired from Smith & Wesson (38-200), also in .38-caliber.

| | Webley | Enfield | Smith & Wesson |
|---|---|---|---|
| **Years of manufacture:** | 1923–1945 | 1932–1945 | 1940–1945 |
| **Caliber:** | .38/200 | .38/200 | .38/200 |
| **Magazine/ capacity:** | Cylinder, 6 | Cylinder, 6 | Cylinder, 6 |
| **Length:** | 266 mm (10.4 in.) | 260 mm (10.2 in.) | 258 mm (10.2 in.) |
| **Barrel length:** | 127 mm (5.0 in.) | 127 mm (5.0 in.) | 127 mm (5.0 in.) |
| **Weight:** | 0.765 kg (1.69 lb.) | 0.765 kg (1.69 lb.) | 0.82 kg (1.80 lb.) |

A Smith & Wesson .38-200 revolver. *Gianluigi Usai*

An Enfield No.2 Mk1 revolver in .38-200 caliber. *Scott Benedict*

A Webley Mk VI top-break revolver in .455 Webley caliber; the Webley 38-200 Mk IV was externally almost identical in appearance. *NRA Museums*

## Profile 20 *France*

# SACM 1935A and 1935S Semi-Automatic Pistol

Using the classic Colt-Browning design as a starting point, Swiss designer Charles Petter developed a new weapon for the *Sociètè Alsacienne de Constructions Mècaniques* (SACM) that was adopted by the French army in the odd 7.65 Longue caliber—a caliber unique to French weapons. In addition to the 1935A, another pistol was developed (1935S) that was less expensive and easier to produce. The pistols were produced by various French arsenals, with designations varying according to the manufacturer (MAS, MAT, MAC, etc.).

Following the occupation of France by Axis forces, many examples fell into partisan hands through various channels, but they were used only briefly because of the uncommon ammunition, which was used only for these pistols and the MAS 1938 submachine gun.

**Years of manufacture:** 1935–1940
**Caliber:** 7.65 Longue
**Magazine/capacity:** Detachable magazine, eight rounds
**Length:** 193 mm 7.6 in.)
**Barrel length:** 110 mm (4.3 in.)
**Weight:** 0.735 kg (1.62 lb.)

A 7.65 longue SACM Mle. 1935A pistol. *Colin Doane*

A 7.65 longue Mle. 1935S pistol. *Colin Doane*

## Profile 21 — *Spain*

# "Ruby" Type Semi-Automatic Pistols

During WWI, several nations, including Italy, came to the realization they did not have enough sidearms to meet their requirements. The solution to the problem was the fledgling Spanish arms industry which, among various models, offered a copy of the turn-of-the-century Browning semi-auto pistol design produced without a license from Fabrique Nationale. Production was undertaken by about thirty different manufacturers who in turn used a myriad of subcontractors, not all of whom were able to provide quality products. This accounts for the widely varying quality of these pistols, running the gamut from good to extremely poor; parts interchangeability was dubious at best, and each pistol had to be issued with two magazines to avoid problems.

At the end of WWI, these pistols were removed from service, but as many had been privately purchased, numerous soldiers took them home, so it is not uncommon to find them in partisan hands.

**Years of manufacture:** 1915–1918
**Caliber:** 7.65 × 17 Browning
**Magazine/capacity:** Detachable magazine, 7, 8, or 9 rounds
**Length:** 157 mm (6.2 in.)
**Barrel length:** 87 mm (3.4 in.)
**Weight:** 0.875 kg (1.93 lb.)

A Ruby pistol in 7.65 mm Browning. *Gianluigi Usai*

This partisan with disheveled hair appears to be holding a Ruby pistol. *Don Angelo Siri*

Detail of the presumed Ruby pistol. *Don Angelo Siri*

# Bolt-Action Rifles

Profile 22 *Italy*

## Mod. 1870, 1870/87, and 1870/87/16 Rifle (Vetterli and Vetterli/Vitali)

This was the first bolt-action rifle adopted by the Italian army, modifying the Swiss Vetterli system. It was updated in 1887 by adopting the Vitali clip feed system.

In 1916, to help meet the Italian army's need for weapons, it was once again modernized by modifying its caliber from the original 10.35 mm to the standard Italian 6.5 mm and issuing it to second-line troops. At the end of WWI, these rifles were issued to Italian colonial troops. This led to the saying among the partisans that rifles of this type supplied by the British had come directly from Abyssinia, but there is no proof this assertion is true.

**Years of manufacture:** 1870–1916
**Caliber:** 10.35 × 48; 6.5 × 52
**Magazine/capacity:** 1–4 rounds (10.35 mm versions); 6-round clip (6.5 mm)
**Length:** 1349 mm (53.1 in.)
**Barrel length:** 860 mm (33.9 in.)
**Weight:** 4.1 kg–4.62 kg (9.0–10.1 lb.)

A Vetterli-Vitali Model 1870/87/16 rifle. *Ralph Riccio*

Partisans entering Reggio Emilia; all appear to be armed with the very old but still useful Vetterli rifle in 6.5 mm. *M. Becchi*

## Profile 23 *Italy*

# Model 1891 Rifle and Derivatives

The Model 1891 was the Italian soldier's individual rifle during both world wars and in the conflicts between those wars. Opinions differ concerning this rifle: there are those who praise it as an excellent weapon and those who consider it little more than scrap iron. A version of this rifle was used to kill President John F. Kennedy: its selection for that purpose was likely not due only to the fact that it was the cheapest rifle on the surplus market at the time.

There were many versions of the basic rifle—long rifle, short rifle, carbine—and each of these had numerous variants identified by the year of modification. Initially, it was the only weapon available to the partisans, yet the partisans tended to abandon this old warhorse in favor of a more modern submachine gun without taking into account the advantage of a rifle capable of long-range engagements.

**Years of manufacture:** 1892–1945
**Caliber:** 6.5 × 52; 7.35 × 51
**Magazine/capacity:** Clip, six rounds
**Length:** from 919 mm to 1282 mm (36.2 in to 50.5 in.), depending on model
**Barrel length:** from 441 to 790 mm (17.4 in to 31.1 in.)
**Weight:** from 3.16 kg to 3.78 kg (7.0 to 8.34 lb.)

The Model 1891 Carcano rifle, Italy's standard rifle in WWI. *Ralph Riccio*

The 6.5 mm Model 1891/38 cavalry carbine; this was the most widely produced Italian long arm of WWII and was widely available to the partisans. *Ralph Riccio*

A 6.5 mm Model 191 TS carbine also frequently used by the partisans. *Ralph Riccio*

A 7.35 mm Model 38 short rifle; because of its caliber, its use by the partisans was relatively limited. *Ralph Riccio*

Profile 24 — Germany

## Mauser System Rifles

The following is a general description of Mauser rifles, as until at least WWII, the Mauser was the most widely used rifle in the world.

The Mauser could be found in the inventories of most major armies, and as the Wehrmacht occupied nations in Europe, it disarmed their armies and then incorporated captured weapons—consisting mostly of Mausers—into its own inventory. The Polish army's inventory consisted largely of Mausers, many of which were supplied as war reparations following WWI; Czechoslovakia produced Mauser pattern rifles considered even better than the original German Mausers. Other countries that used the Mauser were Yugoslavia and Belgium (which used a 7.65 mm cartridge). The Germans also used rifles earmarked for export but whose delivery was not completed, as was the case of Mausers ordered by Portugal.

Because these weapons were generally in the same caliber used by the Germans, it posed no problem to issue them immediately. In addition to arming German troops, Italian RSI units trained in Germany were also issued the Mauser, and a large number of them subsequently fell into the hands of the partisans.

The following specifications refer to the Kar98k standard German service rifle:

**Years of manufacture:** 1935–1945
**Caliber:** 7.92 × 57
**Magazine/capacity:** Clip, five rounds
**Length:** 1110 mm (43.7 in.)
**Barrel length:** 600 mm (23.6 in.)
**Weight:** 3.9 kg (8.59 lb.)

The classic German Kar98k service rifle. *Ralph Riccio*

A Yugoslav Model 1924 rifle; large quantities of this Mauser pattern rifle were captured by the Italians and stored in armories, where they were later seized by partisans for their use. *Pat Egan*

A studio photo of a partisan from Savona. *B. Chionetti*

Profile 25 *Austria*

## Model 1895 Rifle

At the end of WWI, Italy obtained large numbers of this rifle from Austria as captured weapons and war debt repayment.

These weapons—similarly with ex-Austro-Hungarian Schwarzlose machine guns—were mainly used to equip Italian colonial troops, but a significant number remained in army storage facilities and fell into the hands of the partisans immediately following the chaos within the Italian army caused by the armistice in September 1943. The nonstandard caliber rather quickly led to these rifles being removed from partisan service because of a lack of ammunition.

**Years of manufacture:** 1895–1918
**Caliber:** 8 × 50R
**Magazine/capacity:** Fixed magazine, five rounds
**Length:** 1000 mm (39.4 in.)
**Barrel length:** 499 mm (19.7 in.)
**Weight:** 3.34 kg (7.36 lb.)

Austrian Model 1895 carbine. *Courtesy of James D. Julia Auctioneers, Fairfield, Maine, www.jamesdjulia.com*

## Profile 26 *USA*

# Model 1903 and 1903A3 Springfield Rifle

In the early 1900s, the United States became aware of the need to equip its forces with a modern rifle; the country decided to produce an unlicensed copy of the best weapon then on the market, namely the Mauser '98. It is somewhat amusing to note the US court system later allowed Mauser a large award for patent infringement.

The Springfield was used by the Americans during WWI, and was still largely issued during the early stages of WWII, to second-line troops and Brazilian and French allies. Stocks were still available for supply to partisan units, mainly to those detachments operating in close proximity to the front lines and able to draw weapons directly from the Americans.

**Years of manufacture:** 1903–1944
**Caliber:** .30/06 (7.62 × 63)
**Magazine/capacity:** Internal, five rounds
**Length:** 1105 mm (43.5 in.)
**Barrel length:** 609 mm (24 in.)
**Weight:** 3.69 kg (8.14 lb.)

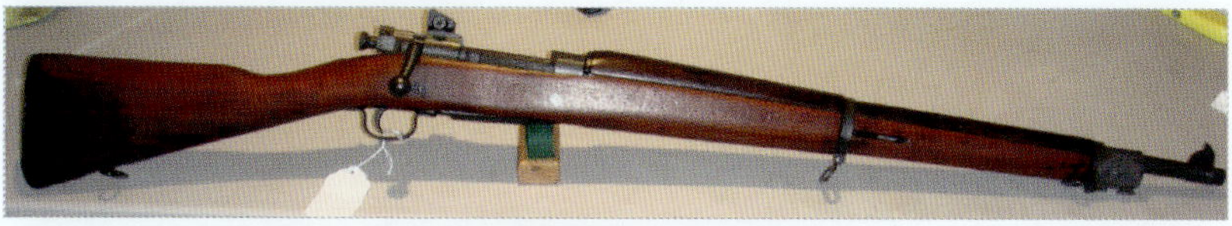

A US Springfield 1903A3 rifle. *Scott Benedict*

A partisan of the "Fumagalli" Division armed with a Springfield 1903A3 rifle. *G. Toscani*

Profile 27 *Great Britain*

## SMLE Enfield Rifle

Introduced in 1903, this rifle experienced continuous development and modification, with many variants identified as Marks using numbers and asterisks to designate them. Quite often these modifications, designed to speed up production, were achieved by converting previous models. The components remaining practically unchanged throughout the years were the action itself and the .303 caliber, known in Italy as 7.7 mm. In addition to being produced at various arsenals in England, it was also produced at numerous factories throughout the British Empire—India (Ishapore), Canada (Long Branch), and Australia (Lithgow)—as well as in the United States (Savage). During WWI, the most common model was the SMLE Mk 3, which was still largely issued at the beginning of WWII; beginning in 1942, the Number 4 Mk 1 began to be produced.

Photographs of Enfields in the hands of partisans generally show older models.

**Years of manufacture:** 1903–1945
**Caliber:** .303 (7.7 × 56)
**Magazine/capacity:** Detachable box, ten rounds
**Length:** 1,132 mm (44.6 in.)
**Barrel length:** 640 mm (25.2 in.)
**Weight:** 3.71 kg (8.18 lb.)

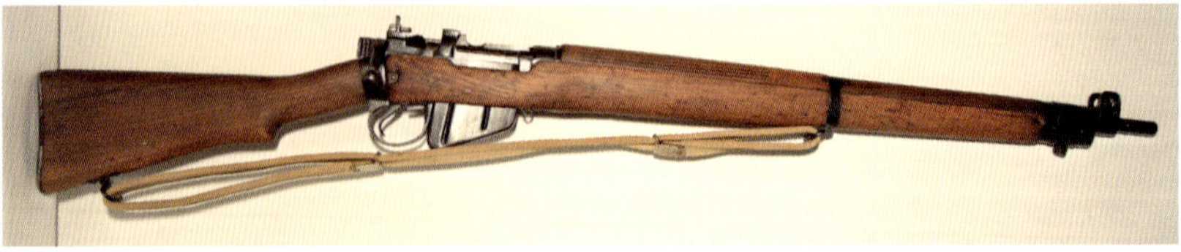

Enfield No.4 Mk1 rifle supplied by British missions to the partisans. *Gianluigi Usai*

A partisan of the "Amendola" Brigade armed with a No.4 Mk1 Enfield. *G. Toscani*

An earlier model Lee-Enfield—likely a Mk III—in the hands of a partisan of the "Fumagalli" Division. *G. Toscani*

## Profile 28 — USSR

# Mosin-Nagant Model 1891 Rifle

In 1891, the Czarist army adopted a new rifle based on the Belgian Nagant system as modified by the Russian Mosin. This rifle had a very long life, being produced in various versions—rifle and carbine—until 1945, with modifications introduced in 1930 and 1938, and carbine versions in 1938 and 1944.

Large quantities were available in the west following WWI and the civil war in Spain; these were augmented by weapons captured by the Germans during their invasion of Russia in 1941. These weapons were used to arm Cossack and Mongolian divisions created by the Germans; consequently, when these units were transferred to the Italian front their armament sometimes fell into partisan hands.

**Years of manufacture:** 1891–1945
**Caliber:** 7.62 × 54
**Magazine/capacity:** Internal, five rounds
**Length:** 1,016–1,304 mm (40–51.3 in.)
**Barrel length:** 512–802 mm (20.2–31.6 in.)
**Weight:** 3.54 kg to 4.43 kg (7.8 to 9.77 lb.)

A Mosin-Nagant Model 1891 rifle, a contemporary of the Carcano Model 1891 rifle. *Richard Percy*

A partisan woman armed with a Mosin-Nagant carbine and several hand grenades. *Gianluigi Usai*

# Semi-Automatic and Automatic Rifles

## Profile 29 *Germany*

## Gewehr 41

The first semi-automatic rifle employed in large numbers was the US M1 Garand, even though unsuccessful attempts to develop a semi-automatic rifle had been made in the very late 1800s.

Research on the German response to the Garand was undertaken by various well-respected companies, including Walther and Mauser. The best attempt turned out to be the Walther design designated the Gewehr 41 (also referred to as the Gew. 41 or G41), which was produced in modest numbers. The weapon did not live up to expectations and it was soon removed from combat units and reassigned to second-line units. When it became necessary to equip Italian units being trained in Germany, the Germans chose to issue them this rifle. As a result, it is not difficult to find these weapons in the hands of Italian partisans, especially in areas where the "San Marco" and "Monterosa" divisions of the RSI fought.

**Years of manufacture:** 1941–1942
**Caliber:** 7.92 × 57
**Magazine/capacity:** Internal, ten rounds
**Length:** 1,130 mm (44.5 in.)
**Barrel length:** 545 mm (21.5 in.)
**Weight:** 4.98 kg (10.98 lb.)

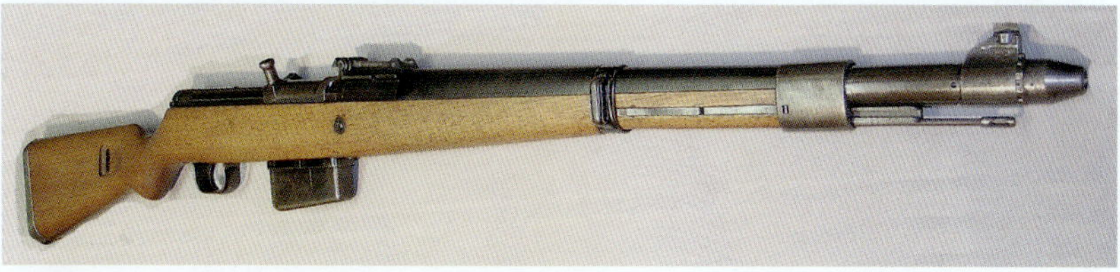

A Walther Gew 41 semi-auto rifle. *Edward McClean*

This well-armed partisan of the "Gin Bevilacqua" Division is carrying an abundance of ammunition and a German "potato masher" grenade in addition to his Gew 41. *E. Biggi*

A "Fumagalli" Division partisan armed with a Gew 41. *G. Toscani*

## Profile 30 — Germany

# Gewehr 43

The next attempt at developing a German semi-automatic rifle was also undertaken by Walther, heeding lessons learned from the Gewehr 41 and avoiding the most serious shortcomings that had manifested under combat conditions. The delicate gas operating system was modified, a removable magazine was fitted, and production was simplified to increase production rates. The result was designated the Gewehr 43 (also referred to as the Karabiner 43, Gew. 43, G43, Kar. 43, or K43).

Due to the introduction of more suitable models (see StG44), this rifle did not achieve the scale of issue it might have otherwise experienced. Despite that, it continued to be used until the end of the war and provides an example of how the inability to shift all production capabilities to the best design available can lead to a dispersion of resources.

**Years of manufacture:** 1943–1945
**Caliber:** 7.92 × 57
**Magazine/capacity:** Detachable box magazine, ten rounds
**Length:** 1,117 mm (44 in.)
**Barrel length:** 545 mm (21.5 in.)
**Weight:** 4.33 kg (9.55 lb.)

A German Gew 43 semi-auto rifle. *Scott Benedict*

This partisan from the Emilia region armed with a Gew 43 is outfitted with a significant amount of captured German clothing and equipment. *M. Becchi*

Profile 31 **Germany**

## FG42

Designed as a weapon for paratroopers, the selective fire FG42 is an example of a weapon that, had it been designed around the proper cartridge, would have been really innovative. Unfortunately, it was designed around the old 7.92 × 57 standard German service cartridge and was not completely successful. There are two versions of this weapon, the second of which is simply a development of the first version; less than 7,000 copies were produced. Many of the innovative features of this weapon were later applied to postwar weapons.

The FG42 made its combat debut in Italy in September 1943, during Otto Skorzeny's raid at Gran Sasso to free Mussolini; subsequently, it was used throughout Italy and the south of France, where it was used by German paratroop units. Given the small number of this weapon used in Italian territory, relatively few fell into partisan hands, although documentation does attest that some were indeed captured.

In the Tosco-Emiliana region of the Apennines the weapon acquired an odd nickname ("fislinger"), likely a corruption of the weapon's full designation *Fallschirmjägergewehr 42*.

**Years of manufacture:** 1942–1943
**Caliber:** 7.92 × 57
**Magazine/capacity:** Detachable box magazine, 20 rounds
**Length:** 937 mm (36.9 in.)
**Barrel length:** 483 mm (19 in.)
**Rate of fire:** 800 rpm
**Weight:** 4.5 kg (9.92 lb.)

The FG42 was an innovative design that made its combat debut in Italy. *Gianluigi Usai*

## Profile 32 *Germany*

# StG.44 or MP43

Following a very contentious evolution, the archetype of one of the most widely produced weapons in the contemporary world was born. The contention was based largely on a matter of semantics and opposition by Hitler, who did not want to hear any discussion of rifles, but rather "machine pistols," which in his judgment he considered assault weapons. A compromise was finally reached by adopting the term *sturmgewehr*, or assault rifle. Meantime, technical development had been completed, resulting in the StG.44, from which the Russians would develop the AK47.

Produced from stampings and using highly advanced techniques at the time, the StG44 quickly showed itself to be a winning horse; it is somewhat amazing that all other small arms production was not immediately canceled to shift all available resources to the production of this weapon. The weapon was chambered for the 7.92 mm *kurz*, which would provide the standard for all modern weapons of this type.

A number of examples ended up in the hands of Italian partisans. There are some who hypothesize the nickname "Mayerling" referred to the StG44 rather than the MG42.

**Years of manufacture:** 1943–1945
**Caliber:** 7.92 × 33
**Magazine/capacity:** Detachable box magazine, 30 rounds
**Length:** 940 mm (37 in.)
**Barrel length:** 418 mm (16.5 in.)
**Rate of fire:** 500 rpm
**Weight:** 5.1 kg (11.24 lb.)

The StG.44 was the first practical assault rifle. *Willam Cogger*

A group of partisans from the Emilia region; the partisan on the left has a StG.44 slung over his shoulder. *M. Becchi*

## Profile 33 — USSR

# Tokarev SVT38 and SVT40

The Soviet design by Tokarev of the US Garand. Many examples were captured by the Germans during the early stages of the invasion of Russia. Photographs show German soldiers using this weapon, as well use by Mongolian and Cossack collaborators as a sign of acceptance by soldiers of the *Wehrmacht*.

The Model 1938 proved to be somewhat fragile, leading to development of the Model 1940, which overcame all of the teething problems of the early version. A variant was developed that was fitted with a scope and was well received by snipers; a full-automatic version (AVT40) was also developed that was only produced in limited numbers.

Despite problems obtaining ammunition, some examples ended up in the hands of Italian partisans (see reference to a "Russian semi-automatic" in the document on page 22).

**Years of manufacture:** 1938–1945
**Caliber:** 7.62 × 54
**Magazine/capacity:** Detachable magazine, ten rounds
**Length:** 1,226 mm (48.3 in.)
**Barrel length:** 610 mm (24 in.)
**Weight:** 3.9 kg (8.6 lb.)

A Tokarev SVT 40 semi-auto rifle. *Scott Benedict*

Although not immediately recognizable, there are at least two SVT 40 rifles in the group: one being held by the partisan sitting at the left of the first row, and another by a partisan standing in the last row slightly to the left of the arch support. *Archivio Storico Cristilli Clusone (BG)*

## Profile 34 — USA

# M1 Garand Rifle

This was the first semi-automatic rifle officially adopted by an army produced in large numbers. Its design dates to 1932, and its adoption to 1936; by 1941, most soldiers in the US Army were issued this rifle. Five and a half million examples were produced before production ceased in 1950. If a removable magazine had been incorporated into the design such as those adopted by the Russians and Germans for similar weapons, this rifle would have proven to be an even greater success than it was.

Not many examples were issued to the Italian partisans, as the Allies preferred to furnish weapons that were already obsolete, such as the 1903 Springfield. Some can be found in photographs of units that fought directly behind the lines and were probably furnished directly on the spot, rather than being air dropped.

**Years of manufacture:** 1936–1950
**Caliber:** .30-06
**Magazine/capacity:** Internal, eight rounds
**Length:** 1,103 mm (43.4 in.)
**Barrel length:** 610 mm (24 in.)
**Weight:** 4.37 kg (9.63 lb.)

The US M1 Garand was the most widely produced semi-automatic rifle in WWII. *Scott Benedict*

A group of partisans in Emilia; the third partisan on the left is holding a Garand. *M. Becchi*

A group of partisans assembled and awaiting instructions. Among the eclectic mix of weapons at least two M1 Garands can be seen. *ISREC Savona*

## Profile 35 USA

# M1 e M1A1 Carbine

Conceived as a weapon for troops like machine gunners, artillery and mortar crews, and soldiers in similar specialties who did not have to use a rifle or pistol, it soon proved to be a very successful weapon, so much that over 6,500,000 examples were produced. In Italian it was known colloquially as the Winchester, because the original design was by that company, even though Winchester produced only about ten percent of the total. The weapon was produced by ten different manufacturers, with prime contractors utilizing many small parts and components supplied by a wide array of subcontractors.

In addition to the basic version there were a number of variants: the best known was the M1A1, which had a folding stock designed specifically for use by paratroopers; and the M2, which had a full-automatic fire capability and generally used a larger 30-round magazine.

Because of its light weight it was a preferred weapon of irregular forces supplied by the Allies and many examples were furnished to the Italian partisans.

**Years of manufacture:** 1941–1945
**Caliber:** .30 M1; 7.62 × 33
**Magazine/capacity:** Detachable box; 15- and 30-round
**Length:** 905 mm (35.6 in.)
**Barrel length:** 457 mm (18 in.)
**Weight:** 2.48 kg (5.47 lb.)

An early production version of the US M1 carbine with flip rear sight and lacking the bayonet lug of the later version. *Ralph Riccio*

Partisans armed with the TZ45 submachine gun and a paratrooper model M1A1 carbine with folding stock. *Don Angelo Siri*

Partisans in Modena; the partisan on the left is carrying an M1 carbine. *M. Becchi*

## Profile 36 *Italy*

# Beretta Mod. 18/30 Semi-Automatic Carbine

Following the introduction of the Villar Perosa—the world's first submachine gun—it was realized the paired weapons comprising the Villar Perosa could be separated, resulting in a more manageable weapon. Experiments were carried out by various companies, including Beretta, and by end of the 1930s led to development and production of this semi-automatic carbine that was not adopted by the Italian army, but by the *Guardia Forestale* (Forestry Guards). This weapon is known to have been used during the Italian war in Ethiopia.

Its caliber (9 mm Glisenti) was such a drawback that it was not widely issued, and was presumably relegated to storage in barracks arms rooms, at least until the partisans' desperate hunger for weapons brought it back to the fore. The carbine was known as *il siringone* ("the big syringe") in Italian due to the prominent and distinctive ring-shaped cocking handle at the rear of the receiver.

**Years of manufacture:** 1930
**Caliber:** 9 × 19 Glisenti
**Magazine/capacity:** Detachable box; 25-round
**Length:** 890 mm (35 in.)
**Barrel length:** 320 mm (12.6 in.)
**Weight:** 3.26 kg (7.19 lb.)

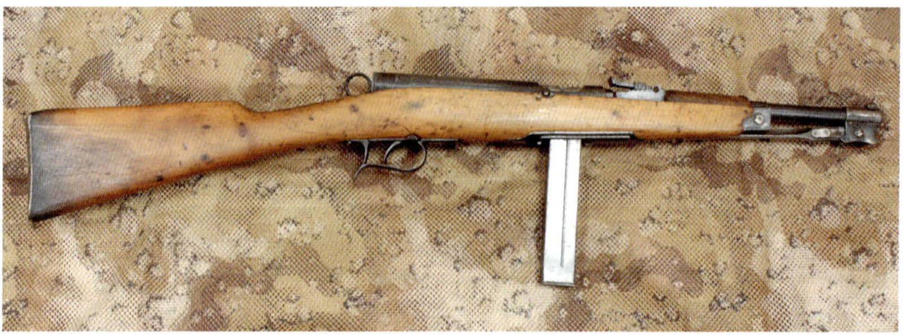

The Beretta Model 18/30 carbine with its characteristic cocking ring at the rear of the receiver. *Museo della Guerra di Rovereto*

The partisan on the left in this group in Emilia is cradling a Beretta Model 18/30 carbine. *M. Becchi*

Partisans participating in the liberation of Turin in late April 1945; even at this late stage of the war the Model 18/30 was still useful. *ILSREC Genova*

# Submachine Guns

## Profile 37 *Italy*

## Beretta Model 38A Submachine Gun

The Beretta Model 38A submachine gun ranks with the Beretta Model 34 pistol as an iconic Italian weapon very much admired by Italy's allies and her adversaries. The weapon's capabilities were not completely appreciated initially, so much so the Italian army did not adopt it until 1941; it reached its peak of perfection during the period of the RSI. The Germans sought to seize as many as they could, and also made arrangements to continue production under German control at a pace estimated at about 32,000 examples a month by March 1945.

The earliest versions were expensive and time consuming to produce, but modifications and simplifications were made continuously to speed up production and lower costs. Enemy soldiers—specifically British and Americans—would willingly file false papers to bring one back as a souvenir.

**Years of manufacture:** 1938–1945
**Caliber:** 9 × 19; 9M38
**Magazine/capacity:** 10, 20, and 40-round staggered row magazines
**Length:** 953 mm (37.5 in.)
**Barrel length:** 320 mm (12.6 in.)
**Rate of fire:** 550 rpm
**Weight:** 3.95 kg (8.7 lb.)

The iconic Beretta Model 38A submachine gun with its distinctive dual triggers and perforated cooling jacket. *Beretta*

A studio photo of a partisan and his Beretta MAB 1938A. *Don Angelo Siri*

Another posed studio photo of a partisan attired in an Italian Army uniform and well armed with two pistols and a hand grenade in addition to his MAB. *Don Angelo Siri*

Profile 38 *Italy*

## Beretta Model 38/42 Submachine Gun

Among the variants of the Model 38A, one of the most easily distinguishable was the version that had a shortened barrel lacking the ventilated barrel jacket. This was one of many modifications made beginning in 1941; the earliest short barrels had longitudinal grooves that were supposed to aid cooling the barrel, but once it was realized they were useless they were initially made thinner and finally eliminated. Generally, these models are referred to as the 38/41, 38/42, 38/43, and finally the 38/44, which departs completely from the preceding models thanks to the introduction of a new receiver end cap from which the spring guide—itself modified—no longer protruded.

It seems the Model 38/42 was first requested by the Germans; beginning in 1942 they took delivery of large numbers. These are recognizable by their markings that differ from the normal Italian markings. With the introduction of a new safety system it remained in use by the Italian army and police forces until just a few years ago.

Logically, partisans took possession of as many of these weapons as they could; in partisan service it was given the rather curious nickname *Balilla* due to its rather small dimensions.

**Years of manufacture:** 1941–1960
**Caliber:** 9 × 19; 9M38
**Magazine/capacity:** 20- and 40-round staggered row magazines
**Length:** 790 mm (31.1 in.)
**Barrel length:** 216 mm (8.5 in.)
**Rate of fire:** 550 rpm
**Weight:** 3.26 kg (7.19 lb.)

The Beretta Model 38/42 was a simplified version of the MAB 38A, but retained the hallmark reliability of Beretta weapons. Note the fluted barrel in lieu of the cooling jacket. *Courtesy of James D. Julia Auctioneers, Fairfield, Maine, www.jamesdjulia.com*

This well-attired partisan woman with a Beretta 38/42 is holding a group of Fascist women prisoner. As was customary, women accused of collaborating with the enemy had their hair shorn when captured. *Don Angelo Siri*

A partisan armed with a Beretta 38/42 in a victory parade in 1945. *Gente magazine insert, "Guerra Civile," 1965*

Profile 39 *Italy*

## FNAB43 Submachine Gun

During the final years of the war, Italian designers finally grasped the importance of the new weapon whose use was becoming increasingly widespread and began to look at a wider share of the market. The FNAB43 is an example of a good technical solution that made its appearance too late. In effect, it seems only a few examples were produced; some sources claim a total of about 6,000 were made, but other sources note known serial numbers are only in the 5000 and 6000 blocks, so possibly only less than 1,000 examples were made. During the final years of the war Beretta produced more than 10,000 submachine guns per month, reaching a high of 32,000 in March 1945, FNAB43 production was merely a drop in the ocean. Further underscoring its limited production, pictures of this weapon are almost completely lacking in photos of partisan and RSI forces; surviving examples are only found in museums. Curiously, there are photos of this weapon in the hands of Algerians fighting against the French in the 1960s.

**Years of manufacture:** 1944–1945
**Caliber:** 9 × 19; 9M38
**Magazine/capacity:** 20- and 40-round staggered row magazines
**Length:** 790/527 mm (31.1 in/20.9 in.) stock extended/stock folded
**Barrel length:** 200 mm (7.9 in.)
**Rate of fire:** 400 rpm
**Weight:** 3.25 kg (7.17 lb.)

Right and left side views of the FNAB43 submachine gun. *Ralph Riccio*

A partisan in Modena with an FNAB43 submachine gun; he is also wearing an ammunition pouch with spare magazines for the weapon. The pouch was issued to Italian paratroopers beginning in 1941 and was referred to as the "Samurai" by the paratroopers, as well as later by the partisans. *Don Angelo Siri*

Profile 40 *Italy*

## Tonon-Zorzoli TZ45 Submachine Gun

The TZ45 was another submachine gun introduced during the period of the RSI that was used to equip units such as the Black Brigades and a few others. Only about 6,000 examples of this weapon were made. The TZ45 did, however, introduce a novel feature that would be copied on other submachine guns produced: a safety on the magazine housing blocked the bolt and had to be squeezed to enable firing (or at least that was the hope, see page 47).

In contrast to its contemporary the FNAB43, the TZ45 is well documented in photographs of RSI and partisans. At least a couple of these weapons were still in use in 1978, during the ambush on Via Fani in Rome, when Italian Prime Minister Aldo Moro was kidnapped by Red Brigade terrorists while killing five of his bodyguards.

**Years of manufacture:** 1944–1945
**Caliber:** 9 × 19; 9M38
**Magazine/capacity:** 20- and 40-round staggered row magazines
**Length:** 851/546 mm (33.5 in/21.5 in.) stock extended/stock folded
**Barrel length:** 215 mm (9 in.)
**Rate of fire:** 550 rpm
**Weight:** 3.26 kg (7.2 lb.)

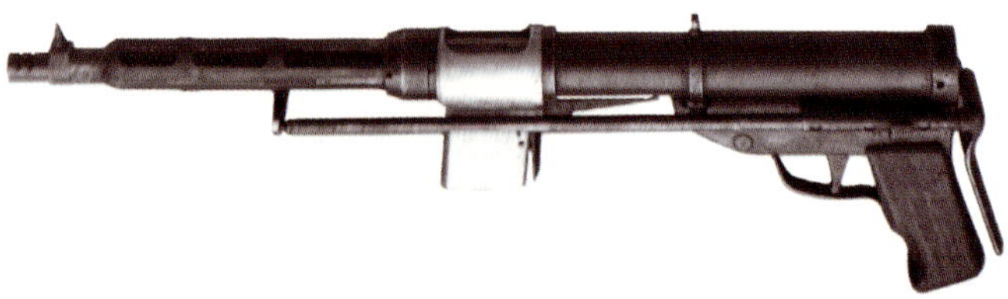

Right and left side views of the 9 mm TZ45 submachine gun. *Ralph Riccio*

Studio photograph of a young partisan with a TZ45. *B. Chionetti*

A partisan armed with a TZ45. *G. Toscani*

Profile 41 *Italy*

## Variara Submachine Gun

The Variara is a somewhat mysterious weapon; only a small number of examples are known to exist (ten to twelve), all in museums. There is no information concerning who designed the weapon, where it was produced, nor how many were made. Speculation suggests the name Variara belonged to a partisan from Piedmont, while other sources speak of a Fiat designer. Some sources claim the weapon was produced in Val d'Ossola, while others maintain it was assembled in Fiat factories from parts produced clandestinely.

The Variara was a mix of different design features; it is hard to understand why, if the intent was to produce a partisan weapon, a more practical approach was not taken, such as simply making a copy of the Sten, as other European resistance movements did. Because it was compact and easily concealable thanks to its magazine housing that could be folded forward and its folding stock, it had the potential to become a more successful weapon than it was.

**Years of manufacture:** 1944–?
**Caliber:** 9 × 19; 9M38
**Magazine/capacity:** 20- and 40-round staggered row magazines
**Length:** 820/560 mm (32.3 in/22 in.) stock extended/stock folded
**Barrel length:** 300 mm (11.8 in.)
**Rate of fire:** 550 rpm
**Weight:** 2.8 kg (6.2 lb.)

The unique Variara submachine gun was produced clandestinely by the partisans; the folding stock and hinged magazine housing made it a very compact weapon. *Ralph Riccio*

A Variara with its stock extended; actual photos of this weapon in partisan use are virtually impossible to find. *Museo della Guerra di Rovereto*

This rather well-dressed individual who looks more like a businessman than a partisan is nevertheless formidably armed with a Variara and a German Model 24 *Stielhandgranate* "Potato masher" hand grenade. *Giovanni Sanguineti*

Profile 42 *Germany*

## MP38 and MP40 Machine Pistol

This weapon is almost an icon associated with the WWII German soldier, even though in actuality it was not in as widespread use as some movies and documentaries would have one believe. Introduced in 1938 after prototype testing as early as 1936, it was later modified and simplified, leading to its definitive configuration. Some 900,000 examples were produced thanks to the use of stamped parts and phenolic resin in its manufacture.

This was a "second generation" weapon; that is, one utilizing methods allowing for more rapid production and the use of less sophisticated machinery than needed for earlier types of submachine gun. For example, to produce an MP18 or MP28, manufacture began with a piece of steel that had to be machined, while for these weapons sheet steel or tubes could be used, and not necessarily of the highest quality either.

This generation of weapons included the British Sten, the US M3, and the Soviet PPSH41, while weapons such as the Thompson or the early Beretta MAB 38A were first-generation weapons. Captured MP38 and MP40 machine pistols were highly sought after by partisans.

**Years of manufacture:** 1938–1944
**Caliber:** 9 × 19 Parabellum
**Magazine/capacity:** 32-round magazine
**Length:** 832/629 mm (32.8 in/24.8 in.) stock extended/sock folded
**Barrel length:** 247 mm (9.7 in.)
**Rate of fire:** 500 rpm
**Weight:** 3.97 kg (8.75 lb.)

The MP40 is probably one of the best known submachine guns used during WWII. *Centro documentazione e Ricerche Storiche Gotica Toscana*

Hans was a German deserter who joined the ranks of the independent division commanded by "Poli"; it is no surprise he is armed with an MP40. *L. Balbo*

***Il Biondino.***

One of the leading partisans in the Savona area was nicknamed *Biondino* ("Blondie"). *F. Sasso*

Profile 43 *Austria/Germany*

## MP34, MP34(o) Machine Pistol

To circumvent the clauses of the Treaty of Versailles, this German-designed submachine gun was initially produced in Switzerland as the Solothurn SI 100; it was later produced by Steyr in Austria, which sold it to various countries. Beginning in 1938, it was also issued to German army units with the designation MP34(o). Because of its sophisticated design and the quality of workmanship it was considered the "Rolls Royce" of submachine guns at the time. It is easily distinguishable from similar weapons due to its forward angled magazine housing with a slot allowing the magazines to be reloaded using stripper clips.

Based on eyewitness statements (second photo), the weapon being held by a relative of Piero Balbo is the "Czechoslovak parabellum" previously described (see glossary).

**Years of manufacture:** 1934–1940
**Caliber:** 9 × 19 Parabellum
**Magazine/capacity:** 32-round magazine
**Length:** 820 mm (32.3 in.)
**Barrel length:** 220 mm (8.7 in.)
**Rate of fire:** 500 rpm
**Weight:** 4.536 kg (10 lb.)

The MP34(o) submachine gun. *Max Popenker*

Partisans belonging to the independent division led by "Poli," one of whom is armed with the easily recognizable MP34(o). *L. Balbo*

Two partisans with their German submachine guns. The individual on the right is "Moretto," Poli's driver and bodyguard, while on the left is a relative of Piero Balbo ("Poli") with the MP34 that was the probable "Czechoslovak parabellum" he carried as war booty from Crete. *L. Balbo*

## Profile 44 *Germany*

# Bergmann MP35 Machine Pistol

This submachine gun had a difficult gestation because of the limitations placed on Germany by the Treaty of Versailles. Designed by German Emil Bergmann, it was first produced by the Danish company Schultz & Larsen, then contracted to Walther as the MP34/I, and later to Junker & Ruh as the MP35/I. It enjoyed modest sales success; some examples were captured by Italian soldiers fighting in Abyssinia in 1936, as the Ethiopian army had acquired a fairly large number. Other Bergmanns went to Denmark and Sweden. As was common, the caliber could vary depending on the wishes of a particular client; the weapon was furnished in 7.63 Mauser, 7.65 Parabellum, .45 ACP, and various 9 mm.

An estimated 40,000 examples produced by Junker & Ruh were furnished to the SS, and production continued until 1945.

**Years of manufacture:** 1934–1945
**Caliber:** 9 × 19 Parabellum
**Magazine/capacity:** 24- and 32-round magazines
**Length:** 840 mm (33.1 in.)
**Barrel length:** 196 mm (7.7 in.)
**Rate of fire:** 600 rpm
**Weight:** 4.05 kg (8.93 lb.)

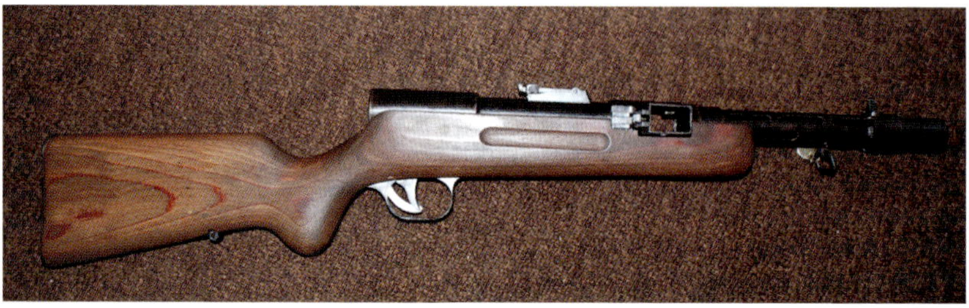

The Bergmann MP35 submachine gun. *Gianluigi Usai*

A member of the partisan division led by "Commander Poli." *L. Balbo*

## Profile 45 *Germany*

# Schmeisser MP41 Machine Pistol

Other than the MP18/28, this is probably the only weapon that can trace its origins to Hugo Schmeisser, even though he is credited with many other designs, not the least of which the MP38/40, which is universally known as the "Schmeisser," although he had nothing to do with its design. Merging the mechanical components of the MP40 with an MP28-style stock, he developed this robust machine pistol produced by Haenel.

The gun was not adopted by the German Army, but was largely exported to friendly nations such as Romania and various Slavic allies. Despite this, some examples managed to find their way to Italian resistance fighters.

**Years of manufacture:** 1941–1944
**Caliber:** 9 × 19 Parabellum
**Magazine/capacity:** 32-round magazine
**Length:** 863 mm (34 in.)
**Barrel length:** 251 mm (9.9 in.)
**Rate of fire:** 500 rpm
**Weight:** 3.7 kg (8.16 lb.)

Although the Schmeisser MP41 appears to be an MP40 with a wooden stock, it is in fact a completely different weapon. *Max Popenker*

A female partisan armed with an MP41 carrying a holstered Beretta Model 34 pistol.
*Don Angelo Siri*

## Profile 46 — *Germany*

# MP18 and MP28 Machine Pistols

The MP18 vies with the Italian Villar Perosa as the first submachine gun ever designed and used in war, although the Villar Perosa was born more as a light machine gun rather than a submachine gun. The MP18 design by Hugo Schmeisser dates to 1916; in light of its effectiveness, following the war, its production in Germany was prohibited, so manufacture had to be transferred to Belgium and Switzerland. During those years weapons were chambered to customer request, so the MP18 and follow-on MP28 can be encountered in a wide range of calibers, such as 7.63 Mauser, 7.65 Parabellum, various 9 mm calibers, .45 ACP, and even in Japanese 8 mm Nambu.

In addition to the few examples in the hands of the Wehrmacht allowed by the Treaty of Versailles, examples could be found captured in countries occupied by Germany in calibers different than 9 mm Parabellum. Reproduced without license, they could also be found in Spain during the Spanish Civil War (the so-called *Naranjero*); when the anti-Franco forces surrendered they were furnished to the French, who initially used them against the Germans until they were eventually captured by the German occupiers. It is also interesting to note that in 1940, when the British realized they had no submachine gun in their inventory, they remedied the situation by producing the Lanchester, which was nothing more than a slightly altered and unlicensed copy of the MP28.

**Years of manufacture:** 1918–1930
**Caliber:** 9 × 19 Parabellum, but other calibers upon customer request
**Magazine/capacity:** 20-, 32-, and 50-round magazines
**Length:** 838 mm (33 in.)
**Barrel length:** 200 mm (7.9 in.)
**Rate of fire:** 400 rpm, (MP18); 500 rpm (MP28)
**Weight:** 4.19kg (9.24 lb.) MP18; 3.97 kg (8.75 lb.) MP28

The MP18/MP28 with its distinctive snail drum magazine. *Max Popenker*

Profile 47 *France*

## MAS 1938 Submachine Gun

Stemming from a long line of models dating to 1924, in 1938, the Saint Etienne Arsenal unveiled this new, modern weapon. It was short and relatively light, differing in many respects from other submachine guns produced at the time (63 cm [24.8 in] long and weighing 2.3 kg [5.07 lb.], compared to the 95 cm [37.4 in] length and 4.2 kg [8.26 lb.] weight of the Beretta MAB 38A), but could not compete with weapons such as the German MP38, especially regarding new production techniques. The chief difference and major fault lay in the caliber that was adopted (7.65 Longue), a uniquely French caliber that went against the trend followed by most other countries.

Between 1938 and 1940, a small number were produced (less than 1,500), and production continued under German occupation, as well as postwar. In Italy, it is most well-known as the weapon used to kill Mussolini—at least according to the official version of the event—and recent news articles have claimed the actual weapon used in the assassination has resurfaced in a museum in Tirana, Albania.

**Years of manufacture:** 1938–1949
**Caliber:** 7.65 Longue
**Magazine/capacity:** 32-round magazine
**Length:** 630 mm (24.8 in.)
**Barrel length:** 224 mm (8.82 in.)
**Rate of fire:** 600 rpm
**Weight:** 2.83 kg (6.24 lb.)

The French MAS 1938 submachine gun used a unique cartridge that the partisans had difficulty procuring. *Courtesy of James D. Julia Auctioneers, Fairfield, Maine, www.jamesdjulia.com*

Partisans of the "Revetria" detachment "Gin Bevilacqua" Division at Calizzano, in the province of Savona. *ILSREC Savona*

A partisan armed with a MAS 1938 on a rooftop, searching for snipers. *Don Angelo Siri*

Profile 48 — USSR

## Shpagin PPSh 41 Submachine Gun

The PPSh 41 submachine gun is synonymous with the Soviet soldier; until the debut of the AK 47, it was also symbolically associated with protagonists in liberation movements worldwide. Extremely easy to manufacture quickly, more than five million were produced. The PPSh 41 replaced earlier Soviet submachine guns designed by Degtyarev that were much more complicated to produce and almost all of which were lost during the early months of the German invasion. Many examples of this weapon also fell into the hands of the Germans, who then issued them to the Russian divisions that fought for the Germans; when transferred to the Italian front, the Russian divisions provided these weapons to the partisans, either willingly or as a result of capture.

There was a variant of the PPSh 41 introduced by Germany in 9 mm Parabellum that could use MP 40 magazines. Some examples of this weapon made their way to Italy as war booty brought back by Italian soldiers who served on the Russian front.

**Years of manufacture:** 1941–1945
**Caliber:** 7.62 × 25
**Magazine/capacity:** 32-round magazine or 71-round drum
**Length:** 838 mm (33 in.)
**Barrel length:** 266 mm (10.5 in.)
**Rate of fire:** 900 rpm
**Weight:** 4.2 kg (9.26 lb.)

The Russian Shpagin PPSh 41 submachine gun. *Gianluigi Usai*

Commanders of the independent partisan divisions meeting in Cuneo on May 1, 1945: "Mauri" is on the left and "Poli" is in the center, wearing the white smock. *L. Balbo*

Partisans gathered for a souvenir photo; standing in the center is a Russian deserter from the Wehrmacht holding his PPSh 41. *G. Toscani*

## Profile 49 *Finland/Switzerland*

# Suomi M31 Submachine Gun

The Suomi M31 was one of the most widely distributed submachine guns, at least until the introduction of second-generation weapons of the type. This Finnish Lahti product enjoyed considerable export success, especially following the favorable publicity it garnered during the so-called "Winter War" between the Finns and the Soviets. This weapon could be found issued to several nations: in addition to Finland, Germany also took delivery of 3,000 examples; Switzerland acquired a number; and Hispano-Suiza subsequently obtained a production license and called their model the MP43/44.

Examples could be found in partisan hands that were captured from the Germans, as well as some presumably obtained from the Swiss. In actuality, photos of partisans armed with these weapons are almost all of fighters who were near the border with Switzerland, leading to the assumption the weapons were of Swiss manufacture.

**Years of manufacture:** 1926–1945
**Caliber:** 9 × 19 Parabellum
**Magazine/capacity:** various, including 20-, 36-, 50-, and 71-round magazines
**Length:** 875 mm (34.5 in.)
**Barrel length:** 320 mm (12.6 in.)
**Rate of fire:** 900 rpm
**Weight:** 4.87 kg (10.74 lb.)

The Finnish Suomi M31 submachine gun was an excellent weapon. *Max Popenker*

The partisan in the foreground has a Suomi slung over his shoulder. *Don Angelo Siri*

A female partisan with her Suomi M31. *Don Angelo Siri*

## Profile 50 *Great Britain*

# Sten MkII Machine Carbine

The Sten is undoubtedly the iconic weapon of the partisan—the desired weapon of everyone who fought for liberty. The Sten was a weapon born of emergency, practically designed at a dinner table during the soup course and manufactured using assorted types of tubing, so much so it was referred to as the "plumber's nightmare." It was produced in very large numbers (around 4,500,000), surpassed only by the Soviet PPSh41 (more than 5,000,000 copies) and the US M1 carbine (6,500,000 copies).

The Sten was easy to produce and maintain, but it had several faults, such as a lack of a safety and excessive shot dispersion. Attempts were made to compensate for the lack of a safety by introducing several modifications, but the improved models never made it into partisan hands, as witnessed by the fact that after a number of incidents many circulars were issued by partisan commands cautioning that greater attention be paid during use and while simply carrying the Sten.

**Years of manufacture:** 1941–1945
**Caliber:** 9 × 19 Parabellum
**Magazine/capacity:** 32-round magazine
**Length:** 762 mm (30 in.)
**Barrel length:** 196 mm (7.7 in.)
**Rate of fire:** 550 rpm
**Weight:** 3.631 kg (8 lb.)

A Sten MkII submachine gun, much used and favored by the partisans. The weapon pictured—somewhat worse for wear—is known to have seen partisan service. *Gianluigi Usai*

Partisans training with the Sten; it might be a good idea if the safety catch were released, as it is difficult to learn how to shoot with the safety engaged. *Don Angelo Siri*

A German deserter named Amoser armed with a Sten fitted with a silencer during the course of Operation Tombola. *M. Becchi*

A studio photo of a partisan armed with a Sten MkII. *L. Balbo*

Profile 51 — *Great Britain*

## Sten MkIII Machine Carbine

Because the Sten MkII was considered too expensive to produce, during 1941, the MkIII—which was simplified and easier to produce—was introduced. In little more than a year, over 900,000 examples were produced by Lines Brothers Ltd., an English manufacturer of pressed steel toys.

As the war progressed the MkII and MkIII were replaced by more sophisticated models like the Sten Mk5, which never reached the Italian front. Judging from very sparse photographic documentation, it appears the MkIII version was rarely furnished to the Italian resistance movement.

**Years of manufacture:** 1942–1943
**Caliber:** 9 × 19 Parabellum
**Magazine/capacity:** 32-round magazine
**Length:** 762 mm (30 in.)
**Barrel length:** 196 mm (7.7 in.)
**Rate of fire:** 550 rpm
**Weight:** 3.39 kg (7.47 lb.)

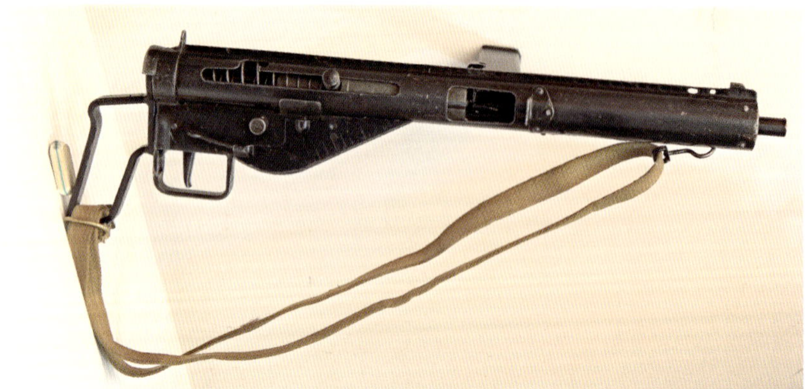

A Sten MkIII. *Gianluigi Usai*

Amidst a profusion of MkII Stens, the partisan on the right is instead armed with a Sten MkIII. *ISREC Savona*

## Profile 52 USA

# Thompson M1928A1, M1, and M1A1 Submachine Gun

The third light automatic weapon chronologically introduced, the Thompson was conceived as a "trench broom" during WWI, but did not make its debut until the war was almost over. After a brief period of negative notoriety as a "gangster weapon," it was finally adopted by the US Army. There were many variants of the Thompson, although only two principal versions (M1928A1 and M1/M1A1) reached notable issue levels.

The weapon was very much sought after by partisan commanders, who showed them off as a sign of their leadership positions. The first Thompsons seen in the hands of Italian partisans were part of the 3,750 M28 version supplied by the United States and captured in France in 1940. It was only later that Thompsons began to be supplied to the partisans by the United States and Britain.

| | **1928A1** | **M1 and M1A1** |
|---|---|---|
| **Years of manufacture:** | 1939–1942 | 1942–1945 |
| **Caliber:** | .45 ACP | .45 ACP |
| **Magazine/capacity:** | 20- and 30-round box | 20- and 30-round box |
| | 50-round drum | |
| **Length:** | 857 mm (33.7 in.) | 813 mm (32 in.) |
| **Barrel length:** | 266 mm (10.5 in.) | 266 mm (10.5 in.) |
| **Rate of fire:** | 600 rpm | 700 rpm |
| **Weight:** | 4.88 kg (10.76 lb.) | 4.34 kg (9.57 lb.) |

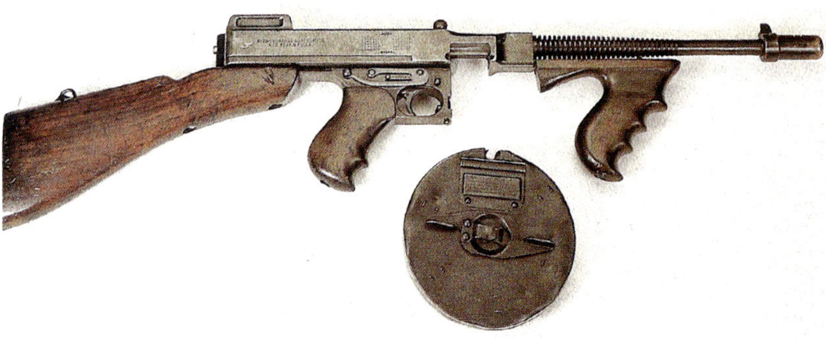

A Thompson M1928—the classic "Tommy gun"—with a 50-round drum magazine; the drum was replaced by a conventional box magazine that was less cumbersome. *Gianluigi Usai*

A simplified wartime production Thompson M1A1. *Gianluigi Usai*

Partisan members of the Savona brigade. *G. Toscani*

A partisan armed with a Thompson entering Savona. *G. Toscani*

## Profile 53 — *USA*

# M3 Submachine Gun

The M3 was the US answer to the British Sten; it could be produced extremely quickly and inexpensively using simple stamping operations, in effect using two shell halves stamped and welded that contained all of the moving parts. The characteristic cocking handle on the right side—present only on the first version (M3)—was said by some Italian partisans to resemble the handle of a coffee grinder. The simplified version (M3A1) that lacked the cocking handle never reached the Italian front.

A version chambered for the 9 mm Parabellum cartridge was developed that could use 9 mm ammunition by simply changing some parts—the barrel, bolt, and recoil spring—and using a Sten magazine. Although still open to question, it appears Italian partisans were furnished with at least some of the 9 mm version.

**Years of manufacture:** 1942–1945
**Caliber:** .45 ACP and 9 × 19 Parabellum
**Magazine/capacity:** 30-round (.45 ACP) or 32-round (9 mm) magazine
**Length:** 762/577 mm (30/22.7 in.) stock extended/folded
**Barrel length:** 203 mm (8 in.)
**Rate of fire:** 400 rpm
**Weight:** 3.71 kg (8.18 lb.)

The US M3 submachine gun; its overall appearance gave rise to the name "grease gun" among US troops, while the cocking handle reminded the Italian partisans of a coffee mill. *NRA Museums*

A salute and thanks to the arriving American liberators. *G. Toscani*

Canadian Capt. Robert MacDonald of the 2nd SAS in Castino. *L. Balbo and E. MacDonald*

**Canadian Capt. Robert "Buck" MacDonald**, 2nd SAS, was born on November 4, 1920, in Westville, Pictou County, Nova Scotia; his family moved to nearby New Glasgow about a year later. Robert was a good student and a natural athlete, winning the Canadian junior 400 meter dash championship in 1937. Robert was also high school cadet captain and won the Cadet Shield as best overall student when he graduated in 1938. From 1939 to 1941, he attended the Royal Military College and graduated early due to the war in Europe. He was commissioned as a lieutenant in the Royal Canadian Dragoons (tanks), but in 1942, he applied and was accepted into the newly created 1st Canadian Parachute Battalion. Circa 1943, he was posted to England and trained for the D-Day invasion, but due to an injury suffered during the winter of 1944, he did not participate in the D-Day pre-invasion airborne assault. MacDonald—still in England assigned to training duties—was very anxious to get to the fighting in France to avenge the death of his fellow officer and best friend, Maj. Murray "Hugh" Macleod, so he made his way to the English Channel, where he hired a fisherman to take him to France. Upon reporting to duty in France he was initially charged with deserting his post, but charges were soon dropped when his superiors realized he was attempting to join the battle rather than avoid it. He was then reunited with the 1st Canadian Parachute Battalion fighting near the town Honfleur. In November 1944, Robert was recruited by the British SAS and sent to Scotland to train with 2 SAS, where he quickly gained the trust of British NCOs. MacDonald was sent to Livorno, Italy, and in February 1945, he was assigned as second in command of the ill-fated Operation Cold Comfort, an airborne drop north of Verona whose aim was to block the Brenner Pass between Italy and Austria to hinder the movement of German reinforcements to Italy. MacDonald was subsequently attached to Maj. Ballard and led Operation Canuck; on April 11, the main SAS party was dropped into the landing strip at Vesime. Along with Ballard and Mauri, MacDonald planned the successful attack on Alba in conjunction with Mauri's partisans. After the war MacDonald returned to Nova Scotia and went to Dalhousie University in Halifax to study law. He graduated in 1949, and after a brief period spent in Venezuela he returned to establish practice in New Glasgow. He was later a Crown prosecutor, and in 1948, was named a judge of the provincial court. In 1985, he was elevated to the Supreme Court of Nova Scotia, where he served until 1995. He died of natural causes in his cottage on the Northumberland Strait in Pictou County on August 16, 1995. (The authors wish to thank Capt. MacDonald's son, Robert Stephen "Steve" MacDonald, for graciously providing the above information pertaining to his father.)

## Profile 54 — *USA*

# United Defense M42 (UD M42) Submachine Gun

In 1940, the United States began to realize sooner or later they would be drawn into war and they began to consider new weapon designs. Among these was a .45-caliber High Standard design that, when tested, was judged to be superior to the Thompson currently in use. The design was set aside until an order for 15,000 copies in 9 mm was placed by the Dutch government to equip troops in the Dutch East Indies. Production was contracted to Marlin Firearms, but the markings on the weapon reflected the name of the consortium that had marketed it: United Defense Supply Corporation. Meantime, the political situation had changed and Holland had fallen to the Germans, so the entire Dutch order for the M42 was taken over by the OSS (the recently created US special operations branch), which used the guns to arm Allied missions and partisan movements.

**Years of manufacture:** 1941–1942
**Caliber:** 9 × 19 Parabellum
**Magazine/capacity:** 20- and 40-round magazines
**Length:** 820 mm (32.3 in.)
**Barrel length:** 279 mm (11 in.)
**Rate of fire:** 700 rpm
**Weight:** 4.11 kg (9.1 lb.)

A United Defense UD M42 submachine gun. *Gianluigi Usai*

A pair of Genoa area partisans; the partisan on the left is carrying a UD M42. *ILSREC Genova*

The UD M42 seems to have been fairly widely used by partisans from the Genoa area. *ILSREC Genova*

A small altar commemorating the partisan chief from Genoa named "Bisagno"; his jacket and boots form the backdrop for his M42 submachine gun. *ILSREC Genova*

# Light and Heavy Machine Guns

## Profile 55 — *Italy*

## Breda Model 1930 Light Machine Gun

At the end of WWI, the Italian army became conscious of the need for a light automatic weapon that could accompany infantry in the attack and thus, after a prolonged period of study and testing through a series of models including Models 1924, 1928, and 1929, finally settled on approval of the Breda Model 30.

The Breda Model 30 was an extremely finely finished weapon, so much so even a grain of sand was enough to cause it to jam. To this was added the need to lightly oil cartridges before loading them into the feed tray, guaranteeing dirt and foreign matter would be collected by the oily cartridges, and in cold climates the oil would freeze, rendering the gun inoperable.

All of these shortcomings notwithstanding, the Breda 30 accompanied the Italian soldier on all fronts and made its way into partisan ranks; initially, it was the only weapon of its class available, so necessity became a virtue. As soon as Bren guns began to become available via air drops the Breda 30 was set aside or, as a gesture of generosity, passed to even more poorly equipped partisan formations.

**Years of manufacture:** 1939–1945
**Caliber:** 6.5 × 52
**Magazine/capacity:** 20-round charger trays
**Length:** 1,230 mm (48.4 in.)
**Barrel length:** 520 mm (20.5 in.)
**Rate of fire:** 475 rpm
**Weight:** 10.2 kg (22.49 lb.)

The Breda Model 30 was used by the partisans until it could be replaced by more reliable light machine guns, such as the MG42 or the Bren. *Gianluigi Usai*

Profile 56 *Italy*

## Breda 1937 Heavy Machine Gun

The Breda 37 was probably the best machine gun used by the Italian army during WWII, and remained in use for many years following the war. Despite some problems with its feed system, it was much sought after for capture and use by enemy forces. There are numerous photos of British soldiers in North Africa who seem quite happy manning this very reliable machine gun.

Feed problems were due to the fact that empty cartridge cases were reinserted into the charger tray as the tray advanced while firing, and at times the empty cartridge would jam; the use of charger trays was predicated upon the use of this weapon in armored vehicles and the need to avoid spent cases distracting or causing injury to crews in the fighting compartment. The ammunition used by the Breda 37 allowed accurate and effective fire to be brought to bear on targets at long ranges; these qualities were much appreciated by the partisans who, because of the weight of the weapon, primarily used it in fixed positions. Until the advent of the .50-caliber Browning M2 in partisan inventory, the Breda 37 was known as *la pesante* ("the heavy one").

**Years of manufacture:** 1937–1945
**Caliber:** 8 × 59
**Magazine/capacity:** 20-round charger trays
**Length:** 1270 mm (50 in.)
**Barrel length:** 679 mm (26.8 in.)
**Rate of fire:** 475 rpm
**Weight:** 19.4 kg (42.7 lb.) gun + 18.8 kg (42.14 lb.) tripod

What appears to be a particularly well-equipped detachment with two Breda Model 37 machine guns; it also appears the detachment commander is the female standing at the head of the group. The photo was taken in a piazza in Modena as the detachment was ready to move out. *M. Becchi*.

The Breda Model 1937, although heavy, was a highly reliable machine gun. *Ralph Riccio*

The Breda Model 1938 was a modification of the Breda 1937 intended for tank use, but could be used with a ground mount as well; the partisans are known to have used some examples of this variant. *Ralph Riccio*

The most unusual weapon in evidence is the Breda Model 38 tank machine gun with an improvised mount displayed in front of the partisans in the front row. *Don Angelo Siri*

## Profile 57 *Italy*

# Fiat Model 1914 Machine Gun

This machine gun was a totally Italian design introduced shortly before WWI; its performance was hampered by a very complicated charger feed system that was not at all reliable. As with some other Italian weapons, the cartridges had to be lubricated, leading to the collection of foreign matter and jamming. The gun was heavy, but suffered from a 6.5 × 52 caliber; although a perfectly fine caliber for the Model 1891 rifle, it was too light for effective performance in a machine gun of this type.

Most of the Model 1914 guns that survived the war were modified beginning in 1935, although some in the original configuration fell into partisan hands and were used until the end of the war.

**Years of manufacture:** 1914–1918
**Caliber:** 6.5 × 52
**Magazine/capacity:** 50-round chargers
**Length:** 1,180 mm (46.5 in.)
**Barrel length:** 654 mm (25.8 in.)
**Rate of fire:** 400 rpm
**Weight:** 17.5 kg (35.6 lb.) gun + 22.5 kg (49.6 lb.) tripod

A 6.5 mm Fiat Model 1914 machine gun. *Museo della Guerra di Rovereto*

## Profile 58 *Italy*

# Fiat 1914/35 Heavy Machine Gun

In view of feed system problems and the inadequate caliber of the Model 1914 machine gun, it was decided to modify both features, resulting in the Model 1914/35 for remanufactured guns, while newly manufactured guns were designated Model 1935. The water cooling jacket was replaced by an air-cooled barrel; caliber was increased to 8 × 59, which was the same as the later Breda Model 37; and the feed system was changed to a disintegrating metal link belt. Despite these modifications the gun did not prove markedly better than its predecessor and the fact it fired from a closed bolt could lead to unwanted "cook-off" rounds. Although it was used by the partisans throughout the war, it was replaced by more capable machine guns whenever possible.

**Years of manufacture:** 1935–1945
**Caliber:** 8 × 59
**Magazine/capacity:** 300-round belt
**Length:** 1,200 mm (47.2 in.)
**Barrel length:** 625 mm (24.6 in.)
**Rate of fire:** 750 rpm
**Weight:** 17.0 kg (37.48 lb.) gun + 23.0 kg tripod (50.6 lb.)

An 8 mm Fiat Model 1935 machine gun, which was a reworked Model 1914 weapon.
*Gianluigi Usai*

A squad of the Savona Brigade posing with their Fiat Model 1935 machine gun. *G. Toscani*

Partisans of the "Gin Bevilacqua" Division. *ISREC Savona*

## Profile 59 *Italy*

# Breda-SAFAT Aircraft Machine Guns

Breda-SAFAT machine guns were mounted on Italian aircraft; as these aircraft were grounded for various reasons, the guns were stripped and re-used by RSI units and the resistance movement, often using improvised ground mounts. These weapons could be encountered in either 7.7 mm (equivalent to .303 British) or 12.7 × 81 mm (not equivalent to or interchangeable with US 12.7 × 99 mm [.50-caliber]).

| | **7.7 mm** | **12.7 mm** |
|---|---|---|
| **Years of manufacture:** | XXX | XXX |
| **Caliber:** | 7.7 × 56 | 12.7 × 81 |
| **Magazine/capacity:** | belt | belt |
| **Length:** | 1,085 mm (42.7 in.) | 1385 mm (54.5 in.) |
| **Barrel length:** | XXX | XXX |
| **Rate of fire:** | 900 rpm | 700 rpm |
| **Weight:** | 12 kg (26.46 lb.) | 28.9 kg (63.71 lb.) |

A 7.7 mm Breda-SAFAT in RSI service; some weapons of this type were captured and pressed into partisan service. *Giancarlo Garello*

The Breda-SAFAT (foreground) mounted on a tripod is clearly the most impressive weapon belonging to this partisan team. *Gianluigi Usai*

Partisans in action using a Breda-SAFAT 12.7 mm with an improvised tripod. *Don Angelo Siri*

A 7.7 mm Breda-SAFAT mounted on the cab of a Lancia 3Ro truck. *Gianluigi Usai*

Partisans examining a Breda-SAFAT 12.7 mm on an improvised wheeled mount.

## Profile 60 USA

# Colt 1895 Machine Gun

This machine gun was another product from the fertile mind of John M. Browning, and was also referred to as the Colt-Browning. Although already obsolete by the beginning of WWI, some 1,600 were acquired to equip the Italian army, which at the time was experiencing a weapons shortage. The gun continued to be used after the war and some examples were still in inventory at the beginning of WWII, then fell into partisan hands after the September 1943 armistice.

**Years of manufacture:** 1895–1917
**Caliber:** 6.5 × 52
**Magazine/capacity:** 250-round cloth belt
**Length:** 1,016 mm (40 in.)
**Barrel length:** 711 mm (28 in.)
**Rate of fire:** 600 rpm
**Weight:** 10.2 kg (22.49 lb.)

The Colt 1895 machine gun, nicknamed the "potato digger" in US service. *Courtesy of James D. Julia Auctioneers, Fairfield, Maine, www.jamesdjulia.com*

A Model 1895 machine gun on an anti-aircraft mount. *Gianluigi Usai*

## Profile 61 *Austria*

# Schwarzlose M1907 Machine Gun

The Schwarzlose was an excellent Austrian machine gun whose design dates to 1907; it was modified in 1912 and 1916 (for aircraft use). At the end of WWI, Italy captured or acquired thousands of these guns as war reparations and used them to equip second-line units. Almost all were later transferred to colonial troop units, although some did remain in Italy, and it was these guns that were grabbed from arms rooms by partisans at the time of the armistice as they began to form operational units.

**Years of manufacture:** 1907–1918
**Caliber:** 8 × 50R Mannlicher
**Magazine/capacity:** 250-round cloth belt
**Length:** 1,066 mm (42 in.)
**Barrel length:** 526 mm (20.7 in.)
**Rate of fire:** 400 rpm
**Weight:** 17.2 kg (37.92 lb.) gun + 18.5 kg (40.79 lb.) tripod

A Schwarzlose M1907 machine gun. *Courtesy of James D. Julia Auctioneers, Fairfield, Maine, www.jamesdjulia.com*

A photo taken in Savona on April 26, 1945; the partisan with the Schwarzlose and its tripod and ammunition on his back is bearing a load of around 35 kg [77 lbs]. *ISREC Savona*

## Profile 62 *France*

# Saint Etienne 1907 Machine Gun

Many examples of this French heavy machine gun reached Italy during WWI. As it had a certain tendency to jam under dirty conditions, the French quite happily rid themselves of the gun by providing it to nations that were their allies at the time.

During the years immediately following the war many guns of this type were used to equip units of the GAF (*Guardia alla Frontiera* – Border Guards) and anti-aircraft units. As with many other weapons, at the time of the September 1943 armistice they were taken from military armories by partisans and references to them can be found in many reports.

**Years of manufacture:** 1907–1918
**Caliber:** 8 × 50 Lebel; 6.5 × 52
**Magazine/capacity:** 24- or 30-round chargers
**Length:** 1,180 mm (46.5 in.)
**Barrel length:** 710 mm (28 in.)
**Rate of fire:** 400–500 rpm
**Weight:** 25.73 kg (56.73 lb.)

A Saint Etienne Mle. 1907 machine gun on its tripod. *Courtesy of James D. Julia Auctioneers, Fairfield, Maine, www.jamesdjulia.com*

The centerpiece of these partisans is the Saint Etienne machine gun.
*ISREC Savona*

Profile 63 *France*

## Hotchkiss Model 1914 Machine Gun

Substantial numbers of this French heavy machine gun were supplied to the Italian army during WWI, and others were obtained as war booty during the Italian occupation of France early in WWII.

The gun was used extensively by the partisans, who liked the fact it could use either 30-round strips or 250-round belts. Some examples have recently been unearthed that were hidden since the end of the war (partially disassembled).

**Years of manufacture:** 1914–1918
**Caliber:** 8 × 50 Lebel
**Magazine/capacity:** 30-round magazine or 250-round belt
**Length:** 1,310 mm (51.6 in.)
**Barrel length:** 787 mm (31 in.)
**Rate of fire:** 500 rpm
**Weight:** 25.26 kg (55.69 lb.) gun + 26.5 kg tripod (58.42 lb.)

The French Hotchkiss Mle. 1914 machine gun. *Courtesy of James D. Julia Auctioneers, Fairfield, Maine, www.jamesdjulia.com*

Partisans manning a Hotchkiss 1914. *E. Scarone*

Among the weapons in a cache recently discovered by the Carabinieri are two partially disassembled Hotchkiss machine guns. *Marco Raffa, La Stampa*

Profile 64 — *France*

## Chatellerault Model 1924 M29 Automatic Rifle

This excellent weapon was designed with an eye toward the Browning Automatic Rifle (BAR); at the time of WWII, it could be encountered in several versions, including the automatic rifle (described), as a fixed fortress machine gun, or a tank machine gun (M31) with a modified feed system and a heavier barrel.

The Italian army obtained a substantial number when France capitulated in 1940, and many were also used by the Germans following their occupation of France. The partisans managed to seize some Chatelleraults from Italian army depots and put them to their own good use.

**Years of manufacture:** 1924–1940
**Caliber:** 7.5 × 54 French (Model 29)
**Magazine/capacity:** 25-round magazine
**Length:** 1,070 mm (42.1 in.)
**Barrel length:** 505 mm (19.9 in.)
**Rate of fire:** 500 rpm
**Weight:** 9.95 kg (21.94 lb.)

The Chatellerault Model 1924 M1929 automatic rifle was available in some numbers to the partisans. *Gianluigi Usai*

A group of partisans heavily armed with automatic weapons. The linked belt of machine gun ammunition is obviously a theatrical touch, as the Model 1924 M1929 automatic rifle in the foreground is a magazine-fed weapon. *G. Toscani*

## Profile 65 *France*

# CSRG Model 1915 (Chauchat) Light Automatic Rifle

CSRG refers to the gun's producer and multiple designers (Chauchat-Sutter-Ribeyrolle-Gladiator). It was probably one of the worst weapons of WWI, but enjoyed considerable commercial success, probably because at the time it was the only light automatic rifle available. Produced in France, it was also manufactured in the United States and was sold to other countries (Poland and Greece—where it was known as the Gladiator), resulting in the capture of many of these guns when those countries were invaded in 1939 and 1941.

Despite its bad reputation, some examples were used by Italian resistance forces, probably having been retrieved from arms rooms in which they were stored since the end of WWI, or from stocks taken by Italy after the fall of France.

**Years of manufacture:** 1915–1918
**Caliber:** 8 × 50 Lebel
**Magazine/capacity:** 25-round magazine
**Length:** 1,143 mm (45 in.)
**Barrel length:** 469 mm (18.5 in.)
**Rate of fire:** 250 rpm
**Weight:** 9.07 kg (20 lb.)

The Chauchat CSRG was an unreliable weapon, but was nevertheless pressed into service by the partisans. *Courtesy of James D. Julia Auctioneers, Fairfield, Maine, www.jamesdjulia.com*

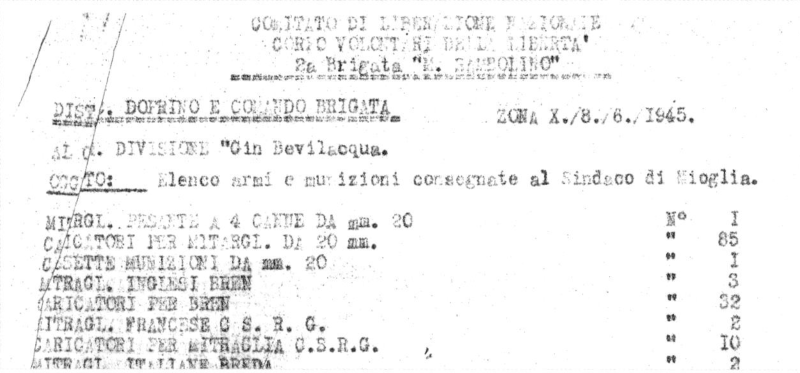

COMITATO DI LIBERAZIONE NAZIONALE
CORPO VOLONTARI DELLA LIBERTA'
2a Brigata "M. SAMBOLINO"

DIST. DOPRINO E COMANDO BRIGATA ZONA X./8./6./1945.

AL C. DIVISIONE "Gin Bevilacqua.

OGGETTO: Elenco armi e munizioni consegnate al Sindaco di Mioglia.

| | |
|---|---|
| MITRGL. PESANTE A 4 CANNE DA mm. 20 | N° I |
| CARICATORI PER MITRAGL. DA 20 mm. | " 85 |
| CASETTE MUNIZIONI DA mm. 20 | " I |
| MITRAGL. INGLESI BREN | " 3 |
| CARICATORI PER BREN | " 32 |
| MITRAGL. FRANCESE C S. R. G. | " 2 |
| CARICATORI PER MITRAGLIA C.S.R.G. | " IO |
| MITRAGL. ITALIANE BREDA | " 2 |

COMMITTEE OF NATIONAL LIBERATION
VOLUNTEER CORPS FOR LIBERTY
2nd Brigade "M. SAMBOLINO"

DOPRINO DETACHMENT AND BRIGADE HEADQUARTERS ZONE X/8/6/1945.

TO HQ "Gin Bevilacqua" DIVISION

SUBJECT: List of weapons and ammunition handed over to the Mayor of Mioglia.

| | |
|---|---|
| 20mm 4 BARREL HEAVY MACHINE GUN | No. 1 |
| MAGAZINES FOR 20mm MACHINE GUN | " 85 |
| CASES OF 20mm AMMUNITION | " 1 |
| ENGLISH BREN MACHINE GUNS | " 3 |
| MAGAZINES FOR BREN | " 32 |
| FRENCH C.S.R.G. MACHINE GUN | " 2 |
| MAGAZINES FOR C.S.R.G. MACHINE GUN | " 10 |
| ITALIAN BREDA MACHINE GUN | " 2 |

There is no mistaking the Chauchat; the partisan on the lower right appears to be holding a US M1 carbine. *Don Angelo Siri*

## Profile 66 *France*

# Hotchkiss Model 1926 Light Machine Gun

After WWI ended, Hotchkiss continued to develop automatic rifles and light machine guns based on the Model 1914. These developments did not meet with much success, except for the model known as the Model 1926, of which some 5,000 were furnished to Greece. When the Italian army occupied Greece several thousand were captured and were earmarked for second-line units because of the caliber (i.e., 6.5 × 54), which was slightly longer than and incompatible with the 6.5 × 52 Italian service round.

When the Italian army disbanded after September 8, 1943, and Italian barracks were looted of weapons by the partisans, these guns were used as long as ammunition was available.

**Years of manufacture:** 1926
**Caliber:** 6.5 × 54
**Magazine/capacity:** 25-round magazine
**Length:** 1,214 mm (47.8 in.)
**Barrel length:** 577 mm (22.7 in.)
**Rate of fire:** 450 rpm
**Weight:** 9.52 kg (21 lb.)

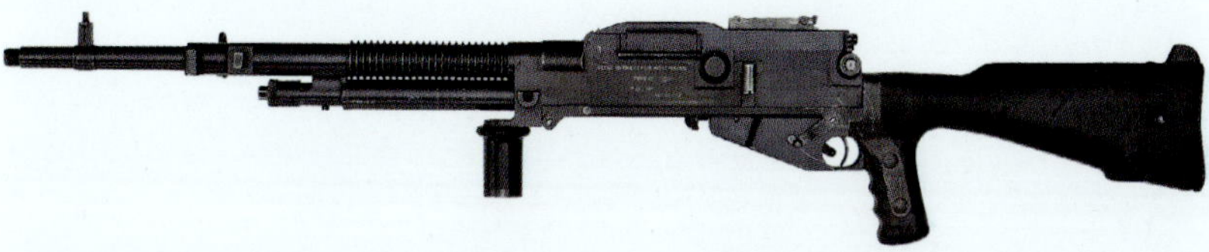

The Hotchkiss Mle. 1926 light machine gun. *Max Popenker*

A partisan lookout on a mountaintop. *Don Angelo Siri*

The partisan holding the Hotchkiss would seem to have no need for the belted ammunition he is carrying, as the weapon is strip fed. *G. Toscani*

Profile 67 *Czechoslovakia*

## ZB vz/26 and ZB vz/30

The excellent Czech ZB vz/26 produced by Zbrojovka Brno (ZB) enjoyed healthy export sales until Czechoslovakia was invaded by Germany. Substantial numbers of the vz/30 were sold to Yugoslavia; when photographs of these weapons in the hands of Italian partisans are found there is always some doubt as to whether the weapons pictured are the ZB30 captured by the Italians in Yugoslavia in 1941, or if they are German ZB26 war booty from Czechoslovakia put into German service and subsequently captured by the partisans (both models used the same ammunition). Changing only the caliber resulted in the British Bren gun (see profile 72).

Because of a widespread linguistic misuse, this gun was often referred to by the Italians as a "Skoda," even though Skoda ceased production of weapons immediately following WWI and had nothing to do with the development or production of this light machine gun.

**Years of manufacture:** 1926–1945
**Caliber:** 7.92 × 57
**Magazine/capacity:** 20-round magazine
**Length:** 1,161 mm (45.7 in.)
**Barrel length:** 602 mm (23.7 in.)
**Rate of fire:** 500 rpm
**Weight:** 9.6 kg (21.16 lb.)

The Czech ZB30 was an excellent weapon produced in several versions and derivatives, most famously the British Bren gun. *Courtesy of James D. Julia Auctioneers, Fairfield, Maine, www.jamesdjulia.com*

Partisans of the "Bevilacqua" Division in the hills of Vado Ligure. Arms include the ZB26 or 30, a Sten, and a Gew 41. *E. Bigi*

"Bevilacqua" Division partisans with a Czech ZB26 or 30. *E. Bigi*

## Profile 68 *Germany*

# MG34 Dual-Purpose Machine Gun

Due to the clauses of the Treaty of Versailles, Germany was prohibited from producing heavy machine guns; the Germans circumvented this clause by developing the "dual purpose" machine gun that could be used as a light machine gun on a bipod or as a heavy machine gun mounted on a tripod. The weapon was innovative, accurate, and reliable, but it was expensive and required a long production time, which soon led to studies for a simpler and less expensive replacement weapon. Despite its shortcomings, the MG34 was still in production in April 1945.

**Years of manufacture:** 1934–1945
**Caliber:** 7.92 × 57
**Magazine/capacity:** 50-round drum,
twin 75-round drum, or 250-round belt
**Length:** 1,219 mm (48 in.)
**Barrel length:** 627 mm (24.7 in.)
**Rate of fire:** 800–900 rpm
**Weight:** 12.1 kg (26.68 lb.) gun + 19.0 kg (41.89 lb.) tripod

The German MG34 set the pace for dual-purpose machine guns. *Courtesy of James D. Julia Auctioneers, Fairfield, Maine, www.jamesdjulia.com*

Unidentified partisan group; the MG34 gunner might find it difficult to move quickly with the linked ammunition belt. *Don Angelo Siri*

Heavily armed youngsters posing April 25, 1945; there seems to have been no shortage of belted machine gun ammunition for German weapons. *Don Angelo Siri*

Profile 69 *Germany*

## MG42 Dual-Purpose Machine Gun

Probably one of the best machine guns ever produced, variants of the MG42 still equip many armies, although in updated calibers. The MG42 was nicknamed "Hitler's buzz saw" because of its characteristic noise while firing; it was the dream of every partisan to have one and a nightmare for supply officers, as its 1,200-round per minute rate of fire meant having enough ammunition on hand for protracted use was almost impossible. The MG42 was meant to replace the MG34 thanks to more modern and less expensive production techniques, but production of the MG34 continued until 1945, even while studies were undergoing to update and simplify the MG42, although nothing was ever achieved in that respect.

**Years of manufacture:** 1942–1945
**Caliber:** 7.92 × 57
**Magazine/capacity:** 50-round drum or 250-round belt
**Length:** 1,120 mm (44.1 in.)
**Barrel length:** 533 mm (21 in.)
**Rate of fire:** 1,200 rpm
**Weight:** 11.5 kg (25.35 lb.) gun + 19.0 kg (41.89 lb.) tripod

The MG42 dual-purpose machine gun was a rather fearsome weapon; its high rate of fire earned it the nickname "Hitler's buzz saw" among Allied troops. *Centro documentazione e Ricerche Storiche Gotica Toscana*

Unidentified partisan group likely from the Langhe area. *Don Angelo Siri*

Partisans from the "Pinan-Cichero" Division operating in the hinterland of Genoa; in this case the MG42 gunner seems fortunate to have someone else carrying his ammunition. *ILSREC Genova*

## Profile 70 *Germany*

# MG13 Machine Gun

Based on a WWI gun that was modified during the early years of German rearmament, the MG13 was considered a second-line weapon, especially following the introduction of the far superior MG34 and MG42. The gun was widely used, consequently many examples fell into partisan hands.

**Years of manufacture:** xxxx–1938
**Caliber:** 7.92 × 57
**Magazine/capacity:** 25-round magazine or twin 75-round drum
**Length:** 1,466 mm (57.7 in.)
**Barrel length:** 717 mm (28.2 in.)
**Rate of fire:** 650 rpm
**Weight:** 10.89 kg (24 lb.)

The German MG13 (introduced in the 1930s) dates back from the Dreyse of WWI, but was nevertheless an effective weapon. *Gianluigi Usai*

Partisans in action in Venice armed with an MG13. *Gente, special issue, 1965*

Profile 71 *Germany*

## MG15 Machine Gun

The MG15 owes its development to two factors: originally designed as an aircraft weapon, at the time it became obsolete for that role due to its relatively small caliber the requirement arose to equip ground troops with a greater number of automatic weapons. A bipod and skeleton shoulder stock were added to the gun and the result was the MG15 for ground use. The weapon was used as second-line armament; despite that many copies ended up in the hands of the partisans, who were not too choosy, as long as they had something that fired.

**Years of manufacture:** 1930–1934
**Caliber:** 7.92 × 57
**Magazine/capacity:** twin 75-round drum
**Length:** 1,334 mm (52.5 in.)
**Barrel length:** 595 mm (23.4 in.)
**Rate of fire:** 850 rpm
**Weight:** 12.7 kg (28 lb.)

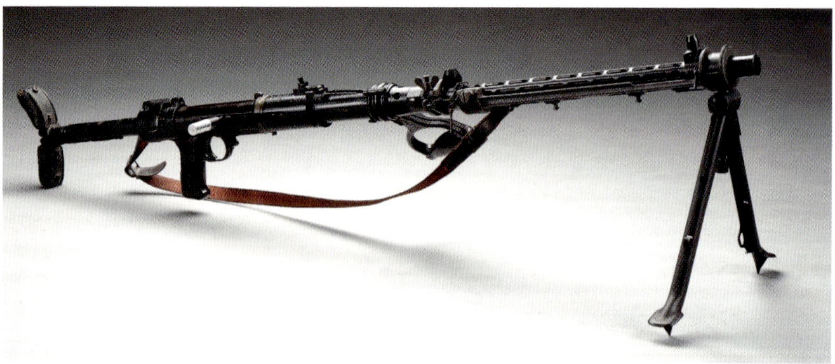

The MG15 was an aircraft machine gun introduced in 1932. *Courtesy of James D. Julia Auctioneers, Fairfield, Maine, www.jamesdjulia.com*

The individual with the MG15 is wearing a fireman's cap and uniform; the grossly overloaded light truck also belongs to the Bologna fire brigade. *Don Angelo Siri*

Profile 72 Great Britain

## Bren Light Machine Gun

Based on the Czech ZB 26, it is immediately recognizable by its top-mounted curved box magazine that held its .303 British cartridges. With modifications to its caliber and other minor changes it remained in use by the British army until only a few years ago. Its name stems from a combination of the initials of Brno and Enfield, the names of the two locations in Czechoslovakia and England that were associated with its development. It was considered one of the best weapons in its class, although there are some who preferred the bipod version of the German MG42 because of its belt feed instead of the Bren's magazine feed.

After the Sten, the Bren is one of the most widely seen weapons in photos of partisans thanks to significant numbers that were air-dropped to all of the partisan units that received aid from the SOE (Special Operations Executive, the British espionage and sabotage organization).

**Years of manufacture:** 1937–1971
**Caliber:** .303
**Magazine/capacity:** Detachable box magazine, 30 rounds
**Length:** 1,155 mm (45.5 in.)
**Barrel length:** 635 mm (25 in.)
**Rate of fire:** 500 rpm
**Weight:** 10.45 kg (23 lb.)

British missions supplied the Bren gun in large numbers to the partisans. *Courtesy of James D. Julia Auctioneers, Fairfield, Maine, www.jamesdjulia.com*

This partisan of "Poli's" group seems to have a large selection of weapons at his disposal, including the Bren resting on the roof parapet, the Beretta submachine gun he is holding, and a holstered pistol. *L. Balbo*

The Fiat 508C automobile (armed with two Bren guns, only one of which is visible) belonging to "Poli" being refueled from airdropped nylon fuel bladders. *L. Balbo*

Profile 73 *Great Britain*

## Vickers Heavy Machine Gun

Based on the early Maxim machine guns from the end of the nineteenth century, the Vickers was the standard machine gun of the British Army during WWI, and continued to be used throughout WWII, although by 1944, it was considered obsolete. It was probably for this reason that the Vickers could be found equipping partisans and the SAS and commando units with which they operated, as the guns were considered "expendable." The Vickers was an extremely reliable weapon and saw much use as a machine gun for fire support.

**Years of manufacture:** 1915–1944 (?)
**Caliber:** .303
**Magazine/capacity:** 250-round cloth belt
**Length:** 1,092 mm (43 in.)
**Barrel length:** 720 mm (28.3 in.)
**Rate of fire:** 450 rpm
**Weight:** 14.97 kg (33 lb.) gun + 22.7 kg (50 lb.) tripod

The .303 Vickers heavy machine gun had an enviable reputation as a reliable weapon.
*Courtesy of James D. Julia Auctioneers, Fairfield, Maine, www.jamesdjulia.com*

Members of the 2nd SAS in action in the vicinity of Vesime. *Courtesy E. MacDonald*

Members of 2nd SAS with a potent lineup of machine guns, including the Vickers and two .50-caliber Browning M2HBs. *Courtesy E. MacDonald*

Profile 74 | *Great Britain*

## Browning MkII Machine Gun

The MkII was an aircraft machine gun that initially equipped many RAF aircraft until replaced by other machine guns and light cannon of larger caliber. Whenever an aircraft was shot down or crashed over partisan territory, there was a race to salvage weapons and ammunition; the weapons were then fitted with various makeshift mounts or tripods for use on the ground.

**Years of manufacture:** 1939–1945
**Caliber:** .303 (7.7 × 56)
**Magazine/capacity:** metal belt
**Length:** 1,041 mm (41 in.)
**Barrel length:** 610 mm (24 in.)
**Rate of fire:** 500 rpm
**Weight:** 14.05 kg (31 lb.)

The Browning MkII aircraft machine gun was used by partisans who adapted them to ground use. *Courtesy of James D. Julia Auctioneers, Fairfield, Maine, www.jamesdjulia.com*

Period photos of the Browning MkII in use by partisans are not to be found, but the makers of this film about the partisans managed to come up with one for the main character. *Cover of Il partigiano Johnny by Giuseppe Fenoglio*

## Profile 75 *USA (also Belgium and Poland)*

# Browning Automatic Rifle (BAR)

Born from the experience of mud and trenches and concepts developed during WWI, this automatic rifle is also attributable to the inventive genius of John M. Browning. It arrived barely in time to take part in the final days of fighting in that war; despite the fact that its magazine held only twenty .30/06 rounds, the US Army fielded it in large numbers until after the Korean War.

Evidence of these automatic rifles can be found in the hands of partisan formations that were supplied by the US OSS, such as units in the interior and in the area east of Genoa. It was also possible to encounter the European version of the weapon in German hands, as a result making its way into partisan hands (it was also produced by FN in Belgium in 7.92 mm for the Polish army and 7.65 mm for the Belgian army—see document page 57 for the problems a unit had that tried using inappropriate ammunition for this weapon).

**Years of manufacture:** 1919–1945
**Caliber:** .30/06; 7.92 mm
**Magazine/capacity:** Detachable box magazine, 20 rounds
**Length:** 1,219 mm (48 in.)
**Barrel length:** 610 mm (24 in.)
**Rate of fire:** 500 rpm
**Weight:** 8.8 kg (19.4 lb.)

The US M1918A2 Browning Automatic Rifle (BAR) was a squad-level automatic weapon. *Centro documentazione e Ricerche Storiche Gotica Toscana*

The Belgian FN version of the Browning automatic rifle.

## Profile 76 USA

# Browning Model 1919A1 Machine Gun

Reading through the preceding weapon descriptions, it is apparent the name John M. Browning appears frequently; his fertile mind was responsible for many of the weapons produced by Colt in the United States and FN in Belgium. The 1919A1 is the evolution of a model whose design dates to 1910, but did not reach its definitive form until 1919. In addition to being used with a ground mount, it was used on tanks, vehicles, ships, and aircraft, and was standard US issue for many years.

Many different versions were used by the Italian resistance movement, some of which were turned over by Allied support missions and others that were either air dropped or salvaged from downed aircraft.

**Years of manufacture:** 1919–1945
**Caliber:** .30/06; 7.92 mm
**Magazine/capacity:** 250-round belt
**Length:** 964 mm (37.9 in.)
**Barrel length:** 610 mm (24 in.)
**Rate of fire:** 500 rpm
**Weight:** 14.05 kg (31 lb.) gun + 6.4 kg (14 lb) tripod

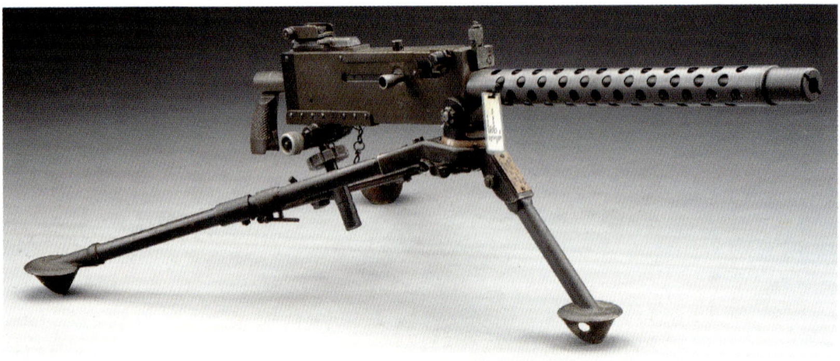

The Browning Model 1919A1 was the standard .30 caliber machine gun of US forces in WWII. *Courtesy of James D. Julia Auctioneers, Fairfield, Maine, www.jamesdjulia.com*

A partisan of the "Fumagalli" Division with a Browning 1919A1; the presence of three Italian helmets suggests the possibility the partisans have just disarmed a small group of RSI soldiers and taken the helmets as booty. *G. Toscani*

## Profile 77 — *USA*

# Browning M2 HB Heavy Machine Gun

The Browning M2 HB was a further development of the earlier .30-caliber model; beginning in 1921, a .50-caliber gun was designed that, with further modifications, ultimately led to the model used in WWII that can still be encountered in many war-torn areas.

A great number of versions of the M2 were developed for ground, air, and naval use; the gun was used by the Italian partisans in various configurations, obtained from air drops and recovered from downed aircraft. The .50-caliber Browning was a defensive weapon on most American bombers, with as many as twelve to fourteen guns per aircraft. Some Allied airmen who were machine gunners aboard aircraft and qualified armorers who survived the loss of their aircraft were very valued by the partisans because of their ability to repair weapons taken from downed aircraft.

**Years of manufacture:** 1921–2011
**Caliber:** .50 (12.7 × 99)
**Magazine/capacity:** 110-round metal belts
**Length:** 1,653 mm (65.1 in.)
**Barrel length:** 1,143 mm (45 in.)
**Rate of fire:** 500 rpm
**Weight:** 38.22 kg (84.26 lb.) gun

The Browning M2 HB heavy machine gun is a long-lived design, still in use in many armies today. *Gianluigi Usai*

Partisans grouped around a Browning M2 HB on a jury-rigged tripod mount. *Don Angelo Siri*

## Profile 78 *USSR*

# Degtyarev DP28 Light Machine Gun

An excellent light machine gun produced in large numbers for the Soviet army, it was simple, robust, and able to function under almost all conditions; even the presence of dust and dirt caused few major problems. Its only weak point was its magazine, which was too large to avoid the risk of dents and damage. Several aircraft and tank versions were also developed.

In widespread use at the beginning of WWII, many examples were captured by the Germans, who used them to arm divisions consisting of Soviet prisoners of various ethnicity, some of which reached Italy.

**Years of manufacture:** 1928–1950
**Caliber:** 7.62 × 54
**Magazine/capacity:** Drum magazine, 47 rounds
**Length:** 1,290 mm (50.8 in.)
**Barrel length:** 605 mm (23.8 in.)
**Rate of fire:** 500–550 rpm
**Weight:** 9.12 kg (20.1 lb.)

The Degtyarev DP28 was a simple, reliable weapon used by partisans who captured or obtained them from Russian deserters. *Max Popenker*

## Uncommon Weapons

Profile 79 USA

### Guide Lamp Liberator Pistol

The Liberator was quite a strange weapon, conceived and developed specifically to provide resistance movements with an inexpensive and easily produced "tool" to be used in close-in engagements; it had an unrifled barrel. Instructions were provided in "comic book" style. About a million examples were produced, although very few were actually distributed; there is some tenuous information indicating this weapon may have been provided to Italian partisan forces.

**Years of manufacture:** 1942
**Caliber:** .45 ACP
**Magazine/capacity:** Single shot
**Length:** 141 mm (5.6 in.)
**Barrel length:** 101 mm (4 in.)
**Weight:** 0.455 kg (1 lb)

The single-shot Liberator was designed specifically for use by resistance movements; it is not certain if any were supplied to the Italian partisans. The Liberator was produced by General Motors Guide Lamp Division, which also produced the M3 "grease gun" submachine gun. *NRA Museums*

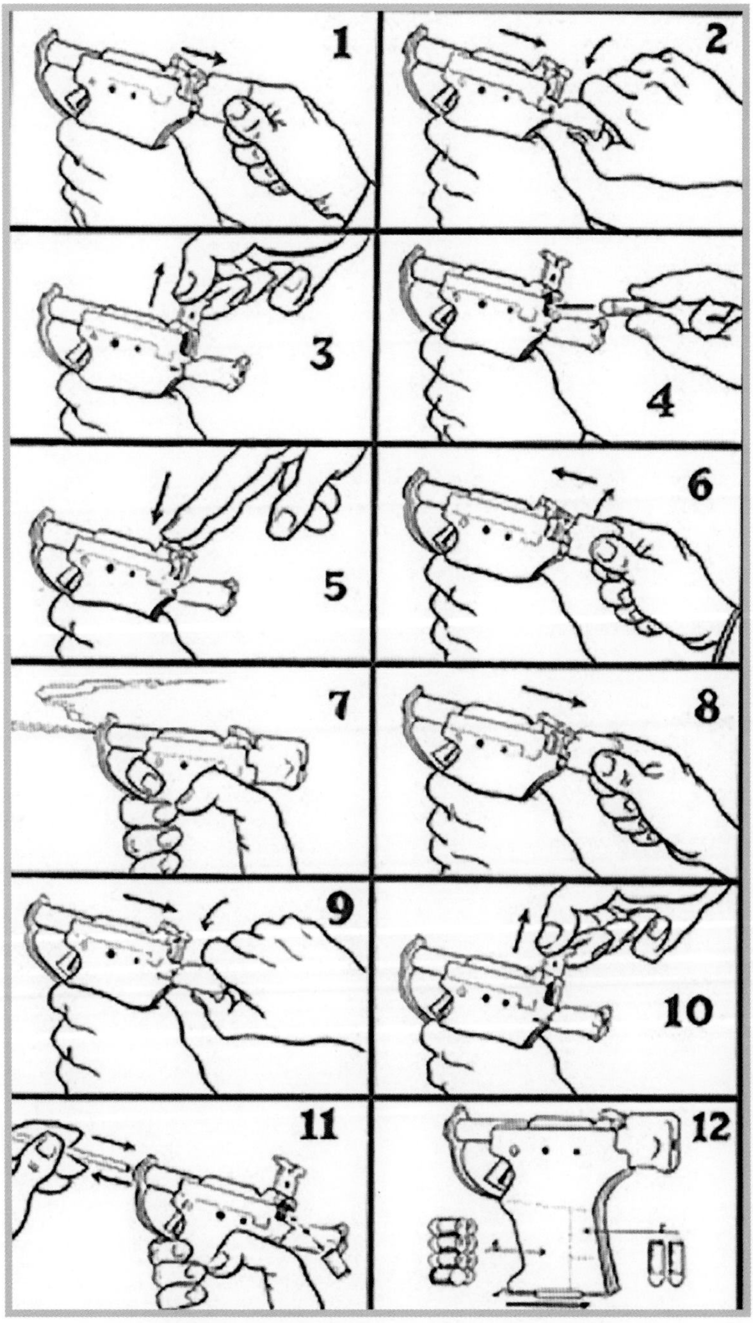


A simple comic book style instruction sheet on how to use the Liberator pistol. *NRA Museums*

## Profile 80 — *Great Britain*

# BSA Welrod Silenced Pistol

We long considered whether or not to include this weapon among the list of those used by the resistance, as the very limited number produced made us believe it would have been unlikely to have appeared in the broad range of weapons employed by the partisans. A report by an expert appointed by a court that places it at the center of a number of killings made us reconsider our thinking.

The Welrod is a manual repeater fitted with an integral silencer that allowed about thirty rounds of special ammunition to be fired before it began to deteriorate. Compared to other devices of this type that reduced sound only to a limited extent, this silencer was capable of drastically reducing noise. Only about 2,800 copies were produced to provide the SOE with a pistol that could be used to eliminate guards and other enemy personnel without alerting anyone nearby. The limited range relegated it to use almost exclusively as a weapon for assassination.

**Years of manufacture:** 1942–1945
**Caliber:** 7.65 mm (.32 ACP)
**Magazine/capacity:** six rounds
**Length:** 312 mm (12.3 in.)
**Barrel length:** 111 mm (4.4 in.)
**Weight:** 1.1 kg (2.43 lb.)

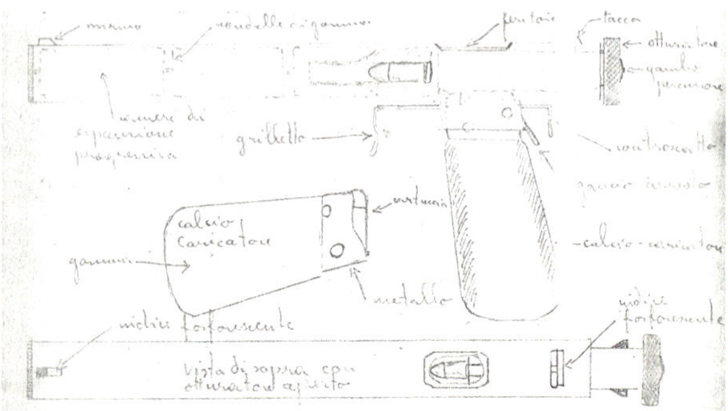

Schematic diagram from 1946 of the Welrod; from the detail pictured it seems obvious that whoever made this drawing had a weapon available to copy from. *ISREC Savona*

BSA Welrod silenced pistol.

## CHAPTER X

# INSTRUCTIONS TO THE PARTISANS

Some attempts were made to instruct partisans how to use weapons and explosives other than by simply learning "on the job."

Following are a pair of circulars issued by the headquarters, one pertaining to weapons and hand grenades:

COMITATO DI LIBERAZIONE NAZIONALE
Corpo Volontari della Libertà

...ando Regionale
...er la Liguria
...EZIONE SABOTAGGI

Zona X, 16 Ottobre 1944

A TUTTE LE FORMAZIONI

OGGETTO: Istruzioni per l'uso delle più comuni armi tedesche

è BOMBA A MANO

I TIPO

Tutti saprete certamente che quelle scatole cilindriche di metallo grigio col manico di legno che vedete appese alle cinture dei soldati germanici sono le bombe a mano.

Questo tipo di bomba a mano si compone di un cilindro di metallo color grigio di cm.10 di altezza e di diametro di poco inferiore e di un manico di lengo che ad esso si avvita.

Vi spiegherò prima di tutto l'impiego della bomba quand'essa è già pronta per l'uso.

Impugnate il manico con la mano destra, si svita con la sinistra il coperchietto di metallo che chiude l'estremeità del manico stesso.

Dal vuoto del manico, cavo internamente, vedrete uscire un bottone biancho di porcellana al quale sta legata una cordicella. Prendete il bottone bianco tra il dito indice e il medio della mano sinistra e dategli uno strappo secco. Poi contate fino a 4; 1,2,3,4...... via! La bomba a mano che ha 8 secondi di sicurezza, scoppierà dopo circa 12 minuti secondi. Così agite quando trovate delle bombe a mano pronte per l'uso/

Ora vedrremo come si fa quando si trovano le casse di bombe a mano non ancora innescate. Le casse di metallo sono molto simili, seppur più piatte e lunghe ai "canister" di benzina. In queste casse troverete delle bombe a mano, cioè cilindro e manico, stivate in due piani e in angolo una scatoletta di capsule. Le bombe a mano si innescano così: impugnate il cilindrocon la mano sinistra e svitate il manico con la destra. Il cilindro si presenterà con una cavità nella quale metterete una capsula presa dalla scatoletta, badando di metterla col pieno in su, Messa la capsula si riavita il manico. Trattate con la massima precauzione le capsule perchè sono molto sensibili.

La bomba a mani funziona così: tirato il bottone bianco di porcellana lo strappo della cordicella incendia l'accenditore a strappo che fa capo alla miccia la quale, dopo 12 secondi, accende la capsula che fa esplodere il tritolo contenuto nel cilindro.

28

-2-

II TIPO

Oltre alla bomba a mano col manico troverete forse delle bombe a mano ovali (simili, se pur con le pareti liscie, alle Sipe) in metallo brunito.

Ad un polo troverete un bottoncino color azzurro avvitato da un dado col quale termina il polo stesso. Svitate con molta attenzione il bottoncino azzurro. Quando sarà completamente svitato noterete che pende una cordicella. Tirate con la mano sinistra il bottoncino, contate fino a tre e lanciate. La bomba a mano che ha sei secondi di sicurezza, scoppierà dopo circa 8 secondi. Così agite quando trovate la bomba a mano già pronta per il lancio.

Ora vediamo come si fa quando si trovano le casse di bombe a mano non ancora innescate.

Le casse di metallo sono molto simile a quelle delle bombe a mano col manico In essa troverete le bombe in un angolo con una scatoletta di capsule e una chiave inglese.

Colla chiave inglese svitate il dado. Nella bomba che vi si presenterà una cavità vilindrica nella quale metterete una capsula presa dalla scatoletta, badando di metterla col pieno in giù. Messa la capsula si riavvita molto stretto il dado. Trattate con molta precauzione la capsula perchè sono molto sensibili.

La bomba a mano funziona così: tirato il bottoncino azzurro, lo strappo della cordicella incendia l'accenditore a strappo il quale fa capo ad una miccia che dopo circa 8 secondi accende la capsula che fa esplodere il tritolo contenuto nella bomba.

---

LA PISTOLA MASCHINE

La p.m. è un'arma automatica (simile come impiego al mitra), lunga circa mezzo metro, tutta in acciaio brunito, con impugnatore a pistola. L'avete vista certamentein mano a sotto'ufficiali tedeschi.

Sarebbe troppo lungo spiegarvi l'arma nei singoli pezzi, perciò vi spiegherò soltanto l'uso pratico di essa, quello che a voi specialmente serve.

Se venite in possesso di una p.m.; come fare per usarla?
Innanzi tutto non scordatevi di prendere anche i quattro caricatori che si trovano in una apposita fondina di tela appesa al cinturone del tedesco. Ogni caricatore ha 32 colpi. la p.m. è di calibro 9 lungo e le cartucce sono uguali a quelle che si usano per i mitra.

Impugnata la p.m.; con la mano destra ed un caricatore con la sinistra mettete il caricatore stesso (facendo attenzione a mettere le punte dei proiettili verso la canna) nell'apposito alveo che si trova nella parte inferiore della p.m.

E che si riconosce facilmente dai pini di invito. Poi col palmo della mano sinistra date un colpo secco alla parte inferiore del caricatore, dopo di che sentirete uno scatto. Il caricatore è a posto.

28

-3-

Poi tirate indietro con forza (col dito pollice e l'indice della mano sinistra) lungo la scanalatura longitudinale il gancio che troverete sulla parte sinistra della p.m. Tiratelo indistro sino in fondo, fino a che, cioè, non sentite che si aggancia. Dopo di che vi basta premere il grilletto per fare partire i colpi.

Se, però; una volta armata la p.m. non avete necessità di pronto impiego, portate il gancio in quella diramazione della scanalatura longitudinale che troverete in fondo e sopra alla scanalatura stessa.
L'arma è in sicurezza. Se volete togliere ppi la sicurezza, non fate altro che portare il gancio nella scanalatura principale.

Quando avete esaurito un caricatore (e ve ne accorgete perchè la massa battente non torna più indietro) dovete togliere il caricatore per rimpiazzarlo con quello pieno. Come si fa?

Prendete col pollice della mano sinistra (impugnate con le altre dita il caricatore) ul bottone a molla che troverete all' altezza dei piani di invito dell' alveo per il caricatore. Il caricatore esce e lo rimpiazzate come sopra descritto con un altro.

Il caricatore vuoto le riempite spingendo le cartucce ad una ad una col pollice nel foro superiore del caricatore, facendo attenzione a metterlo col proiettole verso la parte più stretta del caricatore stesso.

Come funziona la p;M.?

I TEMPO

Tirando indietro il gancio, avete tirato indietro anche la massa battente che, comprimendo la molla si è agganciata al grilletto.

La prima cartuccia del caricatore non più schiacciata dalla massa battente è spinta dalla molla del caricatore si è sollevata all'altezza della camera di scoppio.

II TEMPO

Premete il grilletto si sgancia la massa battente che, spinta dalla molla, scatta in avanti e nella sua corsa trascina nella camera di scoppio la prima cartuccia. Nell'attimo in cui viene la chiusura perfetta il percursore percuote la capsula della cartuccia che incendia la polvere che fa partire il proiettile.

III TEMPO

La forza di rinculo, agendo sulla massa battente che le fa rifare il cammino che al primo tempo le aveva fatto fare
stra mano.

Fino a che premeremo il grilletto la massa battente si susseguirà nei movimenti del 2° e 3° e I° tempo. Lasciato il grilletto la massa battente rimarrà in posizione di p/m. armata.

LA SEZIONE SABOTAGGI

28

COMMITTEE OF NATIONAL LIBERATION
Volunteer Corps for Liberty

Regional Headquarters
for Liguria

Zone X, 16 October 1944

SABOTAGE SECTION

TO ALL FORMATIONS

SUBJECT: Instructions for use of the more common German weapons

HAND GRENADES

TYPE I

You all certainly know that those cylindrical cans of grey metal with the wooden handle that you see hanging from the belts of German soldiers are hand grenades.

This type of hand grenade consists of a grey metal cylinder that is 10cm high and a slightly lesser diameter and of a wooden handle that is screwed onto it.

First of all I will explain to you how to use the grenade when it is already ready for use.

Grab the handle with your right hand, while with your left hand you unscrew the metal cover that closes the end of the handle itself.

From the hollow inside of the handle you will see a white porcelain button emerge to which a string is attached. Take the white button between your index and middle fingers of your left hand and give it a quick yank. Then count to 4: 1,2,3,4...... throw! The hand grenade which has an 8 second safety margin, will explode after about 12 seconds. That is how you proceed when you find hand grenades that are ready for use/

Now we'll see what to do when you find chests of hand grenades that are not yet readied with fuses. The metal chests are very similar, although they are flatter and longer than gasoline "canisters" (Translator's note: the reference is to "jerry cans"). In these chests you will find hand grenades, that is, the cylinders and the handles, stored in two layers and in the corner a small box of capsules. The hand grenades are assembles as follows: grasp the cylinder in your left hand and unscrew the handle with your right hand. The cylinder will have a hole into which you will place a capsule taken from the small box, taking care to insert it with the flat portion facing up. Once the capsule has been placed, screw on the handle again. Treat the capsules with the utmost caution because they are very sensitive.

The hand grenade functions as follows: once the white porcelain button has been pulled the pull on the string lights the igniter that is attached to the fuse which, after 12 seconds, lights the capsule that causes the charge contained in the cylinder to explode.

1

TYPE II

In addition to the hand grenade with the handle you may also find oval hand grenades (similar, although with smooth sides, to the [Italian] Sipe grenade) in blued metal.

At one end you will find a small blue button that is screwed on by a nut with which the end itself terminates. Very carefully unscrew the small blue button. When it is completely unscrewed you will notice that a string hangs out. Pull the small button with your left hand, count to three, and throw. The hand grenade which has a six second safety margin will explode after about 8 seconds. That is how you proceed when you find the hand grenade already set up for use.

Now we'll see what to do when you find chests of hand grenades that are not yet assembled for use.

The metal chests are very similar to those for hand grenades with the handles. In them you will find the grenades along with a small box of capsules and a wrench.

Unscrew the nut with the wrench. The grenade will have a cylindrical cavity into which you will place a capsule taken from the small box, taking care to insert it with the flat part facing downward. Once the capsule has been put in place the nut is screwed on tightly. Treat the capsules with the utmost caution because they are very sensitive.

The hand grenade functions as follows: once you have pulled the small blue button, pulling on the string lights the igniter that is attached to the fuse which, after about 8 seconds, lights the capsule that causes the charge contained in the grenade to explode.

------

THE MACHINE PISTOL

The MP is an automatic weapon (employed similarly as the submachine gun) about half a meter long, all in blued metal, with a pistol grip. You will certainly have seen it in the hands of German noncommissioned officers.

It would take too much time to explain each piece of the weapon, thus I will explain only its practical use, that which is of most use to you.

If you are able to acquire a MP, how do you use it?
Above all don't forget to take the four magazines that are found in a canvas carrying pouch that is hung from the German's belt. Each magazine holds 32 rounds. The MP is 9mm long caliber (Translator's note: 9mm long is the Italian designation for 9mm parabellum) and the cartridges are the same as those used in the submachine gun.

Once you have picked up the MP with your right hand and a magazine with your left hand, insert the magazine itself (making sure to put the points of the bullets towards the muzzle) in the magazine well underneath the MP.

This is easily recognized by the flared opening. Then with the palm of the left hand give a sharp rap to the bottom of the magazine, after which you will hear a click. The magazine is now in place.

1

Then forcefully pull back the handle (with the thumb and index finger of the left hand) along the longitudinal slot that you will find on the left side of the MP. Pull it all the way back until you hear it lock. After that all you have to do is pull the trigger in order to fire the weapon.

If, however, once you have cocked the MP you do not need to use it immediately, move the cocking handle into the cutout located to the rear and above the longitudinal slot.
The weapon is now in the "safe" position. If you want to remove the safety, all you have to do is to move the cocking handle into the main slot.

When you have emptied the magazine (and you will know when you have because the bolt will no longer return) you have to remove the magazine in order to replace it with a full one. How is this done?

With the thumb of the left hand (while using the other fingers of that hand to grasp the magazine) press on the button and spring that you will find on the top portion of the magazine well. The empty magazine will fall out and you replace it with another as described above.

Fill the empty magazine by pushing the cartridges in one by one with your thumb into the open top of the magazine, paying attention to put the bullet pointing towards the narrower part of the magazine.

How does the MP work?

PHASE I

Pulling back on the cocking handle, you will have also pulled back the bolt which, compressing the spring, has attached itself to the trigger.

The first cartridge in the magazine which is no longer compressed by the bolt is pushed by the magazine spring and has raised itself to the level of the firing chamber.

PHASE II

By squeezing the trigger the bolt unlocks which, pushed by the spring, moves forward and in the course of its travel drags the first cartridge into the firing chamber. At the instant in which perfect closure is achieved the firing pin strikes the primer of the cartridge which ignites the powder which causes the bullet to move forward.

PHASE III

The force of the recoil, acting on the bolt makes it retrace the path that it had followed in the earlier phase.

As long as you squeeze the trigger the bolt will continue its movement through phases 2, 3 and I. Letting go of the trigger the bolt will remain in the cocked position.

THE SABOTAGE SECTION

The other document deals with explosives provided by the British.

C.di L.N.
Corpo Volontario d.Libertà
Ca 3 Brigata d'As.Garibaldi
"LIBERO BRIGANTI

-1-

DESCRIZIONI.

1° Miccia di sicurezza (Bickford safety fuze)

La miccia é usata per accendere una carica esplosiva o incendiaria dopo un breve intervallo di tempo.La miccia brucia in ragione di un cm.per secondo,percio per avere un ritardo di 3 minuti é richiesta una lunghezza di cm.180.

Prima dell'uso e meglio tagliare 4 o 5 cm.dalle estremita della miccia che potrebbero essere umide.

La miccia normalmente accesa da un fiammifero controvento o da un tubetto di rame fissato alla miccia o per mezzo di una matita tempo.Puo essere anche accesa da una capsula con meccanismo a trazione.La miccia non accende direttamente l'esplosivo .La miccia non deve essere maneggiata con violenza perché in questo caso tende a bruciare troppo rapidamente.

2° Filo detonante.(Cordtex)

Il filo detonante é una miccia composta di alto esplosivo ed é usato per congiungere un certo numero di cariche in modo che queste esplodano simultaneamente.E'accesa per mezzo di un detonatore messo parallelamente al filo detonante e tenuto ben saldo ad esso per mezzo di nastro adesivo(nastro isolante).Il filo detonante non soffre ad essere maneggiato puo essere tagliato ed annodato.L'umidita potrebbe danneggiare l'estremità lasciata scoperta.

3° Detonatore (Detonator)

Il detona tore é un piccolo tubo lungo circa 4 cm, nell'estremita chiusa é una piccola quantita di esplosivo sensibilissimo. Il detonatore é usato normalmente per accendere un "tappo" che a sua volta accende una carica esplosiva.Il detonatore a sua é acceso dalla miccia di sicurezza.La fine dellamiccia deve essere tagliata a sezione retta e infilata nella estremita aperta del detonatore che viene pinzata su questa miccia.Prima di inserire la miccia accertarsi che non vi siano detriti nell'interno del detonatore stesso,battendolo leggermente sull'unghia dalla parte aperta.Il detonatore deve essere maneggiato con molta precauzione e non essere urtato.Deve essere sempre tenuto separato dagli altri esplosivi.Un detonatore puo essere anche acceso diretta=

7

C.di L.N

Corpo Volontario d.Libertà

52 Brigata d'As.Garibaldi

"LIBERO BRIGANTI

-2-

mente da una matita a tempo.Per fare cio inserire l'estremità aperta del detonatore nell'apposito alloggiamento all'estremità della matita e spingerla al piu possibile senza sforzare.

4° Fiammifero contro vento.(Fuzes.)

Questi fiammiferi sono simili a quelli ordinarii ma bruciano con scintille rosse senza fiamma,sono usati per accendere la miccia di sicurezza.Strofinare la testa del fiammifero sulle pareti laterali della scatola ed avvicinare la parte accesa contro la miccia di sicurezza tagliata a sezione obliqua.

5° Tubetto di rame.(Copper tube igniter)

Questo é usato per accendere la miccia di sicurezza più facilmente che con i controvento.Tagliare nettamente la miccia a sezion retta infilare il tubetto sulla miccia il piu possibile.Qui il tubetto viene pinzato e fissato.Per accendere sfregare la estremita coperta di fosforo del tubetto contro un cartoncino per accensione.Il tubetto di rame deve essere tenuto in luogo asciutto.

6° Cartoncino per accensione(Striker board.)

Puo essere usato come é stato descritto al n.5 per accendere il tubo di rame e puo anche essere usato nello stesso modo per accendere i fiammiferi ecc.Serve pure per accendere la bomba incendiaria M.L.

7° Petardi(Fog signals)

E'usato come sistema schiacciamento nell'accensione di una carica per taglio di ferrovia.Il petardo posto é sul binario per mezzo di una graffa di filo di ferro e in modo che il tubetto di accensione rimanga dalla parte esterna del binario.Un detonatore inserito nel tubetto ed é legato alla miccia detonante che va alla carica?

8° Congegno a pressione (Pressure switch)

Puo essere usato allo stesso scopo del petardo per accendere una carica per ferrovia quando il treno passa sul congegno.In primo luogo l'astuccio di bronzo é avvitato fino in fondo nel centro del coperchio La ghiaia fra due traverse é rimossa da sotto la rotaia;e il congegno a pressione é unito con un detonatore legato al filo detonante.Il congegno

7

C.di L.N
Corpo Volontario d.Libertà
C. 3 Brigata d As.Garibaldi
"LIBERO BRIGANTI

-3-

é allora inserito nella ghiaia in modo che l"estremita dell'asta sia appe= na sotto la rotaia regalandola con la vite.La spilla di sicurezza si puo ora levare e coprire il congegno con ghiaia in modo che ~~sorga~~ sporga solo l'asta.

9° Congegno a trazione.(Pull switch)

Questo puo essere usato per accendere una miccia di sicu= rezza,che é fissata per una capo nell'apposita sede.Per accendere togliere la spilla di sicurezza e tirare l'anello.Il congegno puo essere anche usato per accendere direttamente un detonatore inserito nell'apposito allogia= mento.In questo caso l'anello deve essere tirato da un certa distanza e per mezzo di un lungo filo.Questo mezzo puo essere adottato per il sistema a trappola.

10° Congegno a depressione.(Release switch )

Questo meccanismo é usato per accendere una miccia di sicurezza o un detonatore quando un peso é sollevato e una pressione cessa Il sistema é messo in posizione tale che abbia un peso di almeno due Kg addosso e dopo cio si toglie la sicurezza.Non scatta fino a che il peso non é rimosso.

11° Matite a tempo (Time pencil)

La matita é un tubo di metallo che ha circa le stesse di= mensioni di un lapis ordinario ed é usata per accendere la miccia di sicu rezza o il detonatore dopo un determinato intervallo di tempo.Ad un capo della matita vi é un apposito alloggiamento per inserirvi la miccia o il detonatore.L'altro ~~filo=che~~ capo della matita é un tubo di rame entro cui vi é un'ampolla di acido ed un filo,che trattiene la molla.Per azionare la matita schiacciare il tubo di sicurezza di rame (senza curvarlo)cosi da rompere l'ampolla interna.Togliere poi la sicurezza.Il tempo di ritardo della matita si puo vedere dal colore della sicurezza e puo essere:
rosso=30 minuti-Verde=5 ore e 3/4-Bianco =2 ore -Giallo=12 ore
Questi tempi ~~sarranno~~ sono approssimativi e saranno piu corti per i climi caldi e piu lunghi per i freddi.

12° Tappi (Primers)

Un tappo e un a piccola carica solida di esplosivo sen=

7

C.di L.N
Corpo Volontario d.Libertà
5 Brigata d'As.Garibaldi
"LIBERO BRIGANTI

-4-

sibile di forma conica con un tubo nel mezzo in cui puo infilarsi un detonatore o un filo detonante.Il tappo va inserito nella carica esplosiva e deve essere messo a stretto contatto con questa.I tappi devono essere conservati in luogo asciutto.

13°Esplosivo plastico.(plastic explosive )

Ne esistono di due speci:

a)Stecche gialle brune avvolte in cellofane(p.e)
b) " " " " " " " " carta (808)

In ogni caso la stecca pesa 120 Gr.
L'esplosivo,plastico puo essere maneggiato senza pericolo ed alcune stecche possono essere messe insieme per una grossa carica.L'esplosivo puo essere innescato sia con un tappo sia con il filo detonante in cui siano stati fatti 3 nodi.E'preferibile (specialmente con l'808)usare un tappo che deve essere messo in stretto contatto con l'esplosivo.Se l'esplosivo è diven= tato troppo duro puo essere reso malleabile imbastandolo con vaselina. E'preferibile non impastare l'808 con le mani perche in questo caso provo= ca mal di testa.

14° Miccia istantanea.(Istantaneous fuze )

Questa miccia è simile alla miccia di sicurezza, ma di color arancio e brucia quasi instataneamente. Non deve mai essere accesa direttamente con fiamiferi o con controvento, ma con una matita tempo e con una miccia di sicurezza. Può essere usata simultaneamente per accendere più bombe in= cendiarie unendola a tutte le micce di sicurezza di quaste ultime. PER far questo incidere su tutte le micciedi sicurezza e i in corrispondenza sulla miccia istantanea degli incavi a doppio taglio in modo da scoprire la povere. Legare insieme le due micce in modo che le poveri vengono incontatto. Ripere ciò per tutte le micce di sicurezza finche tutte le bombe incendiarie siano legate insieme sollo stesso pezzo di miccia istantanea. Accendere la miccia istanta= nea ad uno dei capio a tutti e due con uno dei metodi su menzionati.

15° INCEDIARIA TASCABILE TEMPO (POSHET INCENDIARY)

QUesta è una piccola bomba incendiaria che contiene in se stessa un ri= tardo. Il contenuto è fattodi sostanza di combustibile e in due tubi esterni sono pieni di questa miscela. 7

C.di L.N

Corpo Volontario d.Libertà

C. 8 Brigata d'As.Garibaldi

"LIBERO BRIGANTI

-5-

IL ritardo che è simile a quello delle matitetempo è posto nel tubo cen= trale .Per azionare la bomba alzare il nas(ro adesivo sul tubo centrale e tagliare lo stechino di legno di sicurezza(se questo non,viene via facil= pente vuol dire che il meccanismo di ritardo e danneggiato).
Spingere quindi un oggetto duro(una moneta)nella fessura in modo da schiac= ciare il tubetto dirame interno e rompere l'ampolla che vi é dantro.
La bomba si accenderà dopo un certo periodo di tempo.Il ritardo é visibile dal colore dello stecco di legno di sicurezza.La corrispondenza fra colori e ritardi é la medesima gia vista per le matite tempe(Vedi n.11)
La bomba tascabile incendiaria brucia per circa un minuto.
Dovrà essere piazzata i, contatto con materiale il pui infiammabile possi= bile(per esempio paglia asciutta,truccioli,stracci oleati,...)Se la bomba incendiaria é legata ad una bottiglia di petrolio e piazzata orizzontalmenete con la bottiglia sopra,le fiamme della bomba romperanno la bottiglia e ac= cenderanno il petrolio.
Cio avverra precisamente quasi senza rumore.

16°incendiaria al magnesio.(Magnesium incendiary)

Consiste in un cilindro di magnesio riempito con termite.Puo essere accesa togliendo il coperchio e strafilando il fiam= mifero centrale con un apposito cartoncino che si trova togliendo il nastro che cinge la bomba.La bomba si inciendia con un ritardo di 7o8 secondi con uno spruzzo di fiamme,dopo di che il magnesio continuerà a bruciare per circa 10 minuti.La bomba puo anche essere accesa con un lungo ritardo attac= cando matite tempo,ai due pezzi di miccia che sporgono in alto della bomba, (tagliare due cm.di miccia prima di attaccare la matita).La bomba al magne= sio é una delle migliori ed é il migliore per dar fuoco al legname ed altro materiale non facilmente infiammabile;

FINE.

7

C. di L.N.
Volunteer Corps for Liberty
Hq. 8 Garibaldi Assault Brigade
"LIBERO BRIGANTI"

-1+

DESCRIPTIONS

1° Safety fuse (Bickford safety fuze)

The fuse is used to ignite an explosive and incendiary charge after an interval of time. The fuse burns at a rate of one cm. per second, thus to have a delay of 3 minutes a length of 180 cm. is required.

Before use it is best to cut 4 or 5 cm. from the end of the fuse that could be damp.

The fuse is normally lit by a windproof match or by a copper tube affixed to the fuse or by a time pencil. It can also be ignited by a primer capsule with a pull switch mechanism. The fuse does not directly ignite the explosive. The fuse should not be handled roughly because in this case it tends to burn too quickly.

2° Detonating cord (Cordtex)

Detonating cord is a fuse consisting of high explosive and is used to join a certain number of charges so that they explode simultaneously. It is lit by a detonator placed parallel to the detonating cord and secured to it by means of adhesive tape (insulating tape). Detonating cord does not suffer from being handled and can be cut and knotted. Dampness could damage the end that is left exposed.

3° Detonator

The detonator is a small tube about 4 cm long, in its closed end there is a small amount of extremely sensitive explosive/. The detonator is normally used to ignite a "plug" which in turn ignites an explosive charge. The detonator is ignited by a safety fuse. The end of the fuse must be cut at a right angle and inserted into the open end of the detonator which is crimped on the fuse. Before inserting the fuse make sure that there is no debris inside the detonator itself, tapping the open end lightly on your fingernail. The detonator has to be handled with much caution and should not suffer any impact. It should always be kept separated from other explosives. A detonator can also be ignited direct-

C. di L.N.
Volunteer Corps for Liberty
Hq. 8 Garibaldi Assault Brigade
"LIBERO BRIGANTI"

-2-

ly by a time pencil. To do this insert the open end of the detonator in the appropriate opening at the end of the time pencil and push it as far as possible without forcing it.

4° Windproof match. (Fuzes)

These matches are similar to ordinary matches but burn with red sparks with no flame, they are used to light the safety fuse. Rub the head of the match on the side of the box and bring the lit part close to the safety fuse that has been cut at an oblique angle.

5° Copper tube (Copper tube igniter)

This is used to ignite the safety fuse more easily than using the windproof match. Cut the safety fuse cleanly at a right angle and insert the tube onto the fuse as far as possible. Then the tube is crimped and secured. To ignite it rub the exposed phosphorous end of the tube against a striker board. The copper tube must be kept in a dry place.

6° Igniter card (Striker board)

This can be used as described in 5 above to ignite the copper tube and can also be used in the same manner to light matches, etc. It is also used to ignite the M.L. incendiary bomb.

7° Petards (Fog signals)

It is used as a crushing system to ignite a charge to cut railways. The petard placed secured to the rail by a piece of steel wire so that the igniter tube remains on the external part of the rail. A detonator inserted into the tube is connected to the detonating fuse that goes to the charge.

8° Pressure device (Pressure switch)

It can be used for the same purpose as the petard to ignite a railway charge when the train passes over the device. In the first instance the bronze case is screwed fully into the center of the cover. The gravel between the two railroad ties is removed from under the rail; and/ the pressure switch is paired with a detonator connected to the detonating cord. The switch

C. di L.N.
Volunteer Corps for Liberty
Hq. 8 Garibaldi Assault Brigade
"LIBERO BRIGANTI"

-3-

is then inserted into the gravel so that by adjusting the screw the end of the case is barely beneath the rail. The safety pin can now be removed and the device be covered with gravel so that only the pin is sticking out.

9° Traction device (Pull switch)

This can be used to ignite a safety fuse, which is attached in the appropriate place. To ignite, cut the safety pin and pull the ring. The device can also be used to directly ignite a detonator inserted into the appropriate opening. In this case the ring must be pulled a certain distance by sing a long string. This device can be adapted for the trap system.

10° Depression device (Release switch)

This device is used to ignite a safety fuse of a detonator when a weight is lifted or pressure ceases. The// system is placed in such a position so that it has a weight of at least two kilos on top of it and after the safety is removed. It will not explode as long as the weight is not removed.

11° Time pencil (Time pencil)

The pencil is a metal tube that has approximately the same dimensions of an ordinary lead pencil and is used to ignite the safety fuse of the detonator after a predetermined time period. One end of the pencil has a place to insert the fuse or the detonator. The other end of the pencil is a copper tube in which there is an ampule of acid and a wire that holds the spring in place. To activate the pencil crush the copper safety tube (without curving it) so that the internal ampule breaks. Then remove the safety. The time delay of the pencil can be seen by the color of the safety and can be: red=30 minutes – Green=5 hours and ¾-White=2 hours – Yellow=12 hours
These times are approximate end will be shorter for warm climates and longer for cold climates.

12° Plugs (Timers)

A plug is a small solid charge of sen=

C. di L.N.
Volunteer Corps for Liberty
Hq. 8 Garibaldi Assault Brigade
"LIBERO BRIGANTI"

-4-

sitive explosive of conical form with a hole in the middle in which a detonator or detonator cord can be inserted. The plug is inserted in the explosive charge and has to be placed in direct contact with it. Primers have to be stored in a dry place.

13° Plastic explosive (plastic xxxxx explosive)

There are two types:

a. Yellow-brown sticks wrapped in cellophane (p.e.)
b. " " " " paper (808)

In both cases the stick weighs 120 grams.
The plastic explosive can be handled without any danger and several sticks can be put together for a large charge. The explosive can be primed with either a plug or with detonating cord in which 3 knots have been made. It is preferable (especially with the 808) to use a plug that has been placed in close contact with the explosive. If the explosive has become too hard it can be made more pliable by coating it with vaseline. It is best not to work the 808 with your hands because it can cause a headache.

14° Instant fuse (Instantaneous fuze)

This fuse is similar to the safety fuse, but is orange colored and burns almost instantaneously. It must never be lit directly with matches or with fuses, but with a time pencil or with a safety fuse. It can be used simultaneously to ignite several incendiary bombs by connecting it to all of the safety fuses of XXXXXXX the bombs. In order to do this cut all of the safety fuses and make a double-cut notch on the instantaneous fuse in order to expose the powder. Tie the two fuses together so that the powders make contact with each other. Repeat this for all of the safety fuses until all of the incendiary bombs are tied together to the same length of instantaneous fuse. Light the instantaneous fuse on one end using one of the methods mentioned above.

15° POCKET TIME INCENDIARY (POCKET INCENDIARY)

This is a small incendiary bomb that contains a delay within itself. The contents are made of combustible substance and two external tubes are filled with this mixture.

C. di L.N.
Volunteer Corps for Liberty
Hq. 8 Garibaldi Assault Brigade
"LIBERO BRIGANTI"
-5-

The delay is similar to that of the time pencil and is located in the center tube. To activate the bomb lift the adhesive tape on the center tube and remove the small wooden safety stick (if this does not come off easily it means that the delay mechanism is damaged).

Then push a hard object (a coin) in the crack so as to crush the internal copper tube and break the ampule that is inside it. The bomb will ignite after a certain period of time. The delay is visible by the color of the wooden safety stick. The relationship of colors and delays is the same as had already been seen for the time pencils (see n. 11).

The pocket incendiary bomb burns for about a minute.

It should be placed in contact with the most flammable material possible (for example dry straw, oily rags…) If the incendiary bomb is tied to a bottle of gasoline and placed horizontally with the bottle on top, the flames of the bomb will break the bottle and igniter the gasoline.

This will happen with almost no noise.

16° Magnesium Incendiary (Magnesium Incendiary)

This consists of a magnesium cylinder filled with thermite. It can be ignited by removing the cover and rubbing the central match with the striker that has been supplied and which can be found by removing the tape that is wrapped around the bomb. The bomb ignites with a delay of 7 or 8 seconds with a spurt of flame, after which the magnesium will continue to burn for about 10 minutes. The bomb can also be ignited with a long delay by attaching a time pencil to the two pieces of fuse that protrude from the top of the bomb (cut two cm. of fuse before attaching the pencil). The magnesium bomb is one of the best and is the best to set fire to wood and other material that is not easily flammable;

END

# CHAPTER XI
# GERMAN CODES

Sometimes while examining a weapon of German origin it is not possible to determine the producer or the particular model. The Germans introduced a strict code system relative to all wartime production, both national as well as in countries they occupied.

Weapons were marked with a dual set of identification codes: one relative to the model and the other relative to the producer; here we can see the markings on a pistol produced by Mauser (byf) in 1944, and accepted by inspector 135 (WaA 135 = *Waffen Amt*, that is, the Armaments Office).

WaffenAmt 135. *Gianluigi Usai*

The "byf 44" is a code on a P38 pistol produced by Mauser in 1944. *Gianluigi Usai*

Following is a partial list of German codes relating to weapons described in this work.

Weapons that are substantially the same but came from the inventories of various nations were assigned different designations after they were captured. For example, the same Mauser 98K-style rifles that were distributed between the end of WWI and the beginning of WWII are given different designations depending on the nations from which they were taken.

Some weapons also received supplemental codes if they were successively captured from other nations, i.e., the ex-Polish Mausers captured in Russia when Russia was invaded bear a different code than the same rifles seized directly by the Wehrmacht in Poland.

The single lower-case letter in parentheses following the alphanumeric code is the initial letter of the German name for a specific country, indicating the country of origin of the weapon. The letter codes are a for Amerika (USA), b for Belgien (Belgium), e for England (England), f for Frankreich (France), i for Italien (Italy), j for Jugoslawien (Yugoslavia), n for Norwegen (Norway), o for Österreich (Austria), p for Polen (Poland), r for Russland (Russia), and t for Tschechoslowakei (Czechoslovakia).

Cover of a German manual describing foreign weapons.

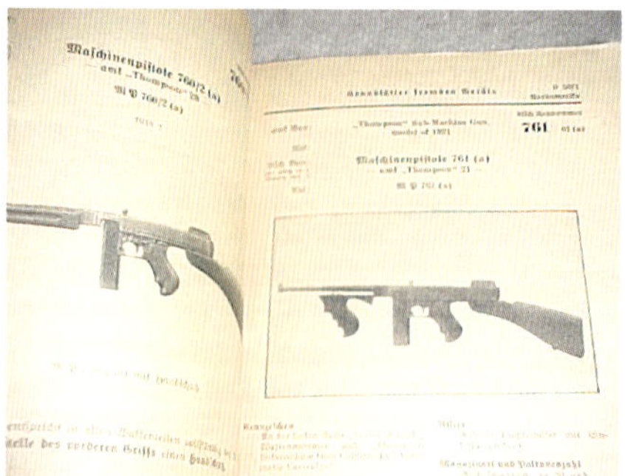

Pages from a German manual describing versions of the Thompson submachine gun.

| Weapon designation | Weapon code | Producer code/WaA |
|---|---|---|
| Mod. 1889 Bodeo | P.680 (i) | xxx |
| Glisenti Mod. 1910 | P.670 (i) | xxx |
| Beretta 1915 | xxx | xxx |
| Beretta 1915/17 | xxx | xxx |
| Beretta 1934 | P.671 (i) | WaA 162 (very rare) |
| Beretta 1935 | P.671 (i) | WaA 162 (very rare) |
| P08 Luger | P08 | S/42 or byf × Mauser, WaA 135 |
| P38 | P38 | ac × Walther, WaA 359 |
| | byf × Mauser, WaA 135 | |
| | cyq × Spreewerke, WaA 88 | |
| Steyr 1912 | xxx | xxx |
| FN HP35 | P.640 (b) | WaA 613, 103, 140 |
| Radom VIS | P.645 (p) | WaA 77 × Radom |
| | P.35 (p) | bnz × Steyr |
| Kongsberg Mod. 1914 | P.657 (n) | WaA 84 |
| CZ 27 | P.M. 27 | fnh × CZm WaA 76 |
| Astra | xxx | WaA 251 |
| Llama | xxx | WaA 251 |
| Star B | xxx | WaA D20 |
| Nagant 1895 | P.612 (r) | xxx |
| TT30. TT33 Tokarev | P. 615 (r) | xxx |
| Colt 1911A1 | P.660 (a) | xxx |
| Ballester Molina | xxx | xxx |
| Colt revolver | P.661 (a) | xxx |
| Smith & Wesson revolver | P.662 (a) | xxx |
| Webley revolver | P.646 (e) | xxx |
| Enfield revolver | xxx | xxx |
| SACM 1935A and S | P.625 (f) | WaA 251 |
| Vetterli-Vitali | xxx | xxx |
| 1891/38 6.5 mm | Gew. 209 (i) | xxx |
| 1891/41 | Gew. 210 (i) | xxx |

| | | |
|---|---|---|
| 1891/38 7.35mm | Gew. 231 (i) | xxx |
| 1891 moschetto | Kar. 408 (i) | xxx |
| 1891 cavalry | Kar. 409 (i) | xxx |
| 1891 TS | Kar. 410 (i) | xxx |
| Mauser, various | Kar98k (Germany) | S/42, byf, svw, ar × Mauser |
| | Gew. 299 (p) Poland | WaA135 |
| | 16/33 Czech | S/147 × Sauer & Sohn |
| | Wz 24 Czech | S/27 × Erma |
| | Gew. 221 (j) Yugo | 660, bnz × Steyr |
| | Gew. 298 (p) Poland | 337 × Gustloff |
| | 29/40 (o) Austria | (this is only a partial list of |
| | Gew. 262 (b) Belgium | codes and producers) |
| Gew. 289 (p) Portugal | | |
| M.1895 rifle | Gew. 306 (i) | xxx |
| M. 1895 moschetto | Kar. 505 (i) | xxx |
| Enfield SMLE | Gew. 281 (e) | xxx |
| Mosin Nagant | Gew. 252 (r) | xxx |
| | Gew 254 (r) | xxx |
| Springfield M1903 | Gew. 249 (a) | xxx |
| Gew 41 | Gew. 41 | ac × Walther, WaA 359 |
| | duv × Berlin-Lübecker | |
| Gew 43 | Gew. 43 | ac × Walther, WaA 359 |
| | Kar. 43 | bcd × Gustloff |
| | duv × Berlin-Lübecker | |
| FG 42 | FG 42 | fzs × Krieghoff |
| | gcy × Vesta | |
| StG 44 | MP43 – StG44 | ce × Sauer |
| | fxo × Haenel | |
| | byf × Mauser | |

| | | |
|---|---|---|
| | ayf × Erma | |
| SVT 38, 40 | Slgew. 258 (r) | xxx |
| | Slgew 259 (r) | xxx |
| Garand M1 | Slgew 251 (a) | xxx |
| M1, M1A1 carbine | Slgew. 455 (a) | xxx |
| Beretta 38A | MP 738 (i) | WaA 162 (very rare) |
| Beretta 38/42 | MP 738 (i) | WaA 162 (very rare) |
| Beretta 18/30 | xxx | xxx |
| FNAB 43 | xxx | xxx |
| TZ 45 | xxx | xxx |
| Variara | xxx | xxx |
| MP38, MP40 | MP38 | 27, ayf × Erma |
| | MP40 | 122, fxo × Haenel |
| | 660, bnz × Steyr | |
| MP34 (o) | MP34 (o) | 660 × Steyr, WaA189 |
| MP35 | MP35 | ajf × Junker |
| MP41 | MP41 | fxo × Haenel |
| MP18 | MP18 | xxx |
| MP28 | MP28 | xxx |
| MAS 1938 | MP 722 (f) | xxx |
| PPSh 41 | MP 717 (r) | xxx |
| Suomi M31 | xxx | xxx |
| Sten MkII | MP 749 (e) | xxx |
| Sten MkIII | MP 750 (e) | xxx |
| Thompson 1928A1 | MP 760 (e) | xxx |
| MP 760 (a) | | |
| Thompson M1, M1A1 | MP 760/2 (a) | xxx |
| M3 | xxx | xxx |
| UD m42 | xxx | xxx |
| Breda 30 | MG 099 (i) | xxx |
| Breda 37 | MG 259 (i) | xxx |
| Fiat 1914 | MG 200 (i) | xxx |
| Fiat 1914/35 | MG 255 (i) | xxx |
| Breda Safat | xxx | xxx |
| Colt 1895 | xxx | xxx |
| Schwarzlose M1907 | MG 261 (i) | xxx |

| | | |
|---|---|---|
| Saint Etienne M1907 | sMG 256 (f) | xxx |
| Hotchkiss 1914 | sMG 257 (f) | xxx |
| M1924m29 | leMG 116 (f) | xxx |
| CSRG Chauchat | Slgew 310 (f) | xxx |
| Hotchkiss 1926 | leMG 104 (n) | xxx |
| ZB26, ZB30 | MG 26 (t), MG 30 (t) | dot × Waffenwerke Brünn, WaA63 |
| MG34 | MG34 | aqx, hhg × Rheinmetall |
| | S/42 × Mauser | |
| | BSW × Berlin-Suhler Waffenfabrik | |
| | 660, bnz × Steyr | |
| | swp, dot × Waffenwerke Brünn | |
| MG42 | MG42 | dfb × Gustloff |
| | ar × Mauser | |
| | cra × Alkett | |
| | as well as a host of other | |
| | subcontractors such as swd, | |
| | svq, ax, bpr..... | |
| MG13 | MG3 | xxx |
| MG15 | MG15 | xxx |
| Bren | MG 138 (e) | xxx |
| Vickers | MG 230 (e) | xxx |
| Browning Mk2 .303 | xxx | xxx |
| BAR (USA) | xxx | xxx |
| BAR (Belgium) | MG 127 (b) | xxx |
| BAR (Poland) | MG 154/1 (p) | xxx |
| Browning 1914A4 | xxx | xxx |
| Browning M2HB | xxx | xxx |
| Degtyarev DP28 | MG 120 (r) | xxx |

The codes listed above represent only a part of those that may be encountered on various weapons, as in many cases the larger firms used parts acquired from subcontractors that had their own assigned codes. Over the course of the war years these codes were changed for security reasons, and for this reason the same factory might display different codes depending on the year of production.

## CHAPTER XII

# SELECTED PHOTOGRAPHS

As a final chapter, a selection of photographs depicting partisans is provided showing many of the weapons described in the profiles; details of these photos have been used to illustrate some of the more interesting weapons.

Considering the weight of the Breda 37 (about 37 kilos [82 lb.] with its tripod), one has to appreciate the strength of the partisan who is holding the weapon as though it were merely a small branch. Among the other weapons are a Bren, a US M3 submachine gun, an M1 carbine, and a machine gun of probable aircraft origin. *M. Becchi*

In this group of partisans the most interesting weapon is undoubtedly the UD M42 being held by the second man on the left. Also seen are a Sten, M3, and a Beretta 38A. *ILSREC Genova*

In addition to several Stens, the partisan on the right is holding what might be a Colt 1911A1 or one of its many clones—possibly a Ballester Molina—that was known to be present in the Valbormida area in numerous examples. *G. Toscani*

The presence of a silenced Sten—recognizable by its long barrel shroud in the hands of the partisan with the white jacket—is unusual; of similar interest is the Mauser C96 held by the individual immediately behind him, although the specific model of the C96 cannot be determined. *M. Becchi*

An abundantly well-armed group; of note are the Beretta pistol in an open-style holster being worn by the partisan on the far right and the Springfield 1903A3 being held by the partisan standing on the far left. There is also a Bren and a plethora of Stens and Mausers. *G. Toscani*

In addition to various types of bolt-action rifles we can also see several Stens, an Italian Breda 30 light machine gun, and an Italian 45 mm mortar. The linked ammunition belt wrapped around the machine gunner's waist is a bit laughable, as the Breda 30 was fed by magazines carried in the ammunition chest strapped to the back of the ammunition bearer lying next to the gunner. *G. Toscani*

The usual profusion of automatic weapons is shown in this photo taken immediately after the end of the war: clearly evident are an MP40, a MAS 38, an M3, and an M1 carbine. *Don Angelo Siri*

Note the TZ45 held by the second partisan standing on the right. As in other posed photos, the presence of ammunition belts draped over the shoulders of partisans carrying bolt-action rifles is somewhat anachronistic. *G. Toscani*

In addition to the common assortment of weapons, the Breda 37 in the foreground is notable. *G. Toscani*

Cuneo, May 1945. The Sten is clearly outnumbered by the M3 in this formation drawn up in a piazza; Brens and MG42 machine guns are resting on the ground. *L. Balbo*

The weapon being held by the individual labeled II is a Beretta MAB 38A that has had its perforated cooling jacket removed, presenting a somewhat curious appearance. The pistols worn by the partisan on the right (labeled VII) seem to be a Steyr 1912 and an FN HP35. *G. Toscani*

A parade marching along a street in Milan; among the less common weapons are the Beretta 38/42 of the partisan on the left and the TZ45 of the partisan on the right. Does anyone who specializes in uniforms have any explanation as to why the alpini hats are being worn backward? *ISREC Savona*

A classic souvenir photo celebrating victory with many automatic weapons clearly evident. The presence of a *siringone* ("big syringe," or Beretta 18/30) carried by the fourth partisan from the left is interesting, as is the MP35 of the individual next to him. *ILSREC Genova*

The usual studio photo taken in the immediate postwar era: everyone is in new clothing and armed with at least four M3s and a MAB. *Don Angelo Siri*

This is part of a posed series taken in the days immediately following April 25, 1945, by photographers of a well-known advertising agency in Milan and have been used in numerous books and magazines, almost always with incorrect captioning. The scene is meant to depict a ferocious hunt for "snipers" over the roofs of Milan, but the individuals shown are photographers who alternated between posing with weapons and taking pictures. The three main weapons used in the war that had just ended—the MP40, MAB38A, and Sten—are pictured. *INSMLI Milano*

Part of the series of staged photos taken on the Milan rooftops; note the individual in the center holding a camera instead of a weapon. *INSMLI Milano*

A parade through the streets of Acqui (Alessandria Province); the commanders of the "Ligure Alessandrina" formation are in the front row, and the individual in the center holding flowers is "Mancini." *G. Toscani*

A somewhat unremarkable group, except for the presence of the Russian PPSh41 being held by the partisan second from the left. *ILSREC Genova*

A posed studio photo of partisans from the "Bevilacqua" Division operating in the Vado Ligure area and commanded by Hermann Wygoda, a Pole. Among the weapons are a "Skoda" and a Gew 41, in addition to the obligatory Stens. *E. Biggi*

A photo that would make any arms collector envious; almost every type of submachine gun described in the individual profiles in this book can be accounted for. Would anyone care to conduct an inventory? *ILSREC Genova*

At times even photographic documentation can give rise to doubt; this photo was taken ony a moment before the photo shown on page 16 that purported to show a full-fledged hunt for "snipers." The presence of a very calm uniformed British photographer to the left leads one to believe quite otherwise. Added to that is the fact that with a Sherman tank close by in the background, was there any reason for so much anxiety? *ISREC Savona*

# NOTES

1. Oral testimony from "Storia e Memoria," year 6, no. 1, 1997, ILSREC Genova, p. 27.
2. Beppe Fenoglio, *Il partigiano Johnny* (Einaudi, Gli struzzi) p. 73–74.
3. The MAS 1938 was the first successful attempt by the French to produce a submachine gun (see Profile 47).
4. Giorgio Bocca, *Partigiani della montagna* (Mondolibri, Bergamo) p. 31.
5. Roy Farran, *Winged Dagger*, Cassel Publishing. Also by W. Fowler, *The Secret War in Italy*, Ian Allen Publishers, p. 106.
6. Pieramedeo Baldrati, *San Marco...San Marco, Storia di una Divisione* (Archetipografia MI, 1989) p. 1,738.
7. Hermann Wygoda, *In the Shadow of the Swastika* (University of Illinois Press, 1998) p. 112.
8. *Maschinen pistole* was the German term for an automatic pistol or submachine gun; all German submachine guns were thus designated, but particularly the MP40 (see Profile 42).
9. Marlin: UD M42 (see Profile 54). The American carbine is likely the M1 (see Profile 35).
10. Giorgio Bocca, *Storia dell'Italia partigiana* (Oscar Mondadori, 2000) p. 342.
11. Fenoglio, *Il partigiano Johnny*, op. cit., p. 92–93. Note the use of "Skoda" and "parabellum."
12. William Pickering and Alan Hart, *I banditi di Cisterna,* translated and commented on by Chiaffredo Bellero, IRSEC, Asti, 2006, p. 203.
13. E-mail correspondence with Ing. Chiaffredo Bellero, Miami Florida. From the description furnished the weapon would be the Italian-produced TZ45 submachine gun (see Profile 40).
14. The first breech-loading rifle used by the Italian army, adopted in 1870 (see Profile 22).
15. Aldo Spinardi, *Mauri e i suoi, Cassa di Risparmio di Cuneo*, 1995, p. 124–125.
16. Lazagna, *Ponte rotto*, Colibri Ed. (Milano, 1946) p. 272.
17. S. Favretto, *Fenoglio*, verso il 2 aprile, Falsopiano Editor, p. 79.
18. See Profile 75.

19. See Profile 41.
20. Fenoglio, *Il partigiano Johnny*, op. cit., p. 291–292. "Scoundrels! – he yelled. – The pigs are disarming the Blues who have scattered, all of the Blues who are returning from the river. They say they did not fight as they should have and that the men who are returning from the river are nothing but deserters, and they are disarming them...But in the meantime they are taking weapons from the Blues, saying they will make better use of them...Listen to me,...if you run across them, shoot first."
21. For example, the Barstone mission of September 1944, which was dropped in error into a Garibaldi formation (see: Morton Paul, *Missione "Inside" fra i partigiani del Nord Italia*, L'arciere, Cuneo, 1979).
22. During WWI, Great Britain placed orders with a number of arms manufacturers in the United States—among them Remington—for production of weapons for the British Army. Remington Arms produced the P14 rifle in .303 caliber for Britain.
23. Savona State Archives, Folder D7-104 Questura.
24. Savona State Archives, Prefecture, Catalogue A4 B S, Folder 140.
25. Savona State Archives, Prefecture, police morning reports 1952.
26. F. Sasso, *Guerra incivile, Griefl* (Cairo M. 2003) p. 192. The following text is transcribed with the author's permission: "Comrade, I am sending you several photos which might be of interest to you in view of the type of research you are conducting. As you can imagine they relate to a cache of arms set aside for a revolution that never happened. I won't tell you where it is located, but I can tell you where the contents came from: we stockpiled it with part of the material we captured from the Fascists who manned the checkpoint at the end of Corso Ricci in a bunker that was underneath the current monument, and also from the nearby GIL barracks. At the end of April, we gathered as much as we could and hid it in anticipation of using it, but the occasion never came. I don't know how much you know about weapons, but what is involved are German Mausers, Italian mod. 91 moschetti, parts of an 8 mm Breda machine gun, parts of a 20 mm cannon, and assorted mortar rounds. I have been unable to track down the complementary material, especially the ammunition. I hope you can make good use of these photos."
27. See "La Stampa" of October 8, 2013, and following days.
28. See Profile 75.

29. This response was reported with different wording in various sources, among them Lazagna, *Ponte rotto*, op. cit p. 199: "…in all operations naturally a lot of ammunition was used; we urgently asked the Allied mission especially for German 7.92 mm ammunition, but the response of the Allied headquarters in Italy was we were much closer to the Germans than they were and thus we could get it ourselves." Or Wygoda, *In the Shadow of the Swastika*, cit, p. 111: "What we needed most was ammunition for the different types of guns we had captured from the Nazis and Fascists. We were continuously short of ammunition as a result of our heavy engagements with the enemy and the continued influx of new men. The Allies were equally short of German ammunition, but they supplied us with British and American weapons instead."
30. Nuto Revelli, *La guerra dei poveri* (Einaudi 1962) p. 137.
31. Piero is Piero Balbo, or "Poli." See Adriano Balbo, *Quando inglesi arrivare noi tutti morti, Blu edizioni* (Torino, 2005) p. 32.
32. According to the testimony of a relative of "Poli" who also made a sketch of the weapon on a paper napkin, this would have been one of the early models of the Steyr-Solothurn SI-100.

To my wife Rosanna, who “enjoys” reading my draft manuscripts and who I thank for all of the corrections she makes to improve the text.